# THE PERMANENT CAMPAIGN

# THE PERMANENT CAMPAIGN

## Inside the World of Elite Political Operatives

### SIDNEY BLUMENTHAL

Beacon Press ☆ Boston

Grateful acknowledgment is made to Paul McGrath for permission to quote from "How I Got Involved" by Jane Byrne, as told to Paul McGrath, *Chicago* magazine, April 1979.

Beacon Press books are published under the auspices of the Unitarian Universalist Association
Published simultaneously in Canada by
Fitzhenry & Whiteside Limited, Toronto
Printed in the United States of America

(hardcover) 9 8 7 6 5 4 3 2 1


Library of Congress Cataloging in Publication Data
Blumenthal, Sid.
   The permanent campaign.

   1.  Campaign management—United States.
2.  Electioneering—United States.  3.  Public relations
and politics.  I.  Title.
JK2281.B63     324.7′0973     79-53755
ISBN 0-8070-3208-5

For Jacqueline B. Jordan

# ACKNOWLEDGMENTS

Writing this book has been a permanent campaign of its own. During its course I have received wide support. Danny Schechter, friend and colleague, was the first person to recognize the book's possible significance. Without him, this book surely would not have been written. MaryAnn Lash, editor-in-chief at Beacon Press, has been flexible and encouraging during my work. Joanne Wyckoff, my editor, took painstaking care with the manuscript. Her thoughtful editing has helped shape the book.

I have been provided with invaluable insights and research material by Alan Baron of *The Baron Report*, Christopher Lydon of WGBH-TV, my friends Ben Gerson and Hillel Schwartz, and Josiah Lee Auspitz, director of the Sabre Foundation's Project on Public Philosophy, whose article (with Clifford W. Brown, Jr.), "What's Wrong With Politics," in *Harper's*, May 1974, was especially provocative.

I owe a special debt to Martin Linsky, former editor of *The Real Paper*, who is now at the Kennedy Institute of Politics at Harvard. Many of the chapters of this book appeared in different form in *The Real Paper*. They were improved by Martin Linsky's editing and his critical judgment.

During my travels I stayed with friends and family. They aided me in writing the book, too. Thanks go to my wife's parents, Frank and Joyce Jordan, to my uncle and aunt, Harry and Alice Novak, and to my friends, William TenHoor and Karen Trais. My parents, Hymen and Claire Blumenthal, as always, provided love and encouragement.

All those who took time to speak with me, consultants and sources, especially deserve thanks.

I am indebted, above all, to my wife, Jackie Jordan, who among other things, has proved to be my best editor. Finally, my son, Max, has been helpful in that he's made everyone happy.

# CONTENTS

# INTRODUCTION

Political consultants are the new power within the American political system. They are permanent; the politicians ephemeral. The consultants have supplanted the old party bosses as the link to the voters. Consultants have the personal contact, possess knowledge of the intimate history of campaigns, and have the voter-catching skills that party bosses once prided themselves on. It is not surprising then that the rise of the consultants has paralleled the decline of the parties. It represents a new stage in American political history as significant as the growth of the political parties. Now, in the 1980s, the business of political consulting has matured so that every major candidate for every major office must employ a consultant in order to have the chance to win.

In their heyday, the political parties, buttressed by vast machines of patronage, seemed permanent. Their slide to an obsolescent state was gradual. The corrosion of party strength began before World War II, during the Depression, when the New Deal assumed many of the social service functions carried out by ward organizations. By taking over these duties the federal government expropriated the machine and rendered impotent the loyalties and obligations people felt toward their parties.

Reform has invariably been an enemy of political parties. In California, during the Progressive Era before World War I, parties were transformed into hollow shells by advanced democratic reforms — for example, allowing candidates to cross-file in both parties. Every new election reform upset the party structure. Political parties could not adjust quickly because they were on the defensive, vested interests attacked by reforms. The world changed around them before they noticed it. When the parties failed to incorporate the new campaign technologies within their operations, they became increasingly useless to politicians. The parties could no longer deliver. A candidate seeking office had to go to a place other than party headquarters to secure the means to get elected. The parties were superseded by the consultants.

With the advent of television and the decline of political machines, politicians needed a new way of garnering public support. How could the public be mobilized if there were no organization to do it? Television provided the answer; it reached everybody. In the beginning, advertising agencies handled election campaigns. The first presidential candidate to hire an advertising firm was Dwight Eisenhower, who did so grudgingly on the advice of his managers. The ad agencies sold candidates like soap. But, by the 1970s, they discovered that political campaigns weren't all that lucrative compared to selling soap. A political campaign ends with an election; a soap campaign can last for years. So the admen mostly cleared out of the field. Sometimes, however, selling a candidate like a soap was very effective, particularly when the candidate's image was too politically charged. Richard Nixon's 1968 campaign, chronicled in Joe McGinniss's *The Selling of the President*, was the last campaign in the first generation of media politics. Nixon desperately needed to be seen as a new Nixon. The admen were perfect for him.

But campaigns today are only occasionally the province of Madison Avenue types. In their place have come the political media consultants, operatives with political sensibilities who understand the new technology and are sensitive to the special qualities of the campaign message. The arrival of new techniques based on computers — direct mail, voter identification methods, sophisticated polling — reinforce the role of consultants. In order to have access to the new technology a candidate needs a consultant. He can't run a viable, much less respectable, campaign without one.

The common image of the consultant is that of a hired gun, a mercenary, available to the highest bidder. Many consultants fall into this category; however, many do not. The smartest and most effective consultants have a highly developed political perspective. Generally they will work only for those candidates with whom they are in basic agreement. There are consultants spread all across the spectrum, from left to right. But they work within circumscribed parameters — as moderate Republicans or liberal Democrats, for instance. Technique, in great part, is neutral. Anyone can learn it, if you have the aptitude, and it can be used for differing political ends. But the uniformity of the means in itself transforms politics.

With the decline of the parties, candidates must wage their own campaigns. Consequently, there is a high value placed on projecting a vivid personality for it makes the politician stand out. But because this *élan vital* is so widely sought after, it becomes common and debased, and the need for consultants becomes that much more intense. Many pols believe consultants offer magic.

Consultants each have their own political grammar, reflected in a particular campaign style. Although consultants dispense the same technique, politicians seek something unique that will permit them to win. Idiosyncratic expression becomes a precious commodity; it makes a campaign distinct, attracting voter attention. The politician's name will begin to be recognized. One classic ad campaign (run, incidentally, by political amateurs), that of U.S. Senator Paul Tsongas of Massachusetts, consisted of a small boy mispronouncing Tsongas's name as "Tickets." Tsongas rose from low in the polls to victory. Most politicians feel that they need consultants to mediate with the public on their behalf. They believe that the consultants know better than they do how to gauge and deal with public opinion. Politicians are dependent on the consultants and some pols are strangely fearful when exposed to the public without intermediaries. The consultants often set the standards of political professionalism that the politicians emulate.

One of the most important facts about consultants is what they don't do: they don't control votes as the old party bosses did through patronage. Consultants can't enforce voter discipline because there is no quid pro quo involved in watching a television commercial. And they can't enforce discipline in those they help elect to office. Consider, for example, New York political consultant David Garth. One Garth client, Governor Ella Grasso of Connecticut, may support Jimmy Carter for president while another Garth client, Mayor William Green of Philadelphia, supports Ted Kennedy. Garth has little influence with either on this matter. Yet they both depend on him to bring out their vote. In this way, parties continue to fragment and the nonalignment of politicians and voters is accelerated.

Political consultants differ from party bosses in other important respects. The party boss might tell a candidate what to do, but he does not instruct him who to be. And the party boss is as concerned with what happens after an election is won as before. The consultant, however, manipulates candidates and voters. His image-making is expressed in a particular kind of strategy, and the politician who is created by it and uses it successfully to win absorbs it as a philosophy of governing. It is the same process by which, years ago, a politician who was created by a party organization and patronage used them as methods of governing as well.

An interpretation of the work of consultants is the royal road to knowledge of underlying elements in our political life. Entering into the world of the consultant gives us entry into the formation of political ideas. By virtue of their central position inside campaigns, consultants, through the use of media, can shape our political thoughts. To the consultant, each candidate is a dream problem, a problem that must be solved consciously. How is this accomplished? The consultant must stimulate the public's wish fulfillment for the candidate through manipulation of symbols and images, enticing voters to believe that the candidate can satisfy their needs. The relationship of dreams to reality is analogous to the relationship between advertising and politics. Ads are condensed images of wish fulfillment. Political commercials are sometimes made to be deliberately irrational in order to reach voters on other than a conscious plane. Image-making, no matter how manipulative, doesn't replace reality; it becomes part of it. Images are not unreal simply because they are manufactured. Comprehending this new image-making is essential to understanding modern politics.

Consultants are more than technicians of mass psychology. They also deal in strategic imperatives, their elective affinities. The Prussian military theoretician Karl von Clauswitz observed, "War is nothing more than the continuation of politics by other means." The converse is true, too: politics is nothing more than war continued by other means. Strategic thinking — software theory with hardware implications — was the sociology of the postwar elite, purveyed in official circles by denizens of the Rand Corporation, the Hudson Institute, and other think tanks. The Defense Department–sponsored intellectuals saw every situation as a problem in itself, unrelated to any other situation; every decision was separate. Politics was a series of scenarios that could be anticipated through computer simulations. Preemptive strikes, escalation of conflicts, and deterrent reactions were key concepts for the player to grasp in order to maximize gains and minimize losses.

What emerged from this was what Richard Nixon called the "game plan," an aggressive strategic outlook that became the dominant brand of politics. The new political technology, readily at hand, provided the tools for implementing this perspective. Polling, especially, supplied a precise navigational guide for mapping out where and when to stage bombing missions on the opponent. As a result, consultants assimilated strategic politics without knowing it; it was so well adapted to their purposes and roles as contemporary operatives.

Traditional politics, unlike strategic politics, was constituency oriented. A tissue of favors and debts connected the voters to politicians and parties. The old-style politician's goal was consensus as a method of controlling conflict and harnessing it to the party's interest. The consultant's goal, on the other hand, is to design a successful scenario, to play the game well. The consultant has no concept of governance, but has the inclination to keep options open. This posture itself is a strategy. In campaigns, consultants focus on those voters not firmly behind their client, the uncommitted voters who might be ticket-splitters. Whereas traditional campaigns concentrated on mobilizing the faithful, modern campaigns ignore them. Party loyalists have no place to go. The fluid voters — those without allegiances — are the objects of consultants' maneuvers, for these voters can be moved decisively in any direction. And if there aren't enough uncommitted voters to swing an election, they can always be created. The committed can be torn from their moorings. Through polling, a consultant can discover what issue will move them into the hazy ground of nonalignment. The candidate can cast appeals to them on the issues on which they are most susceptible to suggestion. The intent of this calculated effort is the destruction of traditional loyalties.

Even given favorable circumstances, however, a politician may not be adroit enough to maintain a swiftly paced campaign geared to keeping up with the fluid voters. So, in order to win over the uncommitted, it helps if the politician is uncommitted as well. Then when he creates issues it can seem to be a breakthrough and he can appear to be a sincere advocate. In this way he can give a winning performance in the play directed by the strategic-minded consultant. The politician's stance on the issues becomes a matter of positioning. Which issues to emphasize and which to ignore must fit the overall scheme constructed by the consultant in order to secure the most competitive spot in the political marketplace. In the art of positioning, advertising and strategy become one.

But just as consultants are not merely mass psychologists, they are not purely technocratic Machiavellians. The consultants, in fact, embody many of the virtues espoused by the turn-of-the-century Progressives. They are usually dispassionate critics of politics, wary of control by party bosses. In the consulting trade these attitudes are institutionalized. Consultants are professionals without binding ties. In an important sense their politics are made possible by their entrepreneurship, their ability to sell themselves to clients. This is the Progressive ideal of individualist middle-class citizen activists in a transmuted form. The consultants are the answer to the Progressives' problems. William Allen White, a Progressive of the Theodore Roosevelt persuasion, argued in his book *The Old Order Changeth* for a "permanent cure" for the political machine system, which Progressives regarded as the bane of democracy. The permanent cure is the permanent campaign.

The permanent campaign is the political ideology of our age. It combines image-making with strategic calculation. Under the permanent campaign governing is turned into a perpetual campaign. Moreover, it remakes government into an instrument designed to sustain an elected official's public popularity. It is the engineering of consent with a vengeance. Popularity, however, isn't demanded for a frivolous reason. The permanent campaign is truly a program of statecraft. It seeks to restore the legitimacy of the state by maintaining the credibility of politicians. Credibility is verified by winning, staying in power. And legitimacy is confused with popularity. A president, especially, may believe that he personifies the government since he was chosen, after all, as the sole representative of the entire country. A loss of his popularity, therefore, can be interpreted as a blow against the American system. As a result, his sense of urgency to better his ratings increases, and so does his reliance on the techniques of the permanent campaign. In doing so, he makes government even more of a permanent campaign. Richard Nixon and Jimmy Carter made this same error in different ways. Nixon's permanent campaign was strategic politics without limitations, abstract military thought carried to paramilitary extremes. Carter's permanent campaign is strategic politics without clear policy.

The permanent campaign is the "game plan" for the embattled politician. He is increasingly beleaguered because he fails to distinguish between governing and campaigning. Having won office by appealing to uncommitted voters makes his base of support weak. He falls back on the calculations that served him so well in the first place. The citizenry is viewed as a mass of fluid voters who can be appeased by appearances, occasional drama, and clever rhetoric. Campaigning never ends. What was once a forced march for votes becomes unceasing forays for public approval.

The permanent campaign, the doctrine of the consultants, is, in a curious way, the American version of Russian revolutionist Leon Trotsky's permanent revolution. In Trotsky's theory the revolution never ceases once it has begun; its fires are stoked until it has engulfed the world. The revolution is built by making the revolution. It goes on forever. Like Trotsky's permanent revolution, the permanent campaign is a process of continuing transformation. It never stops, but continues once its practitioners take power. But unlike the permanent revolution there are not necessarily any idealistic social goals to be realized in the permanent campaign. Because the goals of the permanent revolution were so utopian and the stakes seemed so high, Trotsky was willing to justify the means by the ends. He also depended on a political party to carry out these tasks. In the permanent campaign parties are weak, media is strong, and the means are the ends. Pragmatism unfolds to reveal more pragmatism. The permanent campaign enshrines the pragmatism of the political party without the party. It appropriates the ideology of the American party — to the victor belong the spoils — without any constituency beyond phantom public opinion. This ideology presents itself as objective social science, particularly as polling.

The permanent campaign is unavoidable for a president because winning primaries, rather than securing the backing of party bosses, is the key to the presidential nomination. With the new reforms — an attempt to make democracy more direct and participatory — primaries have proliferated. In 1960, there were very few primaries and they were mainly of symbolic importance. John F. Kennedy used them as vehicles to establish certain campaign themes — that as a Catholic he could beat a Protestant in West Virginia, for instance — not as a technique for gathering delegates. Even up to 1968 the primaries were symbolic. When Lyndon B. Johnson did poorly in the New Hampshire primary against antiwar insurgent Eugene McCarthy his presidency was, in effect, finished. The vote was a blow to the legitimacy of his rule; although he could have won, he could not go on. Shortly afterward, he abdicated. Now, with thirty-five primaries, a candidate can keep going and going, provided there are enough funds. The expanded length of the primary season and the shortened time between primaries has increased reliance on the consultants. With only one or two weeks to blitz a state, a candidate must depend upon the medium that has the most extensive reach. And using television heavily, of course, requires a consultant to program effective commercials.

Years of preparation may be necessary to win an election. For a president to remain credible, he must be powerful, at least powerful enough to win renomination. He must campaign early and often. And the easiest way to do that is to turn governing into a campaign; there is no line of separation. Consultants, then, are brought into the sanctums of government to use the prerogatives of office to further the politician's cause.

Between 1960 and 1980, the permanent campaign thrived mainly on the presidential level. Patrick Caddell, Jimmy Carter's pollster, was the first consultant to serve as a self-conscious spokesman in favor of its implementation. But in the future the method of the permanent campaign will permeate politics down to the most remote legislative district as politicians feel the need to retain consultants to give them the advantage. For different candidates, the permanent campaign will assume different shapes; but whichever candidate triumphs, the permanent campaign will remain. The permanent campaign is not the game plan of any specific politician; it is a description of the new process of American politics.

## CHAPTER ONE

# THE INTERPRETATION OF AMERICAN DREAMS

## EDWARD L. BERNAYS

A common thread is woven through American political campaigns. It is the handicraft of political consultants, often called the image-makers, a new elite in politics. I began my inquiry into their origins, influence, and meaning as near the beginning as I could. I knocked on the massive windowless black door of a white clapboard mansion on elegant Brattle Street in Cambridge, Massachusetts. A short, shoeless old man wearing a knit tie loosened at the collar answered. In a soft voice he apologized for his sore throat. In spite of his infirmity and advanced age of eighty-eight, he was eager to talk. I was invited into his booklined sitting room where he motioned for me to sit on the couch.

Propped comfortably on a pillow was a doll resembling Sigmund Freud.

"I don't know how that got here," said Edward L. Bernays, founding father of American advertising, the first presidential media adviser, and Sigmund Freud's nephew. Bernays is quite literally the Freudian version of the American success story: He is a son of Austrian immigrants who taught the New World its own special techniques of communication. Now wizened, he is an American type from an era that has passed and a prophet to an era that has only recently dawned. He is a seminal figure. He climbed to the top of American society, or at least to the penthouse of the Sherry Netherlands Hotel on Fifth Avenue in New York, where he maintained a luxurious apartment for years. He was enchanted with the certainty of science and the power of the scientific method, trying to do for public relations what Freud did for the human mind. His uncle was his role model.

Bernays sought to overcome the instinctual motive in politics and business, replacing it with rational expertise. In striving for conscious control through the application of technique, he stimulated the mass unconsciousness, which once unleashed by the suggestions and appeals of advertising couldn't be contained. By creating modern advertising, Bernays helped create modern public opinion itself. He was the first person to apply directly Freudian inspired ideas to American conditions.

Everything that Bernays developed in his career can be seen in some form in the politics of the 1980s. Ploys and stratagems may capture the public imagination with their apparent originality; yet whatever is tried is not as novel as it may seem. For it was Bernays who in the 1920s invented the media event, the latent message, appeals of indirection, and initiated market research. He introduced the scientific approach to problems of public opinion, developing a coherent conceptual understanding of advertising that he called the "engineering of consent." This social doctrine has been used to understand and manipulate the psyches of voters as well as consumers. More, Bernays established the role of the media consultant as respectable and essential. The contemporary political image-makers can trace their lineage back to him. In his day he was a master of symbolism. In the political campaigns of today we see an elaboration of Bernays's ideas.

During our talk Bernays padded in his stocking feet to a bookcase, removing a heavy leather-bound tome stamped with gilt lettering. The book is about Edward L. Bernays; it contains all references to him in magazines, newspapers, and books, as well as abstract descriptions of every one of his numerous publications. Bernays has a reputation as a self-promoter, which is like accusing a fish of swimming. It's not surprising that Bernays advertises himself. He also sermonizes. Fortunately, he has something to say. His reminiscences might sound like name dropping to an eavesdropper, but Bernays is merely mentioning in passing the great and near-great with whom he dealt on a quotidian basis. Few of the celebrated men and women he speaks of, however, were as distinguished as members of his own family.

In the old country the Bernays family was one of high culture. Edward's great-grandfather was the chief rabbi of Hamburg, a relation of the poet Heinrich Heine. This great-grandfather's brother was the first publisher of Heine's poetry and was an acquaintance of Karl Marx. The rabbi had three sons, two of whom became university professors; another son, a merchant, moved to Vienna to become the secretary to a well-known economist. His son, Eli, took over this position after his death. Eli was Edward's father. He married Sigmund Freud's sister four years before Freud married Eli Bernays's sister. The Bernays-Freud tie was doubly bound. When Eli emigrated to America to set up a business as a grain dealer, Freud financed him through the difficult transition period. And Edward's sister lived with Freud for a year while the family settled in New York.

In the upstairs study of the Bernays home in Cambridge the walls are covered with memorable photographs from a lifetime of work with presidents and other dignitaries. Bernays points a craggy finger at one picture in particular. It shows the Bernays-Freud brood of cousins, attired in traditional lederhosen and blouses. Standing on the right side of the picture, part of the group but separate, is Freud — a figure of authority, holding his familiar cigar, wearing a tweed suit, and staring with a penetrating gaze directly at the camera. Freud at this time was gaining a notable reputation for his work among scientific circles in Europe. He was virtually unknown in America. Bernays was one of the few Americans who had read his writings, understood them, and had access to Freud on an intimate basis. The closeness of the relationship made assimilation of Freud's work that much easier. Knowing what Freud was up to was important in order to follow the progress of the family. Freud was a household topic. In 1913, after graduating from Cornell, Edward traveled to Europe to spend time with the Freuds. He regarded Freud's daughter Anna, his first cousin, as a "close sister." He and Freud took long walks through the woods together. "I wish I had taken notes and preserved what he said," Bernays says, "but it all seemed so natural that I took it for granted."

Edward admired his uncle and wished to emulate him in some way; but he was not cut out to be a scientist and it was unclear what path his career might take. Freud stood as an intellectual ideal. Bernays wanted to combine worldly pursuit with cultural endeavor. He didn't want to be a mere businessman.

After his European trip, he drifted to Broadway, attracted to the theater. He began to compose publicity for actors and producers. In 1916, he was named the publicity manager of a musical playbill handed out to theater patrons. The *New York Times* duly took note of his new position, but referred to him simply as a "manager," failing to report any connection to publicity. At that time, mention of publicity was forbidden in the pages of the upright *Times*. The reason for its reticence was linked to the development of the paper's image.

In the 1830s, advertising began to become a significant source of revenue for newspapers; as a gesture of good will the papers began to run what were called reading notices in their pages. These articles, run as news, proclaimed the virtues of advertised products. With the rise of the idea of journalistic objectivity as a standard of reliability, leading newspaper publishers joined together in the American Newspaper Publishers Association to ban reading notices. They did not want their papers viewed as grubby commercial vehicles, extensions of their advertisers.

At the same time, another journalistic movement burgeoned, reflecting the reformist, radical tenor of the early twentieth century. Investigative journalists, labeled "muckrakers" by President Theodore Roosevelt, exposed the corruption of newly formed monopolies. Trustbusting became a popular political cause. In defense, the corporations, especially the utility companies, put on their payrolls police reporters, so called because they got their stories by hanging out in police stations. The technique of these unlikely corporate spokesmen was "whitewash," another new term; they offered the public whatever excuses for their employers' avarice they could fabricate.

In 1915, Ivy Lee, a seasoned newspaperman, aide to minor politicians, opened his publicity firm — one of the first. He was promptly hired by the Rockefellers to spruce up their image in the aftermath of the Ludlow massacre in which striking miners and their families were gunned down. His misleading reports about this tragic incident were more clever and contrived than the typical work of the whitewashers. Ivy had advanced the state of the art. He also advised John D. Rockefeller to hand out dimes to street urchins as a way to impress the public with his philanthropy. The Rockefellers rewarded Ivy with a handsome retainer, and he prospered. At a gathering of moguls, he captiously explained his credo: "Crowds are led by symbols and phrases." His most notable symbol was Betty Crocker; his most memorable phrase dubbed Wheaties cereal the "Breakfast of Champions."

In the early 1930s Ivy Lee advised Hitler on how to improve the image of the Nazi government in the United States. His connection to the Nazis was revealed in the press and he was called to testify before a congressional committee. Four months later he died, his health broken. He had died of publicity.

Thus, before World War I, public relations was a phrase known only to those who practiced it. Newspapers like the *New York Times* did not want to reveal cognizance of the trade, which had a seamy reputation. References to publicity, publishers felt, also might recall the unpleasant history of reading notices, dredging up memories of an age when the newspapers were not very authoritative. So, in the *Times*, Bernays was just a "manager."

If Bernays was a shill, it was for truly great artists. His clients included Diaghilev's Ballets Russes and its star dancer, Nijinsky, and the renowned tenor Enrico Caruso. However, Bernays's Broadway fling was interrupted by the war, which opened up for him unparalleled opportunities. He was recruited for the Committee on Public Information, a new branch of government formed to direct a stream of images at the public to inspire patriotism and sacrifice. George Creel, the muckraking reporter who headed the committee, held cabinet-level rank in Woodrow Wilson's administration, so important was this work considered. It was, in fact, the first modern nationwide propaganda campaign. The committee specialized in proliferating stories of pillaging Huns; its products also had a distinctly antiunion tinge. "Creel," says Bernays, "didn't think of it at all as a powerful instrument of war that would inform or provide information. That was far from his mind. He put on this committee newspapermen like himself. I was practically the only one to have had experience with what was called publicity. After the war, I wrote that there was no organized approach to converting people's minds. Creel wrote me a note. 'Don't forget,' he said, 'that we knew nothing of these matters then. We simply gathered together men to do what we thought was the job at the time.' "

During the war Bernays also handled the account of the Ingersoll Company, a manufacturer of wristwatches, which were then regarded as effeminate jewelry. How could this image be overcome? Bernays did some research. He discovered that all soldiers carried pocket watches. In order to see what time it was at night they had to strike matches, which, if they were in the trenches, attracted the attention of snipers. Wristwatches with luminous dials, he reasoned, could save lives. It would also boost Ingersoll. The War Department, convinced by his logic, soon issued wristwatches as standard equipment. With combat soldiers wearing them, the stigma was removed. Bernays tied a watch around the wrist of virtually every male in the country. It was an early instance of the comprehensive advertising approach in which research could help create a consuming public by altering a product's image.

The war provided Bernays with a grand vista of society. He could observe from his vantage point on the Committee of Public Information the roiling shape of public opinion and its response to various appeals. "It was war," Bernays writes in his memoirs, "which opened the eyes of the intelligent few in all departments of life to the possibilities of regimenting the modern mind." The year after the war ended he opened his publicity firm, with his own determined notion of what advertising could do.

One of his first actions was to advise Tomáš Masaryk, the president of the new republic of Czechoslovakia. Masaryk mentioned to Bernays the date on which he planned to declare independence. Bernays objected. The date wouldn't garner maximum publicity. He urged that independence day be proclaimed on a Sunday so that it would make the important Monday headlines. "But, that would be making history for the cables," Masaryk protested. "But," replied Bernays, "it is the cables which make history." Czech independence was announced on a Sunday.

Soon after his publicity firm was opened, Bernays made a splash, establishing himself in the way he wished. In 1920, testifying in a dispute about a fee for his client Caruso, he identified his profession on the witness stand as "counsel on public relations." Nobody had ever heard of this before. The *New York World* headlined a story: FIND NEW PROFESSION IN CARUSO TRIAL.

"Why shouldn't there be an expert on the public, just as there is an expert on health and law and accountancy?" asks Bernays. The idea of being a "counsel" elevated the publicity man into a profession as rigorous and specialized, Bernays believed, as any other. The counsel would do more than whitewash the client or inform the public about the client's good deeds and intentions. The counsel would be an expert on public desires in order best to advise a client on how to make a precise appeal. In Bernays's view, public relations was a branch of the social sciences, blending psychology and sociology; it was a craft requiring arcane skills to deal with the masses. A certain objective stance was necessary, for the counsel was, above all, a professional; his creed was professionalism. The modern advertising executive was born.

In 1923, Bernays published his theory of the public relations counsel in a book entitled *Crystallizing Public Opinion*. He explained in this book how the public was divided into many publics; it was segmented. A "segmental" approach to opinion, it followed, was required. The most efficacious segment to reach was that one which would influence all the others. This was a kind of trickle-down theory of opinion. Bernays called the key segment "group leaders and opinion molders." If you could affect them, they would do your work for you. Bernays spelled out the implications of that argument in his 1928 book, *Propaganda*. "The conscious and intelligent manipulation of the organized habits and opinions of the masses is an important element in democratic society," he wrote. "Those who manipulate this unseen mechanism of society constitute an invisible government which is the true ruling power of this country." In a bluntly titled article, "Manipulating Public Opinion," published the same year as *Propaganda*, he discussed the need to modify attitudes of the public to overcome "the inertia of established traditions and prejudices." He posited this as a great leap forward for the new profession of public relations, business in general, and society, which would reap the benefits of these rational techniques.

Bernays argued his position so strenuously partly because of the backward state of public relations. "There were people who just had the knack of winning friends and influencing people by hunches and insight," he remembers. "But the whole society became more literate through the greater mass distribution of ideas by the new technologies of communications. And with that came a greater awareness of the realities of human life. You could no longer deal with the public on the basis of hunches and insight. You had to deal with it on the basis of scientifically evaluating the hopes, aspirations, ignorances, knowledge, apathy and prejudices of the public. Unless you know what the people want and what their attitudes are you can't move ahead."

He was dismayed when he learned that Joseph Goebbels, the Nazi minister of propaganda, displayed a copy of *Propaganda* in his library. "They were going after the thing on a scientific basis. This had become social science," says Bernays. "I felt very badly, but I couldn't do anything about it. After all, you can take a computer and if you put it into the hands of a crook he can take $15 million out of a bank."

Bernays kept refining his theory over the years. *Crystallizing Public Opinion* begat *Propaganda*, which, in turn, begat *The Engineering of Consent*. Each new formulation was a more comprehensive treatment than the last. In his essay, "The Engineering of Consent," Bernays attained a final synthesis of his thought. He rationalized the use of all the techniques he had developed in the service of an overarching concept. The engineering of consent is "the application of scientific practices and tried practices in the task of getting people to support ideas and programs." By employing the word *engineering* Bernays connoted the scientific method, while the use of the word *consent* implied that the public had to be continually won over, that the appeal had to be constant. Consent, if it was a choice, could be denied. The legitimacy of "ideas and programs" might be at stake. But by assiduous deployment of the arsenal of opinion making, consent could be maintained. This would translate into sales of a product, or perhaps votes for a politician.

But how could consent be engineered? This wasn't an occult mystery, Bernays stated. The methods were at hand: market research, polls, and symbols. The research survey was "a prerequisite to the establishment of policies, strategies, planning and activities." Polling, the principal tool of the surveys, was "the traveler's road map." And symbols were "a shortcut to understanding . . . the currency of propaganda."

Bernays sent his uncle copies of his books, seeking comments and approval. "Freud thought engineering consent was good," says Bernays. "I have some nice letters from him on it. He thought it was very American." Freud was intrigued by his nephew's work. "As a truly American production it interested me greatly," wrote Freud upon reading *Crystallizing Public Opinion*. It should be remembered that after his only visit, Freud called America "a gigantic mistake," meaning the entire culture, not his trip. "To Freud as a scientist," explains Bernays, "to deal with public opinion in the way I suggested in my first book was a completely new idea to a man who lived in a traditional society. After all, he grew up in a city in which the ruling power, the Hapsburgs, had been there since the 1500s. I was applying to the mass what he was applying to the individual."

In the twenties, Freud suddenly became a popular thinker in America. His works were widely read, debated and misinterpreted, used to explain or justify breaking the bounds of sexual puritanism in the Jazz Age. Bernays's contribution to the twenties' eclectic intellectual environment was signal. He had the essential contact, after all. It was Bernays who translated and arranged for the American publication of Freud's *The Introductory Lectures on Psychoanalysis,* which became one of the required texts of the decade.

But Bernays was already familiar with Freud's thinking. He wasn't just beginning to grasp its framework. He wanted to build on it in his own way. He sought more than understanding; he wanted action. "The counsel on public relations not only knows what news value is," he said, "but knowing it, he is in a position to make news happen. He is a creator of events."

Bernays developed his own theory of advertising action, clearly influenced in its formulation by Freud. Bernays would make things happen through what he called the "overt act," what today we call the media event. Bernays's phrase had neat Freudian implications. By making an act overt, he was merely drawing into the open that which was inherent, or perhaps suppressed. He was engaged in acts of desublimation. To wit: George Washington Hill, president of the American Tobacco Company, one of Bernays's clients, had a problem. Women would not smoke cigarettes in the street. It was considered unfeminine. How could this be changed? Bernays consulted the Freudian psychoanalyst A. A. Brill to solve the perplexing case of Lucky Strikes. Brill told Bernays that cigarettes were associated with men; they were hidden symbols, "torches of freedom." To emphasize that point, while dispelling the negative connotations of public smoking, Bernays had his secretary sign telegrams that were sent to a list of debutantes supplied by a friend of Bernays's who worked for *Vogue* magazine. IN THE INTERESTS OF EQUALITY OF THE SEXES AND TO FIGHT ANOTHER SEX TABOO, the telegram read, I AND OTHER YOUNG WOMEN WILL LIGHT ANOTHER TORCH OF FREEDOM BY SMOKING CIGARETTES WHILE STROLLING DOWN FIFTH AVENUE EASTER SUNDAY. WE ARE DOING THIS TO COMBAT THE SILLY PREJUDICE

THAT THE CIGARETTE IS SUITABLE FOR THE HOME, THE RESTAU-
RANT, THE TAXICAB, THE THEATER LOBBY BUT NEVER NO NEVER
FOR THE SIDEWALK. Ten debutantes showed up, marching in a
phalanx under a cloud of smoke emanating from their cigarettes.
It was front-page news everywhere. "Age-old customs, I
learned," Bernays wrote, "could be broken down by a dramatic
appeal, disseminated by the network of media." This overt act was
only one part of the Lucky Strikes campaign. Brill also informed
Bernays that cigarettes were phallic symbols and that "every
normal man or woman can identify" with a man offering a cigarette
to a woman. By using a latent sexual message in the advertising,
resistance to public smoking was finally overcome. The public was
seduced.

By staging overt acts Bernays enabled his clients to present
their dreams as fulfilled. Overt acts weren't distortions of reality,
but attempts to define reality. "The dream is the disguised fulfillment of a repressed wish," wrote Freud. "Actions cannot lie,"
said Bernays. He knew that there was no such thing as a pseudo-
event, however contrived. All events are representations of
reality. Overt acts are accurate events in themselves; they really
happen. They reflect, on a deep level, the substance of dreams.
Although overt acts, because they aren't spontaneous, may seem
artificial, this in no way drains them of meaning. A quality of
artificiality actually might make the overt act more intense and
more powerful because it bypasses the usual barrier of psychic
censorship in which orderly progression is expected.

Bernays's brilliance in choreographing overt acts led eventually
to his most spectacular contract — the grandest overt act of the
twenties, the crowning event of the decade, a paean to prosperity,
technology, and power. On October 21, 1929, with the country
calmly riding the crest of an economic boom, 500 of the most
important people of the time gathered in Dearborn, Michigan, to
honor Thomas Edison on the fiftieth anniversary of the invention
of the electric light bulb. General Electric sponsored the event,

but Bernays toned down any commercial aspects. GE would benefit far more if its sponsorship appeared to be a public service. This was what Bernays called indirection.

President Herbert Hoover was there. So were John D. Rockefeller and the other leading Wall Street tycoons. Henry Ford played host for this Golden Jubilee of Light. He had transformed a nearby town, Greenfield Village, into a reproduction of America as it had been fifty years before. Villagers in rustic clothes greeted the guests; horse-drawn carriages took them on tours of authentic looking Greenfield with its reconstructed general store, tavern, and depot. The barons of success were afforded the opportunity to gaze upon a world they had destroyed and for which they felt a yearning nostalgia. The testimonial dinner for Edison, which took place after the tours and a ride in an old-time train, was broadcast on the radio to a national hook-up. Radio was a new medium then, a new component of technology controlled by the businessmen present at the big event, and Bernays exploited it fully. While Edison recreated his invention of the incandescent bulb millions of radio listeners tuned in. "The lamp is now ready, as it was a half century ago!" the announcer narrated. "Will it light? Will it burn? Edison touches the wire . . . Ladies and gentlemen — it lights! Light's Golden Jubilee has come to a triumphant climax!"

The Golden Jubilee was as much a demonstration of the new techniques of propaganda as it was a celebration of what the free enterprise system had wrought. Bernays carefully staged this epiphany of capitalism as an evocative historic moment, but the event itself was a new kind of invention. Eight days after the Golden Jubilee the stock market crashed. Bernays's overt act was the summation of an era. And he was soon to be hailed in *Time* magazine as "US Publicist Number One." His stock had risen.

When prosperity did not appear to be around the corner, Herbert Hoover, who remembered Bernays from the Golden Jubilee, called him in for advice. "I went to the White House and listened intently, and my advice to him was, I thought, good," says

Bernays. "Hoover said very little. He got out a box of Hoya de Monterrey cigars and offered me one. I should have kept it as a souvenir." Hoover's friend, journalist Mark Sullivan, spoke to Bernays after the encounter. "Ed," he said, "the president has been enthusiastic about what you told him." "How do you know?" replied Bernays. "He didn't say a word."

Later, Bernays attended a dinner where he happened to be seated next to James Farley, the Democratic National Chairman, who was Franklin D. Roosevelt's campaign manager. "I said, 'Why did you nominate Roosevelt at the convention?' He said, 'He had a hell of a good name, he had a good voice, and he had a great smile.' And I said, 'Mr. Farley, what books did you read on politics?' He said, 'I didn't know there were no books.' "

Hoover was not the first president who requested the Bernays touch. Hoover's predecessor, Calvin Coolidge, had an image problem: he appeared to be cold and aloof. Perhaps Bernays could do something about this. A White House aide suggested inviting America's literary lights to dine with the president. Bernays dismissed this idea. He knew what would work. *Mammy!* Before Coolidge could say "Swanee River," Al Jolson and forty vaudevillians were sitting at his breakfast table eating griddle cakes. The *New York Times* headlined: ACTORS EAT CAKES WITH THE COOLIDGES . . . PRESIDENT NEARLY LAUGHS. It was the first overt act initiated by a media adviser for a president.

The last president Bernays personally offered advice to was Dwight Eisenhower. Bernays was invited to the White House to speak about the use of public relations in international affairs. Ike passively listened to Bernays for half an hour and then said, "I agree totally with your people-to-people approach." He flashed his famous grin and retreated to the golf course. "He didn't understand anything I said," recalls Bernays. "It was as if he hadn't heard me speak."

Bernays believed that politicians could profitably use the concept of the engineering of consent. In the 1930s he urged the creation of a cabinet position of secretary of public relations, a prescient prediction, which *Time* magazine termed "bizarre." In an article he wrote in 1928 he laid out the broad outlines of the future to follow. "I said that politics had failed to keep up with business methods in the mass distribution of ideas and products. I recommended a program for remedying the defects. What I said was that there is a terrific time lag between politics and the methods business uses to deal with the public. I said that the emotional content of a campaign must coincide in every way with the basic plans of the campaign and all its minor details. It must be adapted to the many groups of the public to which it is to be aimed. And it must conform to the media in the distribution of ideas. The political campaign must define the various channels through which it can appeal. I said that political supply and demand can be brought closer together and that scientific methods and sales charts will supersede the guesses and the betting that played so big a part in the campaigning then. It's interesting to me that at that time the politician thought he was self-sufficient, that he only had to depend on his insight and personality to win elections. Politicians ran using the spoken word . . . and nothing else. You know that America is a country in which the cultural time lag is one of the dominant elements. In 1928 the politicians were a generation behind. And politicians, who really have to deal with the public, have not caught up yet with the work I did in 1928."

He sees the advent of the political consultant as an expected development, another case of a situation that requires experts. To him, consultants are counsels on a specialized branch of public relations. "I would say that political consultants are advisers on the attitudes and actions of politicians in order to try to gain for them the office they desire," Bernays says. "They approach the problem on the basis of evaluation of the attitudes of the public. They advise on attitudes which presumably will win over 51 percent of the vote. This society has become so complex that just as technicians are needed to advise heads of banks on their practices the modern politician needs somebody to advise him on this complicated public."

But there can be both capable and incompetent technicians. Bernays is not impressed with Jimmy Carter's secretary of public relations, Gerald Rafshoon. "How can people be leaders if they don't know the technique of leadership?" he demands, frustrated that the principles he has enunciated during his career haven't been learned yet. "The advice I would give Gerald Rafshoon would be to get consultants who know more than he does. How can he with limited experience interpret the godhead symbol to over 200 million people unless he's a divine spirit who's learned everything by intuition? But the only danger I can see in Mr. Rafshoon is the danger to Mr. Carter." And that is his final advice to a president.

Edward L. Bernays was the forerunner of the modern political consultant. Without his work American society and politics would not be the same. All his contributions may have been inevitable, but it was he who made them. And that makes the difference. Personal nuances, which can develop into whole professions and systems of thought, affect history.

Bernays's faith in science and his belief in linear progress permitted him to view the growth of literacy and the spreading network of communications as catalysts of a new enlightenment. "The cure for propaganda is more propaganda," he still says. Yet his early-twentieth-century beliefs coupled with his innovative techniques have stunningly set the scene for late-twentieth-century America. In a sense, his life was a prophetic overt act.

Bernays taps the huge book about himself resting on his knees. He looks down at the Freud doll on the couch and says, "Ivy Lee himself told me many years ago, 'This is an art, not a profession. It will die with you and me.' Now look at the damn thing."

## CHAPTER TWO

# THE ALIENATION FACTOR

## PATRICK CADDELL

The office of Pat Caddell, President Jimmy Carter's pollster, is located in the penthouse of the National Permanent Federal Savings and Loan Building at 1775 Pennsylvania Avenue, two blocks from the White House. On the wall is a larger-than-life portrait of the president painted by pop artist Andy Warhol, whose most notable thought is that everybody would be famous for 15 minutes. Caddell's desk is piled high with memos. One of them is his prognosis for the 1980 campaign. One is a numbered list of Jimmy Carter's "strengths" and "weaknesses." Caddell puts his feet up on his desk, careful not to disturb the papers.

He is the *wunderkind* of American politics at age 29, one of the most influential men in the country, a confidant of the president, and a multimillionaire. He is tall, thinner than ever, having recently shed fifty pounds, and he sports a neatly trimmed beard with a gray streak in it, clearly cultivated to make him look older. "It's a little schizophrenic being younger," he says. "You have to act like a grownup even at times when you're not. Growing up when you have to be grownup in a political sense is a little difficult to balance."

No previous pollster has had such an intimate relationship with a president as Caddell has had with Carter. Franklin D. Roosevelt was the first president to employ the services of a pollster, but it was simply to gauge his popularity. The reigning pollster in the immediate postwar era was George Gallup, who incorrectly predicted that Thomas Dewey would beat Harry Truman for the presidency in 1948. While Gallup syndicated his forecasts in the newspapers, he was privately advising Dewey on "the pulse of democracy," as Gallup called it. His technique consisted of asking scientifically selected samples of voters their positions on issues and politicians. The key questions were always answered with a yes, no, or undecided. To Gallup, public opinion consisted of "facts."

Louis Harris, adviser to John F. Kennedy, dominated the profession after Gallup. Harris used the old techniques of forecasting in specifically political ways, testing key districts and states; he advised the candidate where to attack and when to retreat. In 1960, Harris urged Kennedy to enter the West Virginia primary. Kennedy instinctively wanted to avoid this contest because he felt that the Catholic issue would be raised in a damaging way in this overwhelmingly Protestant state. Harris's polls, however, showed Kennedy with a wide lead over Hubert Humphrey. Kennedy entered the race there, but slipped in the polls; he won mainly through exploitation of his vast personal resources. After that, Harris was used as an ornament, not as a strategist. Harris's technique was crude, not sophisticated enough to pick up latent threats. He possessed only horserace numbers, although he used them with a strategic sensibility. But with the Kennedys one mistake was one mistake too many. When Harris began to discuss the mood of the country with the candidate, Kennedy cut him off: "Just give me the numbers, Lou. I can figure them out."

Pat Caddell is the premier pollster of the new generation. His role as a strategist is central to the Carter presidency. Perhaps more than anyone besides Carter, he has defined problems and objectives. Caddell has refined strategic politics into a quantified science, using polls as a weapon. He has forged the era of the antipolitician, the outsider candidate who can inflict piercing wounds on an incumbent, but whose platform is thematic rather than programmatic. The antipolitician emerges logically from Caddell's particular techniques. Crucial to his technique is his theory of voter alienation, which he also calls "malaise." This is also the key to strategic politics because alienated voters are fluid voters, the object of all politicians' desire; alienated voters tend to be the most volatile sector of the electorate, the swing vote to whom carefully calculated appeals are made.

To Caddell, alienation can be roughly defined as a lack of trust in government and politicians. Although alienation is an abstract emotion, it can be measured. Caddell uses an economic metaphor to quantify alienation: the voter as investor. Voting is triggered by self-interest. Voters aren't alienated because they lack civic motivation, but rather because their investment has been debased. Alienated voters are beyond the appeal of party loyalty and beyond idealistic concern. Their preoccupation is with what-have-you-done-for-me-lately, a phrase used as the title of a paper on the subject written by Caddell's business partners for the *American Political Science Review.*

On the basis of this metaphor Caddell constructs "trust indices" to measure alienation precisely. He invents statistical "ladders of confidence." His elaborate polls for his political clients are double-backed profiles of the candidate and his opponent; the same questions are asked about each and the results are contrasted. Through his special techniques Caddell deciphers every weakness and strength of both politicians. He segments the electorate finely so that he knows with which groups points can be scored. He knows the intensity of feeling on any issue by any group. He can tell, for example, if the candidate is perceived as mildly ineffective by thirty-year-old, college-educated white females with children. If he picks that up early in the campaign, the candidate's image can be adjusted. Caddell tests voters on their discontents about American society and through equations can correlate the results to specific politicians. He is especially good working for an insurgent against an incumbent who has a record and established image to attack. Caddell has pushed polling far beyond the one-dimensional survey used to make informed forecasts. He doesn't make predictions, he makes events.

The stage was set for the investment theory of voting by the collapse of the patronage theory of voting. When the New Deal coalition became incapable of servicing all its constituencies during the Vietnam War, creating, as Lyndon Johnson put it, a conflict between "guns and butter," disappointment was rife. Caddell began operating in the aftermath of the Democratic party's fragmentation. By locating the source of alienation in lack of trust of government and politicians, Caddell created the era of the antipolitician. His analysis ultimately leads to a political dead end.

There are glaring contradictions in Caddell's theory. He talks, for example, about alienation as if it could be assuaged by purely political means. But this is not possible given nonmetaphorical conditions in the realm of economics, like the decline of real income. Caddell also neglects to account for a consumption theory of voting, in which voters are consumers who vote for those staging the best show. Caddell's thinking always undermines itself on the basis of its own calculations. By exploiting fluidity, the investment theory of voting becomes circular. Basing politics on appeals to alienated voters — the fluid voters — seems self-defeating, since as a politics without a fixed position, it creates more alienated voters. Carter may have been able to win the presidency on this basis, but he has found it difficult to govern with a permanent campaign. Caddell thinks Carter's political stance is unavoidable. "Jimmy Carter," he says, "is a natural extension of the change in American politics. It'd be crazy not to be."

Patrick Hayward Caddell is the son of a Coast Guard officer from Massachusetts. He attended Catholic parochial schools. When his father was reassigned to the Florida panhandle, which is a conservative, overwhelmingly Protestant region, Pat felt like an outsider. "It's an interesting posture to be in, an Irish Catholic Southerner. There are not very many of them," he says. In school he disliked mathematics, but was intrigued by statistics. When he was seventeen he decided to predict election outcomes for a class project. While the ballots were still being tabulated, he accurately forecast some very close local races. A local newspaper profiled the whiz kid, a story which was read by the Speaker of the Florida House of Representatives, who hired him to do some polling. Pat did polls then for $200, hiring his classmates to assist him. His work came to the attention of Jacksonville television station WJXT, which paid him to perform his magic act of predicting winners on the air; a youngster with a serious mien and a knowledge of the science of polling that was beyond the grasp of most viewers was an unusual attraction.

It was then that Pat discovered the alienation issue. "I remember one of the very first surveys I ever did was in 1968," he recalls. "There were people in Jacksonville, Florida, telling me that they were for either George Wallace or Bobby Kennedy." The desire for change, manifested in support of the two most volatile candidates in the race, implied a new alienation to Caddell. "When voters have little confidence in the ability of the system to produce for them, their attachment to the system and the value of their vote literally declines," he explains. "As it becomes of less value the reasons you will cast it become fewer. As you weaken those bonds you begin to have problems. That 1968 survey was the front end of this alienation issue."

While he was a student at Harvard, Pat borrowed money from a Jacksonville businessman who was impressed with his work to start a polling firm with two friends; the friends supplied statistical expertise, Pat supplied precocious interpretations and election experience. At Harvard his intellectual energies went into a study on the Wallace vote. To Pat, these were the most alienated voters; their disaffection had the potential of fragmenting the Democratic party. More, as an Irish Catholic liberal from the South, Pat had a personal concern with stopping the Wallace trend. Like others before him, he dreamed of a New South, freed from racist politics.

"In this area, Pat was a very passionate and morally concerned student," says Josiah Lee Auspitz, Caddell's tutor at Harvard and former president of the Ripon Society, a liberal Republican group. Caddell labored on the Wallace project through 1970 and 1971. At the time, Richard Nixon was advancing the idea that the South, turning hard right, could be brought into the Republican camp. Nixon's touted "Southern strategy" was an attempt to create a political realignment on a reactionary basis. Caddell doubted that the Wallace vote would become Republican. He postulated that a populist campaign, waged on economic issues, might attract both the Wallace and black voters. He noted, through analysis of recent elections, that Nixon's Southern strategy never really materialized; it was merely a wishful notion. Caddell wondered if Southern politics could change direction quickly, moving from support of Wallace to support of a New South candidate. "If you appeared to be a fresh face, an outsider, that would attract Wallaceites," says Auspitz, summing up his student's work. "This could be called the alienation issue. It is a lack of trust, emptied of content."

The candidate Caddell favored to win the 1972 Democratic nomination was Senator Harold Hughes of Iowa, a liberal and a former truck driver. He was the kind of populist candidate, Caddell thought, who might garner the Wallace vote. But Hughes's candidacy never got off the ground. So when the nascent campaign of George McGovern offered Caddell and his fledgling firm $500 to conduct a poll in New Hampshire in preparation for the primary there, Caddell accepted. In New Hampshire, he discovered that blue-collar workers were not solidly behind Edmund Muskie, the Democratic front-runner; they were fluid. Caddell had a conversation with Muskie's pollster and realized that the Muskie camp was unaware of the weakness.

Caddell urged McGovern to tour the factories of working-class Manchester and unfurl populist rhetoric. On the primary election day, McGovern scored heavily in these wards, demonstrating that he was not merely a liberal suburban protest candidate but also a nationally viable candidate. The campaign always attempted to recapture that moment, although it was never possible to repeat. After the disastrous Eagleton affair, in which McGovern's running mate's history of psychological problems became public and he refused to leave the ticket, forcing McGovern to dismiss him, Caddell informed the candidate that the injury done was almost irreparable. The losses could not be recouped. McGovern, who without the Eagleton incident might have staged a credible campaign, lost in a landslide to Richard Nixon.

That same year, though, Caddell worked in several senatorial races in which he played a major role, sharpening his technique. He was beginning to employ the idea of alienation in antipolitician campaigns with devastating effect. In Delaware he took a key part in the race of Joseph Biden against incumbent senator J. Caleb Boggs. Through his polls, Caddell discovered a latent public antipathy to Washington politicians. Rather than having Biden meet Boggs head-on with that issue, Caddell preferred an indirect approach. Biden did not criticize Boggs, but Washington. He followed a broad theme of establishing himself as the tribune of the taxpayer downtrodden by the federal government. Since there were no specifics mentioned, Caddell's candidate was able to maneuver quickly while the opponent was left behind to deal with the fog cast around him. Biden won.

For his part, Caddell was learning how to quantify alienation through his experiences in these campaigns. He was testing the level of alienation among different segments of the electorate. From this he could detect the weaknesses of incumbents in ways they never suspected. Someone polled by Caddell would be given a card with a rating scale from one to seven. They would be read a list of words, called semantic differentials: honest, cold, warm, trustworthy. How would you rate the candidate on the scale? Other questions would be asked using the one to seven scale. Then you would be asked what you disliked about the candidate, and then what you liked about him. Finally, a key statement, "The candidate really cares about people like me," would be read. "You come up with the worst things you can think of and see if people will buy them," says Jeffrey Smith, a former Caddell polling partner and now political aide to Senator George McGovern. "It helps in the implementation of the campaign. Pretty soon you get to see a pattern developing. How does it look for 18- to 25-year-olds? Blacks? Women? You can say you're in trouble with blue-collar Catholics who have less confidence in the future. So you pick out your campaign themes to see if they'll go."

In the Caddell lexicon themes are called issue levers. In 1976, Cambridge Survey Research (CRS), Caddell's firm, worked on behalf of Westinghouse in California to defeat an antinuclear power initiative. In what CSR called its Public Nuclear Acceptance Campaign, a memo was written urging the nuclear power industry to "find levers" with "emotional intensity." With Caddell's help Westinghouse located these levers.

Smith was one of the CSR people working on the Westinghouse campaign. He explains how the issue levers were pulled: "Say black women were a five on a one to seven scale of opposition to nuclear power. But they were soft on the cost of energy. That was an issue to them. We targeted them and communicated that nuclear power was cheaper. We got black women for nuclear power on television talk shows. It's a small thing. But sure enough black women began to shift. Instead of a five, they've become a three. You can manipulate — that's a bad word — I'll say influence."

Caddell's polling was a systematic attempt to take advantage of alienation. But Caddell was motivated by political objectives that were larger than mere expediency. He still sought to renew the South and stymie Wallace, transforming that alienation vote into a base for a different kind of candidate. Jimmy Carter, therefore, was the candidate Caddell was looking for.

"Pat Caddell is the one key person responsible for inflicting Jimmy Carter on this country," insists Jeffrey Smith. "The key development was in the Florida primary. It was so crucial for Carter to drive a stake in Wallace's heart. In that state Caddell made the difference."

But it was more than in Florida that Caddell tipped the balance. He used his razor-sharp polls throughout the primary campaign, knocking off Carter's opponents one by one, first Wallace, then Henry Jackson, then Morris Udall, until there were none left. Florida was the great experiment; it was a testing site for Caddell's theories. On the basis of Caddell's polls a theme was set early on, expressed in a slogan invented by Gerald Rafshoon, Carter's media man: "This time don't send them a message, send them a president." "Essentially," says Caddell, "we were trying to take votes away from Wallace. Once we were able to establish what the potential vote was we were able to allocate our resources to move those areas in doubt. We were not getting anything out of Dade County. Carter had a fairly good base in central Florida. We were getting tanked in northern Florida. There wasn't much we could do about that. We could go into Tampa Bay and turn that around. What we were really trying to do was to get across the perception that the Wallace vote was weak, that it was no more than a protest vote. We were trying to isolate those people. What we first tried to do was segment the electorate so that we could figure out who was going to be decisive. We could divide it not only geographically and not only by candidate preference but by other dimensions. I'd divide Wallace voters into Wallace voters with a racial component, Wallace voters with intensity, Wallace voters who were happy with things, those who could be dragged away. What we did was take 10 or 12 points away from Wallace in the course of that. We dragged it down from the mid-40s to the low 30s. We found Carter's background was important to people, as well as his general themes, such as being against Washington. We could make in south Florida a more cutting case against Wallace."

There were still difficulties. "Jackson's strategy was not to win but to have Wallace win Florida to deal a blow to Carter. Jackson was running to cut us. Once I was able to make an analysis of that situation, what Carter did, on his own instinct really, was to go at Jackson on the busing issue in north Florida. He just lambasted him for running a racist campaign in the Massachusetts primary. The theory was that if Carter hit Jackson on that issue he could hurt Jackson in south Florida with blacks. And if he did it in north Florida as a Southener he could do it without paying the damage. Everyone thought he had lost his mind. But we had to get that collection of minority votes going to Bayh, Shriver, Udall, who were on the ballot but not campaigning. It was about 15 percent of the votes. We had to get those votes into our column to win, and that's what happened. After New Hampshire, Carter was already a national candidate. But after Florida he never stopped being the front-runner."

By the Pennsylvania primary the Jackson campaign was able to spot the softness in the Carter vote. Carter was perceived as being unclear on the issues. He was, after all, following a thematic approach suggested by his own instincts and reinforced by the uses of Caddell's polls. Jackson prepared to strike directly at Carter on this weakness. But Caddell's polls picked up the same problem. He sought to remedy it before the Jackson response.

Television ads for Carter suddenly appeared to be very specific. "Jimmy Carter on tax reform . . . Jimmy Carter on inflation . . . Jimmy Carter on health care . . ." Before Jackson's television spots went on the air Carter had corrected his posture. "The problem," says Caddell, "was that the fuzzy issue had caught up with Carter. We had a lead we were holding. You could see the potential it had for chopping off a lot of support. Jerry [Rafshoon] simply changed the tag line on the spots. We were polling every day so we could monitor those kinds of problems and see in a tactical way that they had been addressed. We made decisions on where to go, all of the critical tactical things, using polling. We had a lead and we never lost it. There are a lot of things you can use polls for."

Rafshoon said about the episode: "We ran the same type of advertising in Pennsylvania as we had earlier, but we labeled it as issues." The Carter victory in Pennsylvania ended the Jackson candidacy.

Udall was next. "Udall needed to win something before he got to Ohio," says Caddell. "He assumed he was going to win South Dakota because senators McGovern and Abourezk were for him. And the party was for him because the senators were for him. But we outspent Udall in South Dakota. They don't even know to this day that they got outspent. We didn't tell anybody. What happened was that I took a poll in South Dakota. We got Carter to stop in Sioux Falls on the way out to Oregon, and Rapid City on the way back, two media hits. We just bought the state. It wasn't much to buy. And we ended up winning it. It just destroyed Udall as a candidate in Ohio." Which destroyed Udall as a candidate. Carter won an easy first ballot nomination.

President Gerald Ford's camp was keenly aware of the danger Caddell posed. In an internal memorandum on Caddell circulated within the upper echelons of the Ford campaign, tersely written like an intelligence report, Caddell's role in the Carter effort was emphasized: "The close connection between the candidate and his pollster has already had important tactical results. Caddell has polls always in the field on a basis sufficient to disaggregate key states and constituencies from a national sample. Hence there is the possibility of a quick response to any new shifts in opinion and their immediate communication to the candidate. The Ford operation, by contrast, as befits a presidential staff operation, has double or triple the reaction time to new voter moods — a real disadvantage in a short campaign." The Ford campaign memo on Caddell concluded on an ominous note: "On an institutional basis he is a generation ahead of most other techniques. No one has yet devised a system for protecting a GOP incumbent from the Caddell style alienation attack."

The subtleties of Caddell's polls aided Carter immeasurably in the general election campaign. Before the third television debate, for example, the polls telegraphed the information that young mothers were unsure of Carter; he wasn't communicating stability to them. So in the debate Carter had a subliminal message for them. He smiled more than ever and never got excited: Mister Rogers goes to Washington. Yet, in spite of Caddell's polls, Carter dropped 32 points to win only a narrow victory.

He assumed the presidency without a decisive mandate. He had to continue to court public opinion. Governing could not be separate from politics, and politics meant campaigning. After the victory Caddell wrote a 10,000-word memo to the president-elect advising him on the need for a permanent campaign, explaining the death of political parties and the alienation of the electorate, offering a list of symbolic actions, and suggesting a plan for the 1980 campaign. This memo, submitted to Carter on December 10, 1976, entitled "Initial Working Paper on Political Strategy," is one of the essential documents of modern American politics, the Carter administration's very own Federalist Paper.

"In devising a strategy for the Administration, it is important to recognize we cannot successfully separate politics and government," Caddell begins. "Occasionally the result of 'apolitical' government is positive, but most times it leads to disappointing the voters and eventual political disaster. When politics is divorced from government, it often happens that the talented, well-meaning people who staff the administration act without understanding the reasons 'they all' were elected and instead pursue policies which run contrary to public expectations and desires." Caddell comes promptly to his central point: "*Essentially, it is my thesis that governing with public approval requires a continuing political campaign* " (italics mine).

The pollster notes that the support Carter is receiving is superficial: fully half the electorate still doesn't know where he stands on the issues. Carter is viewed as inexperienced, "an individual who often flip-flops on issues and positions," someone about whom there is "considerable skepticism." These are the problems "the political activity of the Administration must try to solve."

In assessing those who supported Carter in the election, Caddell observes that the candidate won the traditional New Deal coalition, although the coalition is shrinking in relation to the overall population. To win, Carter garnered "nontraditional" votes, Bible Belt districts, and some white-collar suburbanites.

Caddell plotted out the political future, arguing that Carter could become the figure to put together a major political realignment. Caddell writes,

While a number of forces have made this possible, the most striking of these has been the decline of partisanship. American politics over the last two decades has observed an historic decline of partisanship. Republicans have gone from more than 30% of the electorate to less than 20%. Democrats have declined from majority status to only about 40% of the electorate. The difference has been made up with increasing numbers of people who think of themselves as Independents and who split their tickets when they vote. The number of Independents is growing because the number of young people in the voting population is growing. The parties are literally dying. Each new cohort of younger voters is less and less partisan than the last. However, those that are partisan are overwhelmingly Democrats. The majority of the young voters, however, do not become partisans. They are disenchanted with issues and ideology in American politics.

Carter's opportunity, according to Caddell, was that of recasting "the old ideology" of the Democratic party by formulating one that bridged older and younger constituencies, especially white-collar professionals — "the largest rising group in the population" — who tend to be conservative on economic issues. These are the crucial fluid voters, the force of the future. To Caddell, the "liberal establishment . . . composed of individuals such as Ted Kennedy" is "antiquated and anachronistic." He believes that opposition to Carter will come from this group, much more than from the Republicans. As for the GOP, he suggests that Carter "co-opt many of their issue positions . . . to take away large chunks of their normal presidential coalition by the right actions in government." In this way, Carter can gain the allegiance of "middle-income, white collar voters."

What we require is not stew, composed of bits and pieces of old policies, but a fundamentally new ideology. Unfortunately, the clear formulation of such an ideology is beyond the intellectual grasp of your pollster. However, I think it can be argued clearly that we are at one of those points in time, when — as Marx or Hegel would have argued — neither thesis nor the antithesis really works. We need a synthesis of ideas. To borrow from the philosophy of science, we desperately need an ideological "paradigm" to replace the "free market capitalist model" that we don't really want. American society does not need another "patch-up" job; it needs some kind of direction.

Despite his misuse of Marx and Hegel and his own self-conscious modesty, Caddell had, in fact, articulated a new ideology of governance, a new paradigm. It was the permanent campaign. But because it seemed so self-evident to him he did not recognize it as such. To him, the permanent campaign was a truism.

He offered to Carter his analysis of the country's mood in terms that were the hallmark of his polling and that would echo throughout the Carter administration:

> On the whole pessimism still reigns. Trust in the government and in our institutions remains at an all-time low. The belief that an individual can influence the government or the political system also remains low. Americans have no real expectation that the government is willing or able to solve the country's problems. Voters are no longer willing to grant authority to leadership; no longer are willing to follow merely because the government suggests that they do so. This skepticism is most visible in the energy and economic areas. The government can promulgate energy regulations, can ask the people to conserve, but as long as the public refuses to believe that there is an energy crisis, they are unwilling to follow.

But "the breakdown of party and the failure of ideology" present opportunities. These conditions are not all bad if new leadership can restructure the nation. How can trust and purpose be restored? In a parenthetical comment Caddell tells Jimmy Carter what to do: "The old cliche about mistaking style for substance usually works in reverse in politics. Too many good people have been defeated because they tried to substitute substance for style; they forgot to give the public the kind of visible signals that it needs to understand what is happening."

As Carter gropes to develop "the new ideology," Caddell suggests that he establish himself as "not ideological," as well as open, compassionate, competent, and "different from other politicians, not part of the establishment." This can be done by following the pollster's recommendations, a list that reads like a chronology of the early days of the Carter administration:

— "I would suggest cutting back on 'imperial' frills and perks. By symbolic actions [you . . . are] sure to excite the public."

— "Fireside chats . . . build a sense of personal intimacy with the people."

— "Town meetings . . . I think it could have a dramatic impact on the public to see the President willing to go out and meet and talk and answer questions from the country."

— "Question periods . . . opportunities for people to question Governor Carter on the media . . ."

Caddell lays out these symbolic actions in what he calls a time frame. A fireside chat for the preinaugural period; "ostentatious use of guests such as Bob Dylan, Martin Luther King, Sr., and perhaps an older conservative to make some points" during the inaugural; a town meeting during the first few months; and carefully staggered fireside chats continuing over time. "If we don't buy time quickly, given their mood today, the American people may turn on us before we ever get off the mark," Caddell emphasizes.

He notes, as part of this comprehensive strategy, the need to keep campaigning. "The Democratic National Committee," he writes, "should immediately begin a nonpublicized working group that begins planning the 1980 campaign. Jerry Rafshoon and I should probably function with this group from the beginning."

Three years later, a year before the 1980 election, Caddell reflected on his "Initial Working Paper," and declared his vision sound. But with the experience of working in the White House he has deepened his perspective. He offers a Hobbesian view of a nasty, brutish world in which political lives can be very short indeed. It is a predatory world in which only the strong survive. "The thesis is right," he says about the permanent campaign. "If you want to be president in these times, with the difficulties of the office and its weaknesses, you just have got to communicate to lead. I think the presidency is a very weakened office because of the attrition of what's happened in the office over a decade or more — assassinations, Watergate, the whole thing. If you could measure power, quantify those things, put them on a graph, the White House would be weaker as an institution than at any other time since 1960, perhaps since World War II. Which then leads you to the question of where you go for allies. It seems to me that it becomes critical to maintain some level of popularity. I don't mean maintaining popularity at the expense of doing anything that's right. You have got to be consistently reinforcing people about where you're trying to go and why. You've got to keep that signal-sending process going. Because the office is what it is, dealing with hostile competitors — the Congress, the press, the interest groups — they are going to be at you all the time. In order to get your message through that, it has to be strong enough to survive. You have to have a strong enough message to penetrate the barrier. If you only negotiate with those groups those negotiations will have little to do with your public out there. Then there is no one to carry your message. You have then denied yourself one of your great strengths. Those barons do not depend on public popularity for survival. Your greatest strength is the pressure you can bring on them. So a critical element of the substance is the ability to communicate what you're trying to do. What I said in that memo was grossly distorted out of context, the statement of style over substance. What I thought was a humorous parenthetical remark ended up becoming legend."

Carter never tried the usual means of effecting a consensus because they had been exhausted by previous presidents. He held himself above constituencies, but not above the general public opinion, which to him is the congregation. In answer to our problems, he offered himself as an upright man. As an engineer the precision of Caddell's polls appealed to his scientific bent; he understood the engineering of consent implicitly. In the polls, trust, a secular word for faith, was central. Caddell's themes of alienation were intuitively grasped by Carter, for Carter's religious faith underlies his politics. He is not only the disciple of Admiral Hyman Rickover, but of Jesus Christ. The faith of the president who tried to convert South Korean dictator Park Chung Hee should not be understated.

For someone who has been reborn, conflict is seen as a process of *psychomachia*, a medieval term for internal battles of the soul. Carter makes analogies between these battles and battles in the social system. He conceives of conflicts as allegories. Caddell's polling puts the public on the other side of the allegory. The polls are not merely a presentation of Carter to the public, but a presentation of the public to Carter. For Carter, Caddell's polls measure the spiritual condition of the congregation, the moral state of the nation. As a pilgrim leading pilgrims, Carter must be continually informed about how many are following.

The major allegorical work that is part of Carter's religious heritage is John Bunyan's *The Pilgrim's Progress*, a book about a Christian hero (named Christian) who is not superior to other people but is more faithful. All around him as he proceeds down the path to the Celestial City are the deadly sins, in all kinds of disguises, which he must learn to see through. And he doesn't see through them easily. He must always pay an emotional toll for his wisdom. He is always on the verge of being deceived. The pilgrim is a one-dimensional, flat character, except when dealing with moral issues, which is his chief virtue. Christian stands out because of his faith.

If people lack faith in government then Carter must personally set himself above institutions to lead the people to the goal of national rebirth. He expects to encounter difficulties like the Valley of Humiliation and the Slough of Despond, which is where alienation resides. A Christian life, he knows, is a beset life, always besieged by doubt and temptation. The Christian hero alternates between jeremiads about the decline of the moral state of society, anxieties about the congregation's flagging enthusiasm, and exaltation when his own evangelic efforts meet success. He has a sense of civic millenialism, that the nation itself is making Christian progress. But a reborn Christian can never relax his vigilance. There are always new tests of faith down the road. It is a deeply personal permanent campaign, for a pilgrim never ends a pilgrimage. "Now," says Christian, commencing his journey of the soul in *The Pilgrim's Progress*, "I begin to reap the benefits of my hazards." Pat Caddell's polls illuminate the path.

Gerald Rafshoon, unlike Caddell, does not understand Jimmy Carter as a pilgrim. Rafshoon always wants to project Carter as a man of achievement. He cannot see Carter as incomplete, a life in progress. Rafshoon's image-making is concerned with action, not character. His public presentation of Carter as fully realized is like a jerky silent movie, a series of disconnected images. The discordance contributes to the idea of Carter as sincere but inept. From an evangelic perspective Carter is predictable. But when Rafshoon presents him he is not the Christian hero, but the fatuous Mr. Worldly Wiseman.

Rafshoon's influence with Carter could never match Caddell's because Rafshoon is a man without ideas. Yet he is more intimate with Carter and is an original member of the Georgia mafia. He rose with Carter from regional obscurity to national prominence. Carter has come to depend upon him. Rafshoon has become a symbol of the idea that the Carter administration emphasizes style over substance.

After Jimmy Carter won a few Democratic primaries Gerald Rafshoon visited the Manhattan office of a high-powered political media consultant, seeking his help in the upcoming presidential campaign. The consultant, who has a reputation for being tough, smart, and pragmatic, asked, "What does the guy stand for?"

Rafshoon replied, "Come on. Be serious. He stands for getting elected to the White House."

"I know everyone wants the election," said the consultant, "but programmatically where would you put him?"

"Be serious," explained Rafshoon.

The consultant shook his hand and said good-bye.

Hanging on the wall of Rafshoon's office is a framed note: "I'll always be grateful that I was able to contribute in a small way to the victory of the Rafshoon agency." It's signed: "Jimmy Carter." Gerald Rafshoon is the Atlanta advertising man who conducted Carter's media campaigns for governor of Georgia and president of the United States. His name has become a verb: to Rafshoon. It means to package a politician's image. CAN RAFSHOONING SAVE THE PRESIDENT? headlined a magazine article, using the word correctly.

The first campaign Rafshoon ran was that of fellow University of Texas student Willie Morris, now a noted writer, for editor of the campus newspaper, *The Daily Texan*. Rafshoon composed a campaign jingle to the tune of Davy Crockett: "Willie, Willie Morris, the king of the ol' Yazoo." Morris, incidentally, won.

After a stint in the army Rafshoon settled himself in Atlanta, where he felt opportunities were boundless. His advertising agency developed into about the fourth or fifth largest in the city; his biggest account was the local Sears Roebuck, until he began to work for Jimmy Carter.

In 1972 Carter was among those at the Democratic convention trying to block the nomination of George McGovern. When that gambit failed Carter attempted to get himself named the vice-presidential candidate. He sent Rafshoon and Hamilton Jordan as his emissaries to McGovern. They were met by high-ranking McGovernite Pat Caddell. Rafshoon said, "The most degrading thing was Hamilton and me standing outside trying to get an audience with Pat Caddell." McGovern's pollster gave them three minutes to make a case. Afterward Rafshoon said, "I remember walking back from the convention the night McGovern was nominated, and Hamilton and I are saying, 'Why can't Jimmy run for president? He's not going to run for Senate. And four years from now we certainly aren't going to go around here trying to curry favor with somebody, asking to put an ex-Georgia governor on as vice president.' " They encouraged Carter to run for the presidency in 1976, to seek the main chance.

In the 1976 campaign, Rafshoon's efforts were effective in the primaries, but not so effective in the general election; he required outside help from other consultants, which he resented. He did not impress many non-Georgians. "I think he's a complete zero," says someone who worked with him in the campaign. "Rafshoon strikes me as being not very bright. I don't think the man reads books. He's way over his head." The non-Georgian consensus about him did not change markedly when Carter became president. A White House insider says, "Who in that business isn't shallow? It isn't a job that draws the Hannah Arendts of the world."

But Rafshoon was not Carter's sole media adviser. Barry Jagoda, a Columbia Journalism School graduate with wide experience in broadcast journalism, also advised Carter. Jagoda worked in the campaign and in the White House, until he was, in effect, forced out by Rafshoon. Jagoda wanted Carter to be spontaneous, which he believed was the most efficacious image-making, whereas Rafshoon wanted to apply the traditional advertising techniques of packaging and promotion.

"My view," says Jagoda, "is that the most critical battlefield in media politics is broadcast journalism. The controlled airtime is not nearly as important as the programming usually thought of as impartial. There are too many government flacks around who don't know what news is: they've been in advertising. It's important in the media age to have observed decision making in television news. To the extent that the television cameras have the function of bringing people where they couldn't otherwise go it's important not to be contrived because you'll be found out."

Jagoda was hired during the primaries in 1976. His job was to coordinate Carter's appearances from 4 P.M. on the day of a primary until noon of the following day. He was one of the first consultants whose expertise was television news decision making. He understood the ways in which a candidate could begin to exercise control over the reportage of the election. "If a candidate physically shows up in a television discussion on, for example, ethnic purity, the candidate controls it," says Jagoda. "It's not manipulation. But if the candidate is there he has the last word." Knowledge of how to do this is not learned by being an outsider; you have to have been inside once to have mastered the techniques of news. This kind of media politics is seamless. It doesn't mimic the news or play off the news. It is the news. It is something Rafshoon never understood except as a threat to his special relationship with Carter.

"Once in the White House," says Jagoda, "the decision was made to increase Carter's standing in the polls. We barely won the election. You needed to do new things all the time. Otherwise it gets boring and it's not news. You have to package your participation in the media so that it's spontaneous and newsworthy. That's what I was doing." He worked on the town meetings, the fireside chats, and other proposed events. He understood that replaying a successful event was just a rerun to the television networks. Why should they broadcast a series of town meetings if they are all the same? Jagoda urged Carter to take risks by initiating news in innovative ways. He believed Carter's great strength was that he would open himself to the American people. "I was saying, within the White House, that the key to Carter was vulnerability. I said he had to take chances."

Jagoda's approach ran against the grain of the thematic presidency advocated by Caddell and Rafshoon, which fit neatly into their polling and packaging techniques. To them, Jagoda's open-ended perspective was a political danger to Carter. But Jagoda made an enemy, through neglect, of someone far more influential than Caddell or Rafshoon. When Rosalynn Carter decided that Jagoda was threatening, his options narrowed considerably. "I should have talked to Rosalynn long ago," says Jagoda. Within the White House, according to Jagoda, her role was that of "the ordinary American." Her opinion was considered by her husband to be a bellwether. She was perturbed that Jimmy was not perceived as a man of great accomplishment, which she believed to be the case. Maybe his presidency seemed to be too spontaneous, unstructured, and uncontrolled. She thought it ought to settle on a few themes easily accessible to the average American. "After I spouted off about the need for vulnerability, it drove Rosalynn off the wall," says Jagoda. " 'Is he trying to expose Jimmy?' she wondered."

Rafshoon had opposed Jagoda all along. "Jerry was saying to Rosalynn that we should let Jimmy project two or three themes. He complained we weren't controlling the press conferences. It must have bothered Jerry a lot to see me in the papers as Carter's media adviser because Carter was supposed to have only one media adviser — Rafshoon. And that's true. Carter always paid attention to Jerry. But I don't think the President can have just two or three themes. The world is more complicated than that."

Meanwhile, Rosalynn acted. "When Carter was down to 28 percent in the polls Rosalynn was nervous. She talked with Jerry. They agreed Carter needed a consistent image. Jerry decided that his job was to narrow the presidency down to a few themes." It was inevitable that Rafshoon, operating a lucrative advertising agency in Washington, would be drawn back into a more formal relationship with Carter. In May 1978, his appointment as special adviser to the president was announced. Barry Jagoda was roaming the jungles of Panama with an American team involved in the Panama Canal Treaty negotiations. Suddenly, Jody Powell's voice came over a walkie-talkie, telling Jagoda that he was being reassigned and that Rafshoon was hired. "That's impossible," said Jagoda. "He and I don't agree. I want to talk to the President."

"We're announcing it today," replied Powell.

For a while Jagoda worked under Rafshoon. "He thought you could get on television any time you wanted. Jerry started to do a remote control direction of Carter's image. The things he did were unrealistic and absurd. For instance, he wanted Carter to give a July 4th address. I said it wasn't news. I called the networks anyway and they rejected it. Rafshoon didn't understand this process. That was the conflict. Finally, I wrote a memo to Carter saying that if he wanted to continue to get on TV when he wanted he needed to have meetings with the people who own the networks. The airtime was being denied him by the news executives. And they were right. Carter told me: 'I don't want to be a supplicant.' "

Eventually, Jagoda quit. "I went to Carter to talk about it. I said that the President couldn't have two media advisers. He asked me to stay in touch and wished me good luck. It was warm, but there was a philosophical difference." Jagoda considered writing a book about his White House experience. He even wrote a proposal. But he dropped the idea because his feelings about Carter remained confused.

He is clear, though, about why he thinks Rafshoon failed. "The real value of Jerry is that since he's a close friend of Carter's he can work with Rosalynn to get Carter to do things that, being a purist, he would not want to do. But Jerry doesn't have any new ideas. He wants to control the information distribution process which has forty or fifty middlemen, that is, journalists. In public life, you can't buy control of journalism. It's not like selling your product. You can't control it and you shouldn't control it."

Rafshoon tried his best. "I'm going to save the President's ass," he said upon assuming his post. He made many contributions to the administration. Mostly, he urged Carter to rely upon his instincts. "I'm not an ideologue, but I think the times demand a conservative thrust," Rafshoon said. He advised Carter to bring back "Ruffles and Flourishes" and "Hail to the Chief," previously banished in a reaction to the imperial presidency. He put Anwar Sadat and Menachem Begin, embracing in the aftermath of the Camp David summit, on television. He pushed the phrase "New Foundation" as a theme for Carter's 1979 State of the Union address. He supported Defense Secretary Brown's proposal to increase the Pentagon budget — opposed by the president's domestic advisers — because he believed it would enhance Carter's image of toughness. When Carter vetoed a bill, Rafshoon instructed speechwriters to draft "talking points" about the veto, which were distributed to officials who had to make speeches on the subject. He also urged the president to fire Bella Abzug from an advisory committee on women. During Rafshoon's tenure Carter began to climb in the polls until larger events swamped him. Rafshoon could solve an internal crisis, but he could not command external reality. Eventually, Ayatollah Khomeini accomplished for Carter's popularity what Rafshoon never could.

In the meantime, Pat Caddell seemed to be riding high. His polling firm's quarterly reports on the American public's attitudes, with subscriptions costing $20,000 a year, were bought by many Fortune 500 companies. Another subscriber was the Saudi Arabian government; this fact raised a brief flurry of adverse comment in the press about a potential conflict of interest. But for Caddell, living well was only part of his revenge. "He wanted to prove to Boston and Harvard that he was as smart as he thought he was," says a friend. "He said one time: 'Take that, Boston. Finally I proved myself to the world. Maybe I proved myself to Boston.' "

He was the intellectual-in-residence at the White House. But his influence was not constant. "Sometimes he was more on the outs," says a White House insider. "Sometimes he was more on the ins. The source of his power is that Carter likes him a lot. His cycles of influence had to do with Ham Jordan and Jody Powell. On the matter of intelligence Rafshoon and Caddell operate on separate levels. One reason Caddell was mistrusted was that he was not a creation of Carter's like Rafshoon."

Even on the inside, Caddell was not a true insider. "Pat was the one Jody and Ham picked on," says a Caddell friend. "They're known as cutters. They have very sharp acidic wit. When Pat was around them he was the butt of their jokes, although he was a good sport about it."

Caddell was not totally confident about his privileged position. He worried a great deal. His status was too much like a dream. "Pat doesn't believe what's happened to him," says a friend. "He emerged too suddenly. He thinks there will be a knock on the door and someone will say: 'Back to Boston.' He's very fragile. It's funny, he's afraid. He built this very powerful kingdom very quickly. He thinks that if it's that easy to get, it's that easy to lose. While he's got that fear of losing the kingdom, he is just the nicest, most gentle man. His journalist friends would not spend the time of day with anyone else in the White House. For a time, Pat was the only person answering phone calls. The White House wagons were in a circle. God, I'd never seen anything like it. Pat was hiding a little, but he wasn't ducked and covered like Rafshoon and Ham Jordan."

In mid-summer 1979, the Carter loyalists claimed that the president's troubles derived from the intractability of problems like the energy crisis, which could not be solved in a short time; Carter unfairly received the blame. It was "the worst of times," wrote domestic affairs adviser Stuart Eisenstadt in a memo. There is some truth to this analysis. The problems are difficult. But Carter aides compounded their difficulty by running the permanent campaign into the ground. Hamilton Jordan, Carter's chief of staff, when asked why his critics on Capitol Hill didn't know him, replied, "That's not their fault. That's my fault. I have not made the effort to know *them*." His contempt for cultivating traditional constituencies was blatant and ultimately counterproductive.

Caddell was the only one with access to the president who offered constructive criticism about the internal operation. He placed this analysis within his cosmic world view, explaining Carter's conundrum as further evidence of American malaise. "He was the one person in the White House suggesting that the conventional ways of doing things weren't paying off," says a White House insider. "Almost nobody else around Carter would suggest that it was Carter's style of operation that might be his problem. Rafshoon thinks in terms of getting good coverage. He and Powell generally believe Carter is a great achiever. They think it's not a matter of salesmanship, but of clearer projection of truth."

Caddell decided to go to Rosalynn Carter. On April 9, 1978, over a two-hour breakfast he presented her with a disturbing new poll, showing that almost half of the American people were pessimistic about the future and that a third were pessimistic about their own lives. He urged a return to the thematic presidency (when had it been abandoned?) and a return to the campaign style of governing. He suggested that the Carter presidency should be fundamentally altered into a "transforming" one, an idea borrowed from a book he had been reading, *Leadership*, written by an academic close to Ted Kennedy, James MacGregor Burns. Burns contrasted transactional leadership, involving an exchange of goods and services, with transforming leadership. "Leaders can also shape and alter and elevate the motives and values and goals of followers through the vital teaching role of leadership. This is transforming leadership," he wrote. Mrs. Carter was shaken by Caddell's presentation. She promised to relay his ideas to the president.

For almost a year, Caddell had been warning Carter of the impending crisis of his administration. In October 1977, in a long memo the pollster informed the president of his low standing in the polls. Caddell argued that the office of the presidency had become weak and that it needed to rely on public opinion to survive its enemies. In December 1977, in another memo, he told Carter that people approved of him personally but thought him inadequate to the task. With the latest poll data showing growing alienation, Caddell prescribed prompt action.

In Caddell's private campaign to transform the Carter presidency he had been reading extensively. The books he studied confirmed his sentiments about the prevalence of alienation and the crisis of trust. Christopher Lasch's *The Culture of Narcissism* discussed, among other weighty topics, how "the propaganda of consumption turns alienation itself into a commodity." In *The Cultural Contradictions of Capitalism* Daniel Bell stated, "Crises of belief are recurrent in human history, which does not make them less significant . . . The invitation to despair arises because the consequences are real, if not always immediate, and yet no one can do very much about them . . . Once a faith is shattered, it takes a long time to grow again . . ." In May 1979, these authors, and others, were invited to a dinner with the president to offer their ideas in a common forum. Caddell was moving methodically.

His timetable was speeded up when the gasoline shortage and the attendant public outrage drove Carter's approval rating to 25 percent, lower than Richard Nixon's at his lowest ebb. The president himself was in Japan, at an international summit meeting on economics, during the crisis. He returned on July 1, 1979, exhausted. Hamilton Jordan, Jody Powell, and Jerry Rafshoon pushed him into taking to the airwaves to make a new energy speech. Caddell was livid that none of his analysis would be addressed in such a hastily constructed speech. Moreover, Caddell felt that the speech would be ignored because it was not dealing with the deeper problems; it would be seen as yet another dreary Carter performance. He wrote another memo, this one 107 pages long, arguing for a "breakthrough" speech to cut through the "trench warfare" of government. At the heart of his analysis was a description of the nation's malaise. He urged Carter to lead the country and to concentrate less on governing it. He wanted Carter to be a transforming president. Carter read his memo and canceled his speech.

For more than a week Carter closeted himself at Camp David, a dramatic move capturing the attention of the public at last. Mystery surrounded his seclusion. A roll call of leaders — governors, senators, economists, women, blacks, old wisemen — paraded past the president. Tension heightened. This event appeared at the time to be the great turning point of the administration. It was as if Christian of *The Pilgrim's Progress* were held prisoner in the Doubting Castle of Giant Despair, but would surely find the key of Promise.

On July 15, Carter came down from the mountaintop. He delivered a televised address, hammering his fist to emphasize his points, chiding Americans for their narcissism in language lifted almost word for word from a 1975 Caddell speech on alienation. "It is a crisis of confidence," declared Carter. "It is a crisis that strikes at the very heart, soul and spirit of our national will. We can see this crisis in the growing doubt about the meaning of our own lives, and in the loss of unity of purpose of our nation. The erosion of our confidence in the future is threatening to destroy the social and political fabric of America."

After the speech, Carter immediately rose 10 points in the polls. But within forty-eight hours he lost everything he had gained. He asked for the resignations of his entire cabinet — needlessly recalling in the public's mind Nixonian excesses — and dismissed several cabinet members, including Joseph Califano, well-connected with the Washington establishment. Carter, according to Califano's account, told him that he, the president, had to get ready for the 1980 campaign. Califano had antagonized tobacco growing states with his antismoking crusade; he was a liability. The uproar could have been predicted. "A self-inflicted wound," said one Democratic congressman.

The mass resignation idea was raised at the Camp David meeting and was strongly supported by Rafshoon, who believed it would allow Carter to demonstrate his forcefulness. Caddell was interested in the notion because of its dramatic implications, but he was most concerned about getting his message into the president's energy speech. He did not foresee the firestorm the resignations would create.

Rafshoon, for his part, was enthusiastic about everything Carter had done. "We found there was so much looking into issues," he said. "That's not leading the country — that's not what people elected Carter to do. So the president was finding that you're irrelevant when you talk about issues. Remember, in the campaign he was the only one who wasn't talking about issues." Meanwhile, on Cape Cod, Ted Kennedy was deciding to run for president.

Pat Caddell, at the center of power and the apex of his influence, still feels like an outsider. He is the only important non-Georgian admitted into the inner White House council; he is castigated by academics for his theory of malaise; his political consultant colleagues resent his success; he is a young man who rose very fast among those much older than himself; and his ideas themselves are a campaign issue to Ted Kennedy, a candidate whom he respects. Pat Caddell is alienated. More, he recognizes that he has helped create the problem he analyzes; and he doesn't know what to do about it.

"I am no longer concerned with getting people elected," he says. "You only do political work because you care about politics. At some point you have to think about the consequences. In my business you ought to be able to have some kind of unique perspective. I'm sitting here measuring things, serious problems, a decade's long work. It raises serious questions about the country. It's difficult for me not to say, my God, we have all had responsibility for this. I understand some of the dimensions of the problem and I understand that we are part of it.

"Consultants really are serving as preselectors of the candidates. We decide who is best able to use the technology, who understands the technology. It's a self-fulfilling prophecy. What happens is that you want to be able to deal mechanically, use your stuff. Those candidates who don't fit that well are blown away. In apportioning blame for the condition the system is in we certainly deserve a share of it. We replaced the parties and we've shown that candidates can get elected without any party's help, or even any institutional support. In your reflective moments you wonder what the hell you're doing.

"There are consultants I know who are good people who could care less what their clients do or what the outcome is of what we're doing. The system is devouring itself. In every election we disillusion more people. It's like having a fire going in the house. Then we start burning the furniture up. Then we start burning the house itself to keep the fire going. It's going to be a hell of a situation."

In Caddell's estimation, the politicians even less than the consultants provide cause for hope. "I don't think we've necessarily improved the quality of politicians," he says. "I'm not convinced the new politicians are superior to the class they replace. That really troubles me a great deal. I know people in Congress who vote simply to survive. How many people there, regardless of party or ideology, worry about the United States of America? I've had congressmen tell me that they know they're voting for things that are not in the national interest and that they're going to hurt the country. The problem is that they stay there to stay there. I've had young congressmen tell me that they're embarrassed about what happens on the floor of the House. Survival at what cost? We have produced these people. I don't know why they're there and they don't know why they're there. Do these people really care what happens to the country? That's what is so ironic about a Carter and Kennedy face-off. They do care about the country. It's not an election I look forward to."

Caddell sighs wearily. "We've created a system in which there are no rewards for dealing with things that are fundamental," he says. "I'm looking into the void."

## CHAPTER THREE

# CHOOSING SIDES

## JACK WALSH

In the spring of 1979 Jimmy Carter needed Jack Walsh far more than Walsh needed Carter. The president had failed to cultivate any constituency that felt a special tie to him, and every day seemed to bring fresh aggravations. Liberal Democrats clamored for Edward Kennedy to declare his candidacy; Congress scornfully dismissed Carter's energy proposals; an international institute in London issued a report stating that the president didn't exhibit sufficient qualities of leadership to ensure the survival of Western civilization; James Fallows, Carter's former speechwriter, characterized his administration as "the passionless presidency" in a long chronicle of disillusionment in the *Atlantic Monthly;* and Bert Lance was indicted. It was a bad season. In the midst of this turmoil Carter began his campaign for reelection,

hiring thirty-eight-year-old Jack Walsh as his national organizational director on the advice of his pollster Pat Caddell, Tip
O'Neill, and other Massachusetts stalwarts. They thought Walsh
would fit into the Carter circle well.

Walsh emerged on the Carter campaign staff as a top-ranking
outsider. A field marshal with laurels garnered in Boston's
political wars — he organized Boston mayor Kevin White's campaign and former Massachusetts governor Michael Dukakis's 1974
campaign — Walsh's presence in the Carter campaign underscored the president's faltering status within his own party. Walsh
is Tip O'Neill's kind of operative, a crackerjack organizer who
knows the voting habits of every precinct in Boston. Hiring Walsh
represented a gesture by Carter to the industrial Northeast and
Midwest, urban Catholics, liberals, and labor. Walsh understood
the issues that moved these groups; unlike Carter he knew the
appropriate cultural symbols as well. "They recognized they could
use Jack's influence," says political consultant John Marttila, who
worked closely with Walsh on the White campaign. "The other
side of that is that Carter was really in trouble."

Mark Roosevelt — Walsh's aide-de-camp, his hand-picked
assistant in the Carter campaign, and the twenty-three-year-old
great-grandson of Theodore Roosevelt — says, "Jack's appointment showed that they realized they needed a primary campaign.
They needed a technician." Walsh indeed had excellent ties to
regular Democrats and labor leaders around the country. He was
Carter's plenipotentiary to this foreign realm. His success would
be Carter's success; on the other hand, Carter's failures would be
registered as his failures. He would only get credit if he won.

Before Walsh took the job with the Carter campaign he went to
Speaker of the House Tip O'Neill, chief therapist of the Democratic party, to allay his anxiety about Ted Kennedy. A few
months before, Walsh had plotted with a coterie of Boston operatives to promote the favorite son presidential candidacy of U.S.
Senator Paul Tsongas as a way of encouraging Kennedy to run.

Understandably, then, Walsh needed to be assured of continuing Democratic support for Carter. Ted Kennedy is like a son, Tip told him. O'Neill added that he couldn't predict the future, but he felt sure that Kennedy wasn't going to run. Reasonably satisfied that the Speaker gave him as definite an answer as he was likely to receive, Walsh decided to take the post.

Jack Walsh is caught between two worlds — one past, one present. For Walsh it's a question of whether ward politics can be brought into the media age. He's too old to have been molded by the sixties and too young to be a ward heeler. He's in the middle generation, a glorified organizer with some conceptual breadth and knowledge of history — in short, an anomaly.

He didn't enter politics through advertising. He's not in packaging; he's street-smart. He had experience with labor unions, not promoting soft drinks. He's more Saul Alinsky than Gerald Rafshoon. In that sense, he's an anachronism, scrambling to stay in the game. The Carter campaign was a test of his viability. His decision to go with Carter was a case of two well-intentioned men operating under a set of mutual delusions about the way things were.

On his study wall, Walsh has a picture of John and Robert Kennedy; they are silhouetted against the light streaming into the Oval Office. Walsh claims he doesn't have heroes, but the icon of the martyred Kennedys indicates otherwise. Among political operatives, especially Irishmen of a certain generation and particularly those who served the Kennedys in some capacity, the picture on the office wall is a cultural symbol. It tells visitors that he is part of the myth and that he might be part of it again. Walsh never worked for a Kennedy, but the picture represents yearning, ambition, and, most of all, a sense of identity.

Jack Walsh has been educated through politics; campaigns are his school. He has taught a seminar at the John F. Kennedy School of Politics at Harvard, but his best lessons have been learned in action. "If you're in politics you're called a consultant," he says. "But most of my politics has been as a citizen. When you say it isn't a hobby people get tense. The people who come into political consulting as a business don't understand the political world. I grew up in an intense political environment. My family were the kind of people you could call up for help. I worked in a lot of local campaigns when I was in my teens. I learned that it isn't an avocation. In campaigns I got a sense of the economy of time. I think about what campaigns do, not who is in them. On the local level, you learn to get from here to there. That was the good thing about the old pols — they knew that. But they never learned the technical stuff."

Jack Walsh is a child of the Boston of Frank Skeffington, the fictional politician in *The Last Hurrah*. It's not fiction to him. With Skeffiington gone (and with James Michael Curley, the model for Skeffington, gone too), Walsh is one of the legatees, an incarnation of the old pol, but with a difference. He updates the folk tradition, comprehending the new techniques, but still possessing a genuinely gregarious manner and shrewd tactical ability. This brand of politics is more than a summary of component parts: it's a sensibility.

Walsh is an Irish political mystic. His politics, more than anything else, are grounded in ineffable sentiment. An associate recalls meetings with Walsh, Kevin White, and other Irish politicos during which not a single sentence was completed and yet everything was understood. It was as if there was an unconscious language being spoken, a Gaelic political tongue that only true sons of the sod could comprehend.

"My parents believed that if you didn't participate in politics you were evil," says Walsh. The family lived in a public housing project in South Boston. The New Deal relief program that aided his family shaped Jack's world view. As a boy Jack was always involved in some local campaign, learning at the precinct level how things worked. Boston was a political hothouse, and Walsh's early political experience wasn't unusual at all.

When it was time to attend college he scored a startling 790 in mathematics on the Scholastic Aptitude Test (the highest mark being 800) and enrolled in Boston College as a math major. "I didn't know why," he says. "I woke up and realized somebody conned me. I left."

Next port of call: Berlin, Germany. "When Jack Kennedy asked people to sign up for the army, I signed up. The day after the Berlin Wall was built." Walsh requested service in Germany. "I hated it." When he was discharged he got a construction job and began working in political campaigns again; it was as logical as wearing civvies.

At the age of twenty-six he decided he wanted to take graduate courses in government, but discovered that he wouldn't be permitted to sign up until he had an undergraduate degree. So, in two years he completed requirements for a B.A. from Boston University. To subsidize his formal education he labored at a succession of jobs — the night shift at the post office, running a bowling alley, painting lines on highways. When at last he had his sheepskin in hand he felt free to take the courses he wanted. All the while, however, he was politically active.

His first big campaign was Kevin White's gubernatorial race in 1970. "The party was more important then," he says ruefully. His job was to survey delegates to the Democratic nominating convention. White was an insurgent running against a regular Democrat, the state senate president, buttressed by his state house cronies. "I learned a lot about primaries," Walsh says. "The smaller the electorate the more you have to focus on turning out your own voters. I got about one hundred years of experience in two years. I perfected the game to motivate people to participate." White won the nomination, but lost the general election.

The following year White stood for reelection as mayor, a bitter campaign against city councilor Louise Day Hicks, Boston's matron of racial discord. Walsh was field organizer; he knew every player, every nuance of every neighborhood. "The campaign had clear direction," he says. "It was organized around good ideas. *Organization is always about ideas.* And it had an opponent who disagreed with the campaign's fundamental precepts. It was a great campaign." White won resoundingly. This was the heyday of urban liberalism.

"City and state politics are different because of class relationships," Walsh says. "A kid who wanted to be president wouldn't run for the Boston City Council. The suburban/urban schism is fundamental." To Walsh this is a reigning idea, connoting class conflict, ethnic discrimination, and the ancient Yankee-Irish struggle in Massachusetts. He is an urban chauvinist, resentful of suburban noblesse oblige. "The people in the city enjoy politics more," Walsh declares. "The suburbanites see it as business, rational civic responsibility."

When it came time to pick a candidate for the 1976 presidential sweepstakes Walsh selected U.S. Senator Birch Bayh. Walsh's reasons sounded good at the time. Bayh was prolabor, liberal, attractive, billed as the electable alternative to liberal Arizona congressman Morris Udall, who was, to Walsh's way of thinking, the suburban candidate. Bayh banked his hopes on the New York primary, lining up solid support from prominent Democrats, hoarding his money to splurge on New York television. But he never made it past the Bay State, where he was severely underfinanced and dispatched to oblivion by his own campaign slogan: "It takes a good politician to run a country." In the post-Watergate election this wasn't clever. Jack Walsh, who admired this sort of pose, was brought in to salvage the Massachusetts primary for Bayh. It was beyond repair. "We had no money, nothing," says Mark Roosevelt, who met Walsh, his tutor in politics, in the campaign. Bayh sank without a ripple. Walsh then switched allegiance to Jimmy Carter, working to get out the vote in the Illinois primary.

After the Illinois primary, Walsh set up his one-man consulting firm, Jack Walsh and Associates, and principally contracted jobs as an organizer for labor unions. In 1978, he placed his name on the ballot for the first time as a candidate in a Democratic primary, contesting a state senate seat occupied by a very conservative incumbent in West Roxbury, a conservative Boston neighborhood. Walsh ran on economic issues, while his opponent railed against busing and abortion. For his part, Walsh didn't waffle. He believes, after all, that elections are how the voters make up their minds; he holds this idea with schoolboy sincerity. In uncompromising terms Walsh explained that he was in favor of busing to achieve integrated schools and in favor of women's right to have abortions. His earnestness was a liability — he was easily beaten. But he wasn't bitter, even though he had dreamed that the state senate seat might someday propel him into the mayor's office.

Politics always goes on. For a politician a loss can end a career, but for a consultant it's not necessarily a last hurrah. Walsh was still in the thick of things, outlining scenarios and planning maneuvers, when the call came from the White House in the spring of 1979. Walsh carefully toted up the risks before he joined Carter's team. His formulation rested ultimately on imponderables. "I live in a world where dealing with the future means playing your best option," he said. "You play your best card. That's what we're doing."

I visited Walsh the day before he left his West Roxbury home to join the Carter-Mondale Exploratory Committee in Washington. When I rang his doorbell he was writing his first memo on campaign strategy while watching a basketball game on television. His reasons for signing up with Carter were completely political; it was a calculated gamble. Walsh had certain goals he wanted to attain, and the 1980 campaign offered a way to achieve some of them.

"I'm to the left of Carter," he readily admitted. "I have my own integrity. And I'm way to the left of Reagan. It's not a good time for liberals. Liberals are going to lose a lot in the next few years. The decline of the party has had a lot to do with that. There's no place to orchestrate a philosophy. But we're not going to allow somebody who's antilabor to get votes from people when he goes against their life blood. That's the political problem. That's what the campaign has to do. You have to remind people that you're labor's candidate. My major motivation is that I think we're going into a Republican year. Reagan isn't going to leave anything behind if he gets in. The campaign will try to raise that issue early enough so Carter doesn't lose the primaries. Nobody's focused on the alternatives."

The Carter strategy, elaborated by Walsh in the summer of 1979, was essentially defensive. Walsh hoped that by laying down a firm general election strategy Carter would help himself in the struggle within the Democratic party. The general election strategy was itself Carter's primary strategy. It reversed the expected order; it was the tack of a weak incumbent. "You have to organize to win the general election," Walsh said. "You hope you don't blow the primaries. In 1976, Carter operated on the assumption that as a Democrat he would win the general election. So he focused on the primaries." In a Republican year, Carter must direct attention to the external threat posed by right-wing Republicans. By doing this Walsh saw Carter consolidating his position within the party during the primaries. A chain reaction was supposed to occur, with the danger of the right catalyzing the party faithful to back Carter. Making the Democrats look forward to the November finale, according to the plan, buttressed Carter's standing in the party.

There was more than an element of faith involved in this strategy. It depended to some degree on luck, and once an operative relies on luck he's walking in the dark. In the 1964 Johnson-

Goldwater race, fear led many voters to cast ballots for peace candidate Johnson, terrified that Goldwater would start a war. Fear was a basic factor that Walsh was counting on for Carter. He prayed that the Republican primaries would be so volatile that the media concentration on them would alert Democrats to Carter's benign qualities.

Walsh himself is strongly motivated by apprehension of right-wing victories. In particular, the Massachusetts Democratic gubernatorial primary in 1978 between liberal incumbent Michael Dukakis and conservative Edward King, ending in a smashing King triumph, haunts him. "In the Dukakis experience," he reflected, "an incumbent governor with sound policies, personally honest, still lost because he never put forward a broad agenda; he had no grand strategy. Nobody ever sat down and asked what his campaign should do." Carter suffered from a similar affliction in Walsh's view. "Carter hasn't demonstrated his leadership yet," he said. "I know he has great leadership, but he hasn't exercised it by giving the country a sense of direction. In this campaign he's going to have to put forward his perception of where the country's going. This campaign is that opportunity."

Walsh didn't view Carter's 1976 campaign as a model. "His last campaign wasn't used for what a campaign can be used for — educating the electorate," Walsh contended. "The problem with the outsider challenge is that an outsider doesn't explain his perception of the future. It may be endemic to being an outsider." However, reports filtered out of the White House over the summer of 1979 indicating that Hamilton Jordan, whose prescient memo on the 1976 campaign guided much of Carter's movement, had penned another memo on the 1980 race, in which he proposed to embellish the old image. In this scenario Carter would present himself as an insider, able to decisively affect events, *and* as an outsider, fighting Washington's special interests on the public's behalf. In 1979, Carter had the worst of both images, blamed as an outsider for his inability to accomplish things and blamed as an insider for whatever happened. The Jordan strategy read like a rationalization for the president's inconsistency.

By hiring Jack Walsh, Carter implicitly conceded the shortcomings of his media campaign. He placed at Walsh's disposal the vast powers of incumbency — workers and allies secured through the granting of federal largesse. This was traditional politics employed on a grand scale to make up the losses Carter had suffered through years of his presidential permanent campaign. Walsh labored under the permanent campaign, for the permanent campaign and against its grain.

The campaign's technical problem was in great part another side of the administration's policy difficulties. In previous campaigns Walsh hadn't made false distinctions between slogans and policy; he viewed campaigns as extensions of political programs. But in Carter's campaign the whole strategy was composed of a series of delusions, all of them related to a grand delusion that the president as incumbent could control events. However, this time around, external conditions — the price and supply of oil, the inflation rate, Ted Kennedy's and Ayatollah Khomeini's inclinations — dictated whether or not the campaign would be meaningful. The campaign's initial premises were shaky. The delusions surrounding the Carter effort were like the layers of an onion: peeling off one layer simply revealed another.

The first delusion Walsh had was that the campaign could be controlled through a tight organization, which was a worm's eye view of the situation. The crucial factor was not internal control, although that always matters to some degree, but larger social forces and pressures. Hiring Walsh in itself was among the campaign's delusions, for it was still an attempt by Carter to resolve his problems with a technical solution — in this case, employing an organizational wizard. Though it showed some sensitivity on the president's part to his weaknesses, this delusion was a corollary of another delusion, namely that the campaign strategy would put Carter on the offensive, portraying him as the indispensable leader. Through Walsh's skills, Carter's leadership was supposed to be manifest to the voters. In fact, Carter's strategy was defensive. It didn't really require Carter to change a bit. It asked Democrats to support him because he was the best they were going to get. Democrats in 1980, according to the Carter plan, were not to pose the question: Why not the best? They were exhorted to be grateful, to fear that things could be much worse. In no way was this a beneficial challenge to Carter. It depicted him failing to rise to the occasion, implicitly ignoring criticism of his policies. It neatly fit the campaign plan of Carter's inner circle who entertained the insider/outsider themes, and it was a blueprint for inaction.

This delusion, in turn, was predicated on the assumption that Carter's real opponent in the primaries was Ronald Reagan. Reagan was a totem of fear. Actually, Carter was running against Edward Kennedy and those who were disaffected with the president's policies. Reagan was the target of the general election strategy, obscuring the intent of the primary strategy. He was used to scare dissident Democrats into line. For Carter this engendered deeper trouble. It created a temporary constituency around the campaign instead of around substantive issues. By projecting Carter as the only realistic choice for Democrats, his campaign urged them to resign themselves to whatever he might offer. It was a strategy suggesting Carter's leadership was not likely to nurture a genuine coalition that could exist beyond the election to assist in enacting actual legislation. The campaign's ultimate premise wasn't shared objectives but expedience.

The campaign's defensive posture gave Carter room to maneuver politically without taking any real risks or committing himself to any policy changes. Faced with tumultuous opposition within his own party, Carter was inclined to adopt the peculiar position of standing pat, thinking that this was what would win the rebels over in the end. The danger for Carter was his instinct to rest on his laurels, which many Democrats felt he didn't have.

Perhaps Walsh's major delusion was that if Carter won he might move to more progressive positions. In fact, Carter would be more likely to interpret his victory as a mandate to continue his policies unaltered. Since the campaign didn't address the profound crisis facing Carter, it couldn't push him in the direction Walsh preferred. In this way, Carter split policy from campaigning, rendering superfluous an important contribution Jack Walsh might have offered him: the idea of educating the public.

In the meantime, as this strategy was developed, Walsh tried to convince himself that Kennedy wouldn't run. "What's the power of the presidency?" he asked. "You have the power to raise ideas, you control the agenda, at least the new agenda. Kennedy already has power over the agenda, almost as much as the president." As one of the earliest Draft Kennedy partisans, Walsh now offered the most fervent prayers that it wouldn't come to pass. "Jack will blow his brains out if Kennedy runs," said a political colleague. "That's who he'd want to be with." But Mark Roosevelt insisted, "Kennedy won't run. I'm working for Carter because that's where I'd be later anyway."

Walsh assured Hamilton Jordan that Kennedy would not run, although Jordan kept saying that Kennedy was already running. No, Walsh countered, he had it on the very best authority, Tip O'Neill, that Kennedy wasn't going to enter the race. And Teddy was like a son to Tip.

Suddenly, it was clear Teddy would announce his candidacy. Jack Walsh found himself on the opposite side from most of his friends. After the ceremonial opening of the John F. Kennedy Library in Boston, Walsh stood near the box-lunch stands with Pat Caddell, conversing intently. He loped away, running for a limousine, part of the presidential entourage.

"Hell, no, I'm not going to take my picture of Kennedy in my study down," he said, on the run. "I still like Teddy. I mean, you've got to make political judgments. It's politics."

A month later, Jack Walsh quit his position with Carter. "The internal situation was screwed up," he said. "My situation was not what I wanted it to be." Once again, he set up Jack Walsh and Associates and began operating out of his home.

## CHAPTER FOUR

# MACHIAVELLI AND THE MEDIA

## DAVID GARTH

It's the middle of the gasoline shortage during the summer of 1979 and David Garth is on the telephone with New York governor Hugh Carey. "Have you called Fritz?" he asks, meaning the vice president. "You better talk to Ed," he advises, referring to the mayor of New York. "Carter will be at six in the polls when this is over. In New York, Heinrich Himmler could beat him by 20 points tomorrow! I don't understand it from a political point of view. Did you hear Jody Powell's remark knocking Washington today? It's a gimmick, like Carter saying he'll whip Kennedy's ass. Jimmy Nice-Guy becomes Jimmy Balls. Have you talked with Schlesinger?" Garth asks, referring to the Energy Secretary. "Can you get any straight figures from him? If you hear anything, I'll be here all day."

From his Fifth Avenue office in Manhattan, a cockpit of political action, Garth conducts his permanent campaign. Losing is an affront to his pride. He prefers to win and to be known as a winner. He works behind the scenes as successfully as in full public view. During New York's fiscal crisis he was an influential adviser to the main players, although his name rarely surfaced in the press.

When Edward Koch, Garth's candidate in the last New York City mayoralty race, beat Mario Cuomo, Cuomo cried publicly, "What hath Garth wrought?" Garth is one of the few consultants who has become an issue in his campaigns. On his roster of winners are New York mayor Ed Koch, New York governor Hugh Carey, Connecticut governor Ella Grasso, New Jersey governor Brendan Byrne, U.S. senators Adlai Stevenson and John Heinz, Los Angeles mayor Tom Bradley, and Luis Herrera, the new president of Venezuela. Mention of Garth's name is often enough to lift a candidate off the launching pad. In Boston, for instance, even before Garth's television spots for mayoral hopeful Joseph Timilty appeared on the air during the 1979 race, Timilty used them to draw a crowd of big money men to a special screening. Once the ads were shown the checkbooks were opened.

Clearly, Garth's name alone is worth a lot to a candidate. "In 1974," notes writer Jeff Greenfield, who worked with Garth for six years, "when Hugh Carey signed Garth it was taken as a sign that he was serious." Garth's compensation matches his reputation: it's large. He draws about a quarter of a million dollars a year salary. If you were to hire him to run your campaign, he would charge a $10 to $15 thousand monthly fee plus 15 percent for broadcast billings. You had better be serious when you sign Garth.

"Politicians use him as a good luck charm," says a consultant, "part of the sales package when you talk to the press or the money people. Politicians say, 'I've got Garth. How can I lose?' " Jack Newfield, political writer with the *Village Voice*, one of Garth's fiercest critics, concedes, "He's a genius at what he does. He will kill you to win an election. He has no sense of limits. He thinks an election is a war."

In his office, surrounded by memorabilia, framed pictures, testimonials from politicians he has aided, video tapes stacked to the ceiling, and piles of newspapers from Venezuela, Garth is constantly on the telephone. It's an appendage to his ear. "Information is power in politics," says Jeff Greenfield. "There are people who want to plug into him." Garth talks like Damon Runyon, thinks like Niccolò Machiavelli, and clutches his thin Dannemann cigars like Edward G. Robinson. He combines the personal style of the clubhouse boss with the professionalism required in the new era: he has something more potent to dispense than patronage. It's in such demand that he has become powerful in his own right. He embodies the past in his manner, recalling the denizens of Tammany Hall, while possessing the latest in video politics. When the party bosses went into decline, the media masters filled the vacuum with television commercials. They became the new power brokers. The shift from the clubhouse to the video cassette, from Carmine DeSapio to David Garth, was especially rapid in New York City.

Garth acutely expresses the New York idiom — brash, smart, and tough. He has played a large role in New York politics over the last fifteen years. He wants to be street-smart, authentic, and gritty while maintaining his airy Fifth Avenue suite. One without the other would indicate failure or emptiness in Manhattan. It's not enough simply to be a success; in New York success is always complicated. The style in which it occurs is all-important. Money has to be dressed up. Its appearance has to be fashionable to be acceptable. And power is always in fashion. In politics, the Garth style is New York.

He assumes that there is always an inside story, and he wants to know it. When he converses with insiders his words can't get out fast enough; they cascade over each other. He is an original type of inside dopester, though, one who has forged his own inner circle from which he derives his privileged information. He isn't sub-servient to the dominant opinion as are most inside dopesters. When a politician speaks with Garth he doesn't expect deference.

In political campaigns, Garth deploys a full-service blitz. Some consulting firms consist of a small nucleus that expands during the election season and contracts after the balloting. David Garth and Associates is always pumping at maximum strength. His research staff works year in, year out. A candidate taken on by Garth is investigated to establish the veracity of his claims and to ensure that he is impervious to criticism. Then his achievements are highlighted in the ad campaign and stitched into the overall strategy, which includes research into the opponent's record and statements. Any unsubstantiated remark the opponent may have made can work against him, turning his credibility into an issue itself. Polling is done in-house, too. Garth used to rely on out-siders, but now he prefers his own operation. As a campaign goes down to the wire the polling intensifies. In the beginning there are monthly polls, then weekly polls, then a poll every few days, then daily polls. Not a single palpitation in public opinion escapes Garth. By running the polling himself, he controls the interpre-tation of the figures. He insists on consistency. Once the themes are devised the candidate must gallop at Garth's speed. It's a carefully calibrated campaign.

When Garth controls your image you have to watch your weight. He made Ed Koch lose fifteen pounds: it's devastating for flabby liberalism to be represented by a flabby liberal. Garth insists that his candidates engage in some physical exercise. Garth himself — forty-nine years old, of medium height and a trifle stout — runs four miles every morning. He believes a strict regimen makes the candidate more disciplined, ready to take on the world.

Garth's success has a profound impact beyond his immediate campaigns; he deeply affects politicians and political consultants generally. He is an industry leader. "The emphasis placed on his media wizardry is all wrong," contends his former colleague Jeff Greenfield. "The key to David is that he's a first-rate political analyst. If we were back in 1931 David would still be an invaluable political adviser. What's true about television is that it can take someone who's relatively unknown and make him a visible factor. In the past you would have had to have gone through the party machinery. Most of the people who run for office aren't the kind of people who allow themselves to be taken over by a political consultant. David's very strong willed. He insists media is part of the overall strategy." There's always a question of whether Garth and his ads are implementing strategy or setting it.

But if others are confused, Garth understands very well what he's doing. "Politicians have always gone where the voters are," he says. "When the voters turned out at local fairs, the pols were there. When the voters listened to the radio, the pols were there. When the voters didn't leave their houses and sat in front of their television tubes, the pols went on television. So the politicians have always gone where the voters have gone. The result has been a real diminution of the power of the parties. What really strikes me now is that a lot of political writers are nostalgic about the bosses, which is really horseshit. As if the machines ever turned out high-quality candidates. Imagery is nothing new. Most of it hasn't happened by accident. Manipulation by publishers and bosses is nothing new. It's the style of manipulation that's new, except for the fact that the voter is more informed with the lousy commercials than he was before."

Rarely considered, though, is Garth's effect on politicians. They often believe that Garth can provide a short cut to success. They may feel that the narcissistic attention of the media is what counts. They lay money on Garth's desk and request the magic. Garth does not, however, suffer fools. He evicts them from his premises, as he did when a young, handsome, prominent New York politician profiled in the *New York Times Magazine* as a rising star asked Garth to put a spell on him. Garth hexed him instead. To have an image projected by Garth you first have to convince him that you know who you are. If you don't, he's convinced you're ultimately a loser. "We turn down about five out of every six guys who approach us," he says. "We take someone because they're unusually good, because the person they're running against is unusually bad or because there's an overriding issue, like the war. That's the way we get involved. I couldn't care about party. A guy in New York politics came to me and said he had the money. He offered me a quarter of a million dollars to do a small local race. I said " 'Fine, what do you stand for? What's wrong with the other guy?' 'You tell me,' he said. 'That's why I'm hiring you.' 'Get the fuck out of here,' I said. I thought the guy was a total disaster. Terrible."

Politicians increasingly feel that if they hire Garth or another premier consultant they're joining the charmed circle of winners. A pol may be flattered and bedazzled by the idea of the consultant making him a television star. The ads give him credibility with himself. He likes the image he sees — tough, decisive, honest, accomplished, often an improvement on reality. But the ads can be dangerous, freezing the pol's self-perception. Even a candidate who's staked out firm positions on the issues can suffer the shock of recognition. When Ed Koch was campaigning for mayor of New York, a voter on a subway platform recognized him from his television ads. "That's me," Koch clucked. "The commercials — they're me."

Hiring Garth or another high-powered consultant may give a politician a false sense of well-being. He feels he's secure in the hands of a proven professional. There's something inherently passive in this, even when the campaign may be dynamic. Too many politicians believe that the consultant possesses occult powers. The pols don't necessarily want to comprehend the media art, but rather to be possessed by it.

The secret, however, is that there is no secret. Garth's ads are like a televised brochure; their artlessness is artful. Consider his typical commercial: the candidate peers directly into the camera or shakes hands with folks in front of his house; as he speaks or during the voice-over, numerous statistics and written statements flash on the screen; his slogan is almost too long to read for the brief time it's seen. What is Garth doing? This doesn't seem especially clever or creative. But its plainness is deceiving. "Most of our commercials are what I consider quite obvious. We stopped doing cinema verité commercials ten years ago," he says. "Most of our commercials have our candidate looking directly into the camera. We took an obvious thing. I decided in 1968 that the guy on television wanted your vote. That's why he was on television. So the brilliant reasoning was why pull shit? Look into the camera and say: this is what I'm about, this is where I'm going, this is what I want to accomplish. And then we started superimposing a lot of information. This came out of Watergate when the credibility of politicians came into question. We discovered that the more information you put into a commercial there's a kind of disturbed reaction the first time people see it. They say, 'I missed that.' What you then do is have them looking the next time they see it. They don't want to miss anything. And the third time they see something else. Also, these commercials are designed to play several times. In an automobile ad, the first time you see it you get all the information. We wanted to get people involved in the problems, involved in what the candidate has done. We actually compress forty-five seconds of information into a thirty-second spot. The criticism about what we do is: what can you say in thirty seconds? Well, you can say a hell of a lot in thirty seconds if you want to. The ideal time for spots is five minutes. But you really can't get that time. So instead of that we'll do eight spots, ten spots, twenty spots. I'd rather get a deeper message across, but you have to break it up into different spots. If you put together all the spots that we do in a campaign, you've got a pretty good fifteen-minute presentation of what the guy's all about. We don't do mood stuff anymore."

Garth's ads are less an outgrowth of advertising than a bastardization of New Journalism. "A lot of times when we poll we ask people if they saw our commercials," he says. "They say no, we saw you on the news. That was the news. *We use our commercials as a news vehicle.*" Garth's ads are always factual. He presents reality unadorned, yet with completely biased implications. They are thirty-second documentaries reporting facts for partisan purposes. His spots aren't replete with factoids — Norman Mailer's neologism for half-truths — but real facts. He offers information as propaganda, oversimplifying and complicating things. He may lend gravity to the lightweight and importance to the insignificant. He may inflate small facts — for example, portraying a candidate's authorship of a minor bill as a major event.

Even Garth's negative campaigns take on the aura of news, an ersatz muckraking. They have the patina of investigative journalism, reporting moral failures against the public interest. These negative campaigns may work well partly because they seem actually to be a form of investigative journalism. Garth defines political experience through his ads, dramatizing events and issues in a reasoning way. It's objective on the surface, but thoroughly subjective in intent. This propagandistic version of New Journalism also creates stereotypes for easy grasping: the candidate as the man of the ethnic neighborhoods, for example. This too is a journalistic method.

Walter Lippmann, in his 1922 classic, *Public Opinion*, first offered the contemporary definition of the word *stereotype*, explaining it as the difference between "the world outside and the pictures in our heads." This was an advanced notion for its time. Photojournalism, which deals in real stereotypes, was still in its infancy. (It wasn't until two years after the publication of Lippmann's book that the first wirephoto — of the Republican convention nominating Calvin Coolidge — attracted widespread attention.) In 1922, radio didn't report news, newsreels were only about a decade old, and it was fourteen years before the introduction of *Life* magazine, the first picture newsweekly. With the spread of these journalistic vehicles, stereotypes assumed more tangible and actual form.

Lippmann believed that the media, if it adhered to high standards, would enlighten the public, unwrapping the enigma of public opinion. He observed:

> Democracies have made a mystery out of public opinion. There have been skilled organizers of opinion who understood the mystery well enough to create majorities on election day. But these organizers have been regarded by political science as low fellows or as "problems," not as possessors of the most effective knowledge there was on how to create and operate public opinion. The tendency of the people who have voiced the ideas of democracy, even when they have not managed its action, the tendency of students, orators, editors, has been to look upon Public Opinion as men in other societies looked upon the uncanny forces to which they ascribed the last word in the direction of events.

Lippmann believed that disseminating objective news would strengthen democracy, a corollary of the Fabian Socialist idea that education would lead inevitably to reform. Lippmann didn't foresee, however, that media would report events accurately *and* subjectively, shepherding the public. He failed to see that the "skilled organizers of opinion who understood the mystery" might themselves one day employ journalistic methods.

David Garth's television spots imagine politics so well that they become politics. They're not the message; they're the process. The spots allude to issues and candidates in a campaign and are a hidden issue themselves, straddling the chasm between truth and illusion. Everything Garth reports is true, but is it the truth?

His ads aren't political programs, but they're not empty images either. The ads objectify the desires of the candidate. They portray him as he wishes to be regarded by the public at the moment: the best man. This is more subtle than mere packaging. In selling a box of soap, the product is an inanimate commodity. A politician isn't. The relationship between a politician and the public differs from that of a product and the consumer. All markets are not alike.

"It was the money that made the political media experts," says Malcolm MacDougall, partner in Humphrey, Browning and Mac-Dougall, a leading Boston advertising agency, who devised the ads for Gerald Ford's 1976 presidential campaign. "The consultants used to concentrate just on political strategy," he says. "Now they do ads and strategy." MacDougall argues that the political consultants aren't properly part of the advertising business. "The ad agencies didn't really love this business. A political candidate isn't a soap. A politician spends money and then the campaign's over. Then he's not running anymore. This is a one-shot deal. It's a way for an ad agency to get a quick buck, but you don't fight for it. It's better to have an account that spends $1 million every year. Politicians are hard to deal with — they're a pain in the ass. They know nothing about advertising. Advertising agencies have little to do with politics anymore. The consultants are *the* political scene now."

"All soaps are alike," says Jeff Greenfield. "Candidates are different, unless you believe it makes no difference who wins. Politics is the art of explaining the difference. That takes an appreciation of what's on people's minds and what it will take for you to appreciate the candidate. The skill is not to shape a candidate but to make the reality about the candidate as appealing as possible."

For David Garth, video tape is power at thirty frames per second. He uses media as an instrument and a guise. He is a strategist, mentor, and confidant. He isn't bothered with the detailed administration of government, but with the grand outlines of power. He may have more impact on politics than his candidates. Yet hung in his office is a cautionary quotation from

*The Prince* by Machiavelli: "Whoever causes another to become powerful is ruined because he creates such power either with skill or with force; both these factors are viewed with suspicion by the one who has become powerful." Garth asks, "Did you read that quote? One of the reasons that hasn't happened to me is because I have disappeared on the public level after a campaign."

Garth studies Machiavelli, well aware that technique without political insight is ultimately ineffective. He is not a theorist; his intelligence is practical and adaptive. He is very sensitive about being labeled a Machiavellian because it implies that he is without principles. He forgets that Machiavelli himself had principles and that *The Prince* concludes with an idealistic expression of Italian nationalism.

Garth is driven by impulses reaching back into his childhood, leading him to seek mastery in his life. He exhibits all the characteristics of what might be termed the Teddy Roosevelt Syndrome: he was a physically frail child who developed his body and his career out of sheer will. Garth's father was a well-to-do manufacturer and his mother was active in Democratic politics. They lived in a small town in Nassau County on Long Island, which was almost exclusively Republican; Garth knew only one other boy whose parents were Democrats. His mother conducted political meetings in the house constantly. Discussion of Walter Lippmann's latest column was typical dinner-table conversation. As a youngster Garth was stricken with a mastoid infection and rheumatic fever. He was bedridden for five years. A doctor told his parents he would never walk again. "When you're very young and you're in pain for a very long time you really are given a choice," says Garth. "And the choice is whether you succumb to the pain or you beat it. My father and mother would never let me give up. In my mind, I beat the illness. You develop a sense of drive and competition and a love of life and excitement that you never lose. This was forty years ago. You overcompensate. I had to learn to walk again. I picked up marbles with my toes to build my feet back up. Nobody was ever as compulsive as I was. I was in bed for five years listening to kids play outside, and when I was well I played eighteen hours a day. All I cared about was playing ball. That carried on until I was in my twenties. My parents were very intellectual, and they'd look at me with amazement. My father said I was going to be a total idiot. I never did any school-work at all. It's where the competitive instinct came from. I think I've mellowed a lot in the last ten years, after the age of forty. I think success helps quite a bit. You don't have to prove anything anymore. When you don't have freedom of movement, freedom to play, freedom to travel, and then regain that freedom, it means a lot to you. The idea of being able to walk is a big thing. Forty years later it's still a big thing to me. I have the memory of being incapacitated. The thing about having pain when you're very young is that the memory of it doesn't really ever leave you. It developed something else in me that wasn't such a good thing. I decided that I would do what I wanted to do. If something didn't make me happy I wouldn't do it. So that what I am today and what I do today is what I wanted to do. I paid a lot of dues. I probably was ten years behind where I could have been if I had taken *the* job or gone into my father's business. I might have been successful in what society terms success. To say the least, I was a late bloomer."

As a young man Garth felt himself on the edge. He needed existential action desperately. "I read Hemingway. I couldn't stand my mother's meetings. But the idea of action . . ." He found the single most dangerous spot on the globe: a border kibbutz during the Israeli war of independence. Garth toted a gun, waiting for nighttime assaults. After a few months he returned home, where he finished college. He wasn't cured of warfare, though. "I'm very crazy," he says. "I loved being in the army during the Korean War. It was different. I felt I was pampered, indulged. In the army, you're on your own. For the first time in my life I met a cross-section of people. If you come from a gilded ghetto the army is a great equalizer. The idea of getting killed isn't such a great idea, but the people you meet are great. Your money, your background, your degrees don't mean anything. The question is: can you work with the guys, are you a good guy?" Coming from a genteel family, his obsessive search for authenticity makes his gruff, occasionally profane manner understandable.

When he was finished with the army, Garth enrolled in Columbia University's graduate program in psychology. He wanted to be a clinical analyst. But he gave it up because it was too passive. His first postgraduate job was as a television producer. He convinced a New York station to commit itself to broadcast high school football games. It was assumed Garth already had the high schools' agreement. He didn't. It was a bluff — and it succeeded. The station gave him the contract and with it Garth was able to get the schools to provide the action.

When he was thirty, he was anonymous, without influence, and uninvolved in politics. Four of his friends, who congregated regularly in a coffee shop, decided in 1960 that they wanted Adlai Stevenson as the Democratic party's candidate for president. They had no political connections. They approached the local pols, who were waiting for Kennedy, but were given the brush-off. "So," says Garth, "we had a fundraising party in one of our apartments. We invited everyone we knew — and eighteen people showed up. We raised $100. We got a walkup apartment for our headquarters. Since it was the off-season for the television shows, I had some spare time. They made me chairman. We had a press conference. Reporters said, 'Who do you think you are?' I said, 'Nobody.' They said, 'Why should you run it?' I said, 'I'd be happy to join you.' It got bigger and bigger and bigger. Then Eleanor Roosevelt joined. She said she wouldn't chair the Draft Stevenson Committee unless I was co-chair. So I wound up being co-chairman."

Stevenson, as always, played Hamlet, indecisively wavering — to run or not to run. Garth forged ahead. At the convention he gave the Kennedy campaign a fright attack. The Kennedys were cocky about their hardball politics, but Garth played the same game. He tapped their phones and forged gallery tickets, which he distributed to Stevenson supporters. Then Garth packed the gallery for a wild demonstration. Newspaper headlines blared: KENNEDY BANDWAGON FALTERS and KENNEDY TIDE EBBS. Theodore White wrote in his book, *The Making of the President 1960*, "Here now was the greatest and most authentic demonstration of emotion since the galleries of Philadelphia had overwhelmed the Republican delegates of 1940 with their chant of WE WANT WILLKIE." Davey Garth, a punk upstart from New York, almost had the Kennedys on the run. Unfortunately for his plan, Stevenson opted not to run. On Garth's wall is a framed letter from Stevenson dated August 12, 1960: "I hope we can have a proper talk 'when the dust settles' — and I can have a proper chance to thank you in person for contributing so gallantly to my glorious 'demise'!"

Garth's big break came in the 1965 campaign of John Lindsay for mayor of New York. Garth ran his media campaign, helping to usher in the golden age of charisma and pure image. For the Lindsay spots, Garth adopted a cinema verité style, which he later abandoned. Lindsay, the tall, lean, handsome WASP, was filmed walking in his shirtsleeves through New York's poorer neighborhoods expressing concern. "The original Lindsay stuff was very interesting," says Garth. "We started using a nightly news technique. The imagery was that we had a guy who was active. The poster shot of the guy with the coat over his shoulder, which was copied by everyone in the country, was an image spot."

In 1968, at an interlude in Garth's rise, he handled advertising in Eugene McCarthy's campaign for president, teaming up with his old friend and mentor from the Draft Stevenson movement, Tom Finney. After the short-lived Stevenson campaign Finney became the law partner of Clark Clifford, the most influential attorney in Washington, epitome of the capital's elite, adviser to every Democratic president since Harry Truman. "I learned from

Finney that all the cliches about the establishment — I came from a left background, my mother worked for Henry Wallace — were really cliches," says Garth. "You have to know what you're talking about. Just because a guy is a Washington lawyer you can't say he's a bad guy. I watched Finney operate: he was straight, tough, and had a sense of humor. I don't think he did anything he couldn't live with a month or a year later."

During the Lindsay administration Garth helped build the mayor's popularity in the polls through an array of media events. Lindsay was everywhere, doing everything: hosting call-in talk shows, giving special televised speeches, personally intervening in dramatic incidents. "We built people to too high a pitch," says Garth. "We raised expectations too high. People expected him not to screw up. When he did, the result was much worse."

After winning reelection as an independent with few political debts to fulfill, Lindsay squandered an unprecedented chance for accomplishment through a run for the presidency in 1972. "If you elect a matinee idol mayor, you're going to get a musical comedy administration," Robert Moses, the penultimate New York power broker, prophetically remarked after his first meeting with Lindsay.

Garth did the Lindsay for president ads. Lindsay never caught fire. When Dick Aurelio, a Lindsay aide, pulled Garth's ads off the air in the middle of the Wisconsin primary, Garth was incensed. Undeterred by a blizzard in New York, Garth hopped the first available plane to Milwaukee. Upon arrival he charged into a taxi, directing the driver to Lindsay headquarters, where he stormed into Aurelio's office still wearing his overcoat and hat. "Aurelio!" Garth shouted. "Fuck you!" And then he turned on his heels and retraced his route back to New York.

In the meantime, Lindsay prepared the groundwork, through his neglect, for New York City's subsequent financial crisis. In a way, he was the Tom Buchanan of New York politics. "They were careless people, Tom and Daisy," F. Scott Fitzgerald wrote in *The*

*Great Gatsby* about the upper-class swells from fictional East Egg Harbor. "They smashed up things and creatures and then retreated back into their money or their vast carelessness, or whatever it was that kept them together, and let other people clean up the mess they had made."

Lindsay was as careless in his personal relationships as he was in politics. After contracting Garth as his agent, directing him to try to get him a gig as a commentator on CBS television, Lindsay made his own deal with ABC without notifying Garth. "I woke up one morning and CBS said David Garth broke his word," Garth says. "I called up CBS and asked what was going on. They said Lindsay had signed with ABC. I said I didn't know about it. He left me out on a limb. Supposedly, he told someone to tell me who never told me. That was his rationale. Horseshit! I was very upset about it." For a while they didn't speak, which made for certain unpleasantries since they lived in the same building. ("I got *him* into *my* building," Garth says.) But now they are courteous if not exactly cozy.

The period of the early seventies was dominated, of course, by Richard Nixon. For Garth, this was the age of toughness. "We began to use the word tough," he says. "What happened with toughness was that we got involved with a lot of campaigns in 1970 when the right wing was coming on very hard on law and order. We came up with the idea of using the word tough to provide an answer to the right-wing attack. We started to use the word tough in our commercials." The slogans of Garth's candidates from the age of toughness are strikingly similar: "Fighting for the People of Illinois," "Give Yourself a Fighting Chance," "Strong Enough to Speak His Mind, Tough Enough to Get Results," "Tough Young Men for Tough Young Jobs." The key transitional figure for Garth in the passage from the age of charisma to the age of toughness was John Tunney, who ran for the Senate from California in 1970. (That year Nixon campaigned hysterically for John Mitchell's kind of justice, eagerly provoking crowds to pelt him with rocks so that he would have evidence of lawlessness on video tape to show in political commercials.) Tunney was a friend of Ted Kennedy's, liberal and glamorous, son of the former heavyweight boxing champion Gene Tunney, perfect lineage for the moment. Garth's poster of Tunney showed him with his coat clung over his shoulder à la Lindsay. His slogan: "The Big Boys Have Enough Friends. You Need a Fighter in Your Corner."

Perhaps the best campaign Garth ran in the early 1970s was Tom Bradley's for mayor of Los Angeles. Bradley was the ideal liberal candidate for the age of toughness, a moderate black, former police officer and college track star, a walking personification of the American Dream. Bradley had been beaten in 1969 by Sam Yorty, who ran a racist campaign. Nineteen seventy-three was the rematch. Voters were confused about Bradley. He was a hulking figure at six feet four, and he was always surrounded by blacks raising their fists. Garth knew immediately that this wasn't an image that would work. Selling Bradley wasn't hard, though. All he had to do was explain who he was. Hence, this ad in which the candidate speaks into the camera: "The last time I ran for mayor, I lost. Probably because a lot of people weren't sure what I stood for. Maybe you were one of them. Maybe you wondered whether I'd treat all people fairly, or whether I'd only listen to the problems of blacks. Frankly, I couldn't win this election with only one bloc of voters . . ." This time, Bradley won.

The signal that a new period was unfolding came in 1976 when John Tunney was beaten by S. I. Hayakawa. Garth's spots for Tunney were very positive and not very effective. Compounding the problem, Tunney was short of cash. Without money, Garth can't work well for a candidate. It was the end of both the age of charisma and the age of toughness. "Garth is highly creative," Tunney says. "In my first campaign he did a brilliant job. In the second campaign we were terribly handicapped, not having adequate amounts of money to have the spots he had done viewed by the voters. His spots were extremely positive while Hayakawa's were extremely negative. I was outspent four to one. We never had a chance to counter the poison spread on the television screen. When it became obvious we didn't have the dough it became difficult for Garth to do much. By the very nature of his profession he needs money to display his wares and have impact. We never gave his campaign a chance. No image-maker can create an image if you don't have the money to put it on the screen. When we had a lot of money in 1970 it worked superbly. There's no way to tell whether the political climate in California had changed, because we didn't have the money. Television is the only way to go out here. If you're in a large state where you rely on media, if you're up against an opponent who has money to launch a highly negative campaign, you better be able to spend an equal amount of money. Maybe you shouldn't be concerned with creating a positive image for yourself, but attacking your opponent. Jerry Brown did that last time with Evelle Younger. He made Younger the issue. If I could do it over again, based on what Brown did and what happened to me, I'd spend every bit of money I had attacking my opponent."

It was the beginning of the age of lowered expectations. Garth's paradigmatic candidate for the new age was Ed Koch. Garth didn't believe Koch had a chance. He tried to convince him not to run. Garth wanted Mario Cuomo as his man, but Cuomo waffled, only to enter the race later, with Garth in the enemy camp. Under Garth's tutelage, Koch refurbished his image and spent virtually all of his money on airtime. His campaign staff consisted of David Garth's office. Meanwhile, Cuomo, aided by Jimmy Carter's trusted lieutenants, Gerald Rafshoon and Pat Caddell, tried to win the liberal vote by blasting Koch for supporting the death penalty. The issue backfired for Cuomo, who was also wasting his funds on posters, neighborhood storefront headquarters, and bumper stickers. Television was the ballgame. And Garth was far better than Rafshoon, especially on his own turf. Garth mugged him. Koch's slogan: "After eight years of charisma and four years of the clubhouse, why not try competence?" Garth's wording was an implicit self-repudiation.

The most emotionally unsettling incident for Garth during that campaign was an embittering fight with *Village Voice* writer Jack Newfield, who helped a *Voice* reporter pen a damaging article on Koch's pro-death penalty stand. "I don't think Jack Newfield could accept the fact that Ed Koch could beat Cuomo," says Garth. "Little Ed beat Cuomo? If anyone knew the worthwhile things I had done, Jack should have known them. He personified me as a Machiavellian genius. If something good happened for Ed I did it. If something bad happened for Mario I did it. If I was half as powerful as those guys said, it would be the biggest joke in the world. We ran an obvious campaign. Jack just didn't like it. He told a guy to tell me, 'I'm going to get you.' After the campaign he wanted to become friends, make up. I said, 'No, you son of a bitch. You knew me for eight years. You knew of the campaigns I didn't take because the people were just bad guys. A lot of money. You knew it better than anyone in the city. You were the one son of a bitch who knew me. You knew everything. And you let that article get in the paper. I will not forget.' There are a lot of guys I'll have fights with. Jack was different. Jack went on vacations with me. Everywhere I went the guy was there. He was a friend. My feeling is that you do that one fucking time only. There's no going back."

Newfield is as splenetic as Garth about their tiff. "He has no political beliefs that interfere with a well-paying client," he says. "David's weakness is a streak of paranoia, and he's a hater. He wants to establish himself as the boss. He has an authoritarian streak." In 1978, the *Village Voice* listed Garth as one of the hundred greediest people in town. "It wasn't for money, though," says Garth. "It was for power."

Garth is angered and hurt by the repudiation of his former friend. He finds it inexplicable that Newfield should accuse him of having no principles. "Ask him about Moynihan," demands Garth.

When Daniel Patrick Moynihan, former United Nations ambassador, began to put together his campaign for the Senate he approached Garth, asking him to produce the ads. Garth's friends were alarmed. They believed Moynihan's brand of neoconservative politics was dangerous. At a lunch in a small coffee shop on a Saturday afternoon, Jack Newfield, Jeff Greenfield, and David Halberstam — chronicler of the American Establishment in his books *The Best and the Brightest* and *The Powers That Be* — made the anti-Moynihan case. "It was clear Moynihan was going to win," says Greenfield. "We all urged him not to take him." Garth went to Moynihan and told him he couldn't do the campaign. He lost a quarter-million-dollar fee.

In 1978, Garth faced his biggest tests. Two candidates he had directed to previous victories were in deep trouble. New Jersey governor Brendan Byrne was down in the polls 75 to 25 and New York governor Hugh Carey was down 70 to 30. It looked like the long count. Garth's response was to devise a politics of apologetics, presented as a bold stroke of candor and leadership. The pol on the wane would go before the cameras and say he was sorry; this would prove him a leader. This tactic can disarm an opponent, depriving him of a target. If the public accepts the chastened incumbent's apology, the opponent has little to attack. More, a vote for a repentant pol can make the voter feel magnanimous.

"Byrne promised no taxes and there was a tax," says Garth. "So we ran an ad where he said, 'I made a mistake.' Carey had really been an excellent governor and a terrible personality. So we went out in public and said it: 'Look, I'm not a very nice guy, but I've done this and I've done that.' Carey is brilliant in regard to government. Personality? He's black Irish, very moody. He won't do the things most pols will do. He's a split personality. When the chips are down, he gets down to business. The reason he was in trouble was that he didn't take credit for half the stuff he did in the state. He didn't want to cut ribbons. He's very irascible." For Carey's race, Garth became the psychologist of public opinion. He had Carey paternally explain his errors and positions, like a good father, telling the public why they must mature and accept them, because to do so was to accept complexity. A front-page headline in the *New York Daily News* read, CAREY: I'LL CHANGE MY PERSONALITY.

Almost miraculously, Byrne and Carey both won reelection. This style of campaigning placed the burden of change on the public, not the pol. A vote for the repentant pol was a measure of how grownup the voter was. (In fact, this tactic was borrowed from the second Lindsay campaign, when he confessed mistakes, a gambit that resurrected him.)

In 1978, Garth escaped from the age of lowered expectations to enjoy a success harkening back to the age of charisma. All three presidential candidates in Venezuela made bids for his services. From one hopeful, Garth could have cleared a cool million. He passed and took the Christian Democrat, Luis Herrera.

American consultants had been working for Venezuelan politicians for years. To be a contender for president there you must have a gringo image-maker. Garth's man was outspent by more than three to one. It was a high-stakes contest. The governing party laid out about $110 million, while Herrera spent a measly $28 million. "The usual thing in Venezuela is pretty faces and a lot of music," says Garth. "We polled and the polls said the Venezuelan people knew what the problems were. The cliche of the establishment was that you had to tell them only good news. They're happy people. We ran an issue-oriented campaign. We aimed for the lowest economic group, which is called the *marginales*. We got unbelievable criticism. One ad said: 'When Carlos Andres Perez came into office the Venezuelan debt was $1.7 million. The price of oil tripled. The debt today is between $12.2 and $18 billion.' They went wild." Then Garth pulled a number from his collection of golden oldies. He reran John Lindsay, with Luis Herrera playing the part. Herrera was sent into the slums with cameras trailing behind him, much like Lindsay tramping through Harlem. "If you don't use a set and you show conditions and you put the guy where the conditions are, it's obvious. Herrera says to look at the conditions here. He goes into a barrio and asks about the conditions. Our style hasn't changed. The reality of the problems dictates the shots." Garth was propagating the multinationalization of images.

Garth's own image was indelibly imprinted in the public imagination through the movie *The Candidate*, in which a consultant, satirically patterned on Garth, guides a good-looking but vapid pol, played by Robert Redford, to victory. In the film, there is a scene in which Redford debates his opponent. Redford can't answer a question posed by a reporter so he replies, "I don't know." This response is a big hit. The cynical consultant hypes it as refreshingly honest, a new brand of politics.

Jeremy Larner, screenwriter of *The Candidate*, was a speechwriter for Eugene McCarthy during his presidential bid. He met Garth in that campaign.

"Larner really resented the 'ploys' in the campaign," Garth says. "I read the script and I said it was every fucking cliche in the book. What came out was just a cliche. Jeremy went on and on with his cliches: no principles, doesn't give a shit: if it works, it works. It was obvious and it was wrong. There's plenty to criticize in this business. But to portray me as a hack — I resented it."

Garth was given a script to read for a reason. He was offered the part of the Garth character, which would have been life imitating art imitating life. He turned it down. The role went to an actor named Allen Garfield, who copied the patented Garth mannerisms. The image disturbed Garth. "I lost forty pounds," he says, "because the guy they cast was a dead ringer for me."

## CHAPTER FIVE

# ENDING THE MACHINE AGE

## DON ROSE

Death is one of the great agents of reform in politics. When it intervenes you can't make a deal. Death can't be compromised with a favor or bought off with a bribe. Death isn't impressed with how powerful you are. In the race against death the balloting is always rigged. Connections won't help, even when you're the boss.

So it was for Richard J. Daley, mayor of Chicago, chairman of the Cook County Democratic Central Committee, a midwestern Ozymandius, titan of his realm. On December 20, 1976, seated in his doctor's waiting room and dressed in the blue shroud of a patient, Daley was stricken with a massive heart attack. He keeled over onto the carpet and died. Chicagoans were aghast. Daley had promulgated the doctrine that Chicago is "The City

That Works." The political machine he headed never failed to deliver services and favors, and, for the twenty-one years he occupied the mayor's office, he made himself seem indispensable to the smooth operation of the city. Without him, the future was uncertain. His death, not entirely unexpected because he had a chronic heart condition, instilled in Chicagoans fear that the machine might not be eternal. The Boss is dead! Long live the Boss!

Daley's successor was Michael Bilandic, a loyal alderman who had been a corporate lawyer. Bilandic represented the Eleventh Ward, where Daley lived his life from birth to death on a single block. The Eleventh — Bridgeport — is the "Back of the Yards" neighborhood, an immigrant enclave, for years perfumed with the odor of the nearby packinghouses. When the South Side turned into a black ghetto after World War II, Bridgeport remained the same. Daley's ward was frozen in time; the mayor took care of his own. A majority of its residents became city employees, a special legion of soldiers in the vast army of precinct captains who maintained the machine in working order. All of Daley's key men were from Bridgeport. Bilandic was the logical heir.

Yet less than three years after Daley's death, the standard-bearer of the organization bequeathed to him was defeated in the Democratic primary, an unprecedented event. Worse, Mayor Bilandic was beaten by Jane Byrne, who as consumer affairs commissioner had exposed a taxi fare-fixing scandal and had been booted unceremoniously out of office. It was widely assumed that Byrne was a nuisance who would fade into obscurity once she was thrashed in the primary. When she entered the race it was with long odds. She needed help to manage her campaign. So she turned to the best independent political consultant and the best-known radical in Chicago, Don Rose.

Political consulting is virtually an unknown craft in Chicago. Consultants are as rare as blacksmiths. In Chicago, the machine handled all aspects of campaign work. A candidate had no reason to go outside the machine for assistance. Dissenters in the one-party state had great difficulty in cracking the monolith; the machine apparatus was impenetrable and unified. Media campaigns conducted by imported specialists appeared to have no impact. When Bill Singer, an independent alderman, made a run for mayor against Daley in 1975, he hired David Garth from New York. Garth waved his wand over Singer, but to Chicagoans Singer never resembled a prince. Within the borders of the city, the machine was the campaign.

Don Rose defied Chicago's Newtonian laws of politics, transcending the linear dynamics of the machine and ushering in the age of media relativity. The Byrne versus Bilandic contest was a direct clash of the modern and old-style campaigns. The machine had always run its campaigns the same way. It depended on an army of patronage workers to turn out the faithful who were loyal to the machine for its performance of social services. Those not in the machine's orbit seemed irrelevant to politics. Independent activists were mostly isolated individuals without instruments of power. Rose, however, as a political consultant, played the role of activist and discovered the tool of media with which to challenge the machine. "The media was pivotal in this campaign," he says. "In effect, it was the machine versus the media."

The consultant is necessarily a political outsider in Chicago; to be outside the traditional party organization is in itself an act of opposition. "I am fundamentally a social activist," Rose says. "I pick and choose very carefully whom I want to get involved with." In defeating the machine Rose showed how effective a consultant could be in campaigns. The machine lost not only because it failed to uphold its customary efficiency but also because it didn't understand the nature of the campaign waged against it. "Consulting is not heavy in Chicago," Rose says. "We don't have the kind of operations here that there are in New York or Washington." Advertising, on the other hand, is a major industry in Chicago; in fact, the city is the second-biggest center of advertising agencies in the country. The rise of the consultant in Chicago is strictly a function of politics, not of advertising. "The politics are very specialized here, unique in America, much more constricted," Rose observes. "The domination of the machine made the trade almost superfluous."

To most Easterners, Chicago is a place to do business or a way station to points west. They don't comprehend its indigenous culture, political or otherwise. They generally consider Chicago to be the Second City. Chicago, after all, receives the latest trends; it doesn't start them. It follows fashion, and in doing so seems to live up to its billing.

On the other hand, the perception of Chicago by southern Californians is very different from that of Easterners, mainly because many Chicagoans have emigrated to the West Coast. In some ways, the flamboyant style of southern California is an unfolding of the fantasies of Chicagoans forced to repress their more surreal imaginings in the wintry Midwest.

The mythology of Chicago is mostly true: it is "the city of the big shoulders" (Carl Sandburg), where "the masses who do the city's labor also keep the city's heart" (Nelson Algren), and whose unofficial motto is "Where's Mine?" (Mike Royko). It is where "form follows function" and "function follows form," according to the dictum of the seminal Chicago architect Louis Sullivan. Chicago is a city-state with its own standards, its own galaxy of stars, gossip columnists, folk heroes, rebels, and villains. It is neither east nor west. It's more flatly American, and that's a truism, too. Chicagoans have a secure sense of being at the center of the continent. They don't feel themselves at the edge like Californians; Chicagoans don't think they'll fall of the continent or that they've reached the end of the frontier. Chicago remains an inescapably realistic setting, the city of Theodore Dreiser, Richard Wright, and James T. Farrell. Chicago is too distinct to pretend it's something it isn't. And Chicagoans always know the score. (Richard J. Daley was the premier scorekeeper. The license plate number on his car was the exact vote total he received in his first mayoral election — 708,222.)

Don Rose learned the score and never went down for the count. As he worked his way through several professions, each job became part of an apprenticeship, training that stood him in good stead when it was time to confront the machine.

He started out in the late forties as a jazz musician, and he jammed with some of the best. (His son is named for his friend Max Roach.) He played the trumpet, but he hurt his mouth, and picked up a heavy drug habit. "I wanted to get out of the whole gestalt," he says. He abandoned his career as a jazzman, but kept improvising. He soloed in politics; everything else was a riff. Since giving up the horn he has been a newspaper publisher, political columnist, jazz critic, film maker, radio broadcaster, public relations expert, and professional gourmand. While he was conducting the Byrne campaign he maintained the following jobs: writing restaurant reviews for the *Chicago Sun-Times*, *Chicago Reader*, and *Chicago* magazine; hosting a weekly radio show called "Problems of the City"; performing public relations work with the Illinois Housing Development Authority; and writing occasional book and jazz reviews.

Rose is one of those autodidacts who, having mastered one discipline, feels compelled to master others. "A long time ago," he says, "in the early sixties, I started a film production company to do industrial films, with dreams of doing theatrical films. I learned all the ancillary things around it; some self-taught, some at courses. I know sound, I know typography, I know photography. I published my own newspaper, the *Hyde Park–Kenwood Voices*, one of the early alternative newspapers, from 1966 to 1973. I've made it a point to learn about these things. It interests me."

The week before Jane Byrne's inauguration as mayor I met Rose at the Byrne headquarters, housed in the ancient Monadnock Building, one of the first skyscrapers and a monument to the Chicago School of architecture; it was built in 1891, and is sixteen stories tall with, as one architectural critic observed, "severe Egyptian inspired walls." Rose's office was a nook decorated with the predictable maps of key wards and precincts. He stroked his salt-and-pepper beard as he spoke on the telephone; a stack of pink messages requesting him to return calls was on his desk. He's balding and has a paunch, indicating that jogging and tennis aren't among his myriad interests. He wore crepe-bottomed shoes, navy blue pants that didn't exactly match his navy blue sport jacket, an electric blue, white, gold, olive, and pink-striped shirt, and an indescribable blue- and red-patterned tie. Nothing matched but his socks. His trousers were ripped in the crotch. But not once during a long afternoon of meetings and traipsing across the Loop did he concede the existence of the tear. He never glanced downward for a furtive second. Clearly, here is a man of substance.

We spent little time at Byrne headquarters. Rose had to race across town to his job at the Illinois Housing Development Authority in the Prudential Building, located at the base of Grant Park. We walked briskly up Michigan Avenue, a stiff wind in our faces, Rose's unbuttoned sport jacket flapping as though he had wings. Once inside, he collected a pile of phone messages from the receptionist and headed for his desk. "I got a pigeonhole here," he remarked. A young secretary handed him a copy of the autobiography of former Black Panther Bobby Seale, which he had lent her. She didn't care for it. Rose shrugged.

"I've been involved in left politics since I was a kid," he says. "At the age of sixteen I worked with what became the Progressive party. My parents weren't left. They were Roosevelt Democrats. My father managed a shoe store. But somewhere early on I started reading about socialism, and I decided that that was the way the world ought to be run. I read everything — Trotsky, Bakunin, Malraux. The only thing I ever joined was Norman Thomas's Socialist party. It sort of dissolved. I was a promiscuous leftist. I was never a party-line person. I think I'm an ideologue, but a flexible one."

His involvement in the jazz scene and his leftist perspective led him to believe that race was a paramount question in American life. He became a civil rights activist. When Dr. Martin Luther King, fresh from his campaigns in the South, decided to shift the focus of the movement to the northern cities, he chose Chicago as the testing ground. Don Rose became his press secretary. "King was one of the few people I was slightly in awe of," he says. For King he wrote speeches, interpreted them to the Chicago press, escorted King to unproductive meetings with Mayor Daley, and devised some media events. It was important that King appear to be accessible to his constituency in Chicago, which differed from the Southern blacks he had worked with previously. The Southern Baptist preacher image wouldn't do. "Did you ever shoot pool, Dr. King?" Rose inquired one day. "Certainly," came the reply. So Rose directed him to a nearby pool hall, where King ingratiated himself with the patrons and had his picture taken with cue in hand. Rose also convinced King to post his demands on the door of city hall, recalling Martin Luther's act. The Chicago Freedom Movement, however, wasn't a success in the way King had expected. Mayor Daley — who in 1963 had proclaimed, "There are no ghettoes in Chicago" — was polite but unyielding. King's mission drew him away to other battlefields.

Rose then became press secretary for the New Politics conference held in Chicago in 1967. This convention floated publicly for the first time the notion of a "Dump Johnson" movement. Although the conference ended in a shambles when black power advocates demanded half the representation and some white liberals walked out, it helped generate the pressure that led to President Johnson's abdication.

As a result of his involvement in the New Politics conference, Rose was strategically placed for his next phase, as press secretary for the National Mobilization Committee, the sponsor of protests against the 1968 Democratic convention. In his account of the events, Rose wrote:

We had been planning the convention action for most of that year. Twice we almost called the whole thing off — after the King murder and after the Kennedy murder. But we weighed the effect of the two assassinations on young people against the war and black people against the Johnson Administration's position on civil rights and decided that people would still want to come.

On August 26, the first night of the Democratic Convention, youths gathered in Lincoln Park. Police unloaded barrages of tear gas and flurries of nightsticks; they clubbed everyone within reach, including *Playboy* publisher Hugh Hefner, out for a stroll. It was a police riot. The next day the National Mobilization Committee called a press conference. "What the hell can we say, man? It was so horrible, unbelievable," said Rennie Davis, protest spokesman, to Don Rose. "Tell them," Rose answered, "they'll never get away with it because the whole world's watching." And that's what Rennie Davis said. On August 28, the night Hubert Humphrey was nominated, phalanxes of police bludgeoned young demonstrators in full view of the television cameras. The sound-track accompanying the video tape played to a stunned nation. It consisted of a rhythmic chant, uncannily revealing the crowd's self-consciousness about the media dimensions of what they were experiencing. They were chanting Don Rose's slogan: "The Whole World Is Watching."

While the infamous Chicago Eight conspiracy trial proceeded, Don Rose was entrenching himself deeper into the recesses of Chicago politics. He was the behind-the-scenes strategist of the most significant postconvention foray against Daley in the electoral arena: liberal alderman Bill Singer's victory in 1969. "It was the beginning of the rebellion against Daley," Rose says.

In 1971, he produced the media spots and helped devise strategy for the challenge of liberal Republican Richard Friedman against Daley. "Those were the first political ads I worked on," Rose says. "The campaign demonstrated the limitations of lakefront liberalism as a citywide strategy. It lacked ethnic appeal. Friedman had no relationship to the people off the lakefront, where the liberal wards are. That campaign taught me about issues that cut and didn't cut in Chicago. We tried only the litany of antimachine lore. And we got 29.5 percent of the vote."

The following year Rose managed the successful campaign of Bernard Carey, the Republican candidate for state's attorney. It was a cathartic political event. Carey's opponent was Edward Hanrahan who in 1969 had participated in the midnight raid on a house of sleeping Black Panthers. Fred Hampton, the young Panther leader in Chicago who had a considerable reputation in the black community, was gunned down while he slept. Hanrahan self-righteously defended the killing. His law-and-order fervor even created a split between him and the Daley machine. "There were two themes in that campaign," Rose recalls. "In black and liberal areas it was to exterminate Hanrahan, the racist murderer. In suburban areas the theme was that Hanrahan was incompetent." The campaign caught Hanrahan in a vise. Moreover, the election of Bernard Carey laid the groundwork for further reform efforts. It was a crucial victory. "If nothing else," Rose says, "Carey's work on vote fraud made everything else possible. By the end of the 1974 elections he had wiped out two thirds of the vote fraud in the city. That's a major achievement."

Rose seemed to be behind every reform candidate in Chicago, although in 1975 he didn't work for Bill Singer in his race for mayor against Daley. "I didn't think he was ready, that the time was right, that he was the right candidate," he says. Singer lost. ("You don't go for winners all the time," says David Garth, Singer's media adviser.) Meanwhile, Rose continued to assist campaigns that severely weakened the machine's authority. For example, he

ran the campaign of Congressman Ralph Metcalfe, a black legislator who broke with Daley over the issue of police brutality.
Metcalfe's defection was a blow to Daley from which the machine
never fully recovered. Rose's expertise and political savvy helped
make the break a viable option for Metcalfe, who trusted Rose
because of his work with Dr. King. Rose became a one-man
movement, possessing more intimate knowledge of Chicago politics
than any other reformer. By the late seventies he knew he could
provide the campaign to beat the machine. What he lacked were
the proper circumstances and the right candidate.

A friend introduced him to Jane Byrne. Byrne had had a genteel
upbringing. Her father, a former Inland Steel vice president, was
a steel warehouse owner. She attended proper Catholic schools
through college. Immediately after graduation she married a
Marine Corps pilot, a Notre Dame graduate. A year after their
marriage a daughter was born. It was an Irish-American idyll, a
perfect marriage of the fifties. Then William P. Byrne's plane
crashed in heavy fog; Jane was left a widow, with a fifteen-month-
old child to raise and support.

Her sister was a friend of Eunice Shriver, whose husband,
Sargent Shriver, managed the Merchandise Mart in Chicago and
was involved in Chicago politics as chairman of the school board.
When John F. Kennedy ran for president Jane's sister signed on to
do campaign work. Jane, too, decided that she'd like to work for
Kennedy. She was hired as secretary-treasurer of the Chicago
Kennedy for president campaign headquarters. Two years after
the election Mayor Daley called her into his office.

"Why did you go to them? The Kennedys. Why did you go to
them? Why didn't you come to us?" Daley asked her.*

"Well," she replied, "I'm no big political whiz that everybody's
looking for. I went to them because people knew them, and I
wanted to work for the campaign."

---

*This conversation is based on one recorded in the article "How I Got Involved"
by Jane Byrne, as told to Paul McGrath, *Chicago* magazine, April 1979.

"We take care of our people," he said.

"Well . . ."

"What did they do for you?" Daley asked.

"Are you speaking of a job?"

"Yes, I am."

"Oh, they offered me one, but I couldn't take it. I would have had to move to Washington. For your information, I've had a letter of introduction to you for two years. I never used it because I didn't know what I wanted to do."

Daley asked, "Do you look down on the Democratic Organization?"

"No," Byrne replied. "I don't know anything about it."

"Are you averse to being a member?"

"No. I don't know anything about it."

"Have you ever worked in your ward?"

"No, I haven't."

"Would you work in your ward?"

"Yes."

"Do you know how to do it?"

"No."

And Daley said, "Well, you should be a neighborhood type, you know, get out there. People tell you a lot of things about this machine, but we're no different than General Motors or anybody else. We make a product, and we try to sell the product. It fails if you get bad candidates. If they can't be sold, no matter what you try to do you can't sell them. When we come up with poor candidates, it's our own fault when we lose. And that's what it amounts to. So, you would not mind being a volunteer?"

For four years Jane Byrne worked in Chicago's antipoverty program. Then, in 1968, she was appointed consumer affairs commissioner, the first woman commissioner in any major city. In 1975, she became co-chairman of the Democratic party of Cook County with Mayor Daley. He directed her rise, nurturing her along. When he died she was in trouble. The new Bilandic administration quietly began undermining her. She wasn't really one of the boys; she hadn't come up through the organization the way they had. Instead of allowing her to regulate industries as she had done under Daley, the boys were soon making deals without informing her. Bereft of her patron, she was without clout. But she had an ace in the hole, memos proving that the city's taxi fare increase had been fixed by the industry itself with the covert cooperation of the Bilandic administration. When Byrne's political position finally became intolerable, she leaked the memos. Bilandic was only singed by the heat, but Byrne was ousted. It was commonly thought that he had survived his first scandal with only minor burns. In the meantime, Byrne, out of office and privately doubting the efficacy of her action, was buoyed by the supportive public reaction. She was so impressed that she commissioned a poll to test response to the idea of her running for mayor. The poll results were very positive: 40-percent favorable. Her new husband, Jay McMullen, a journalist with the *Chicago Sun-Times*, urged her to run. She took the plunge.

Jay McMullen was an old friend of Don Rose. He was the first reporter to call Rose a political strategist in print. When Byrne's campaign seemed rudderless after the initial splash of the announcement, McMullen invited Rose to meet his wife. "I went to a party where I met Jane," says Rose. Despite the dissimilarities in their backgrounds they are contemporaries; Rose, in his late forties, is even a few years older. "We talked. My impression was that she was slightly afraid of me or a little nervous. She knew my reputation. She looked like she was stiffening. She didn't know what to expect. But it was a pleasant perfunctory meeting. I was called later to a meeting at her office. They asked what I could do for them. I said I would make her spots and all that. They were happy. Jane asked if I would do strategy for them. I said I would as my time permitted." Of course, he rearranged his schedule so that he could manage her campaign. This was the best shot he was ever offered at the machine. "Basically," Rose says, justifying his commitment to the Byrne campaign, "I'm just antifascist."

Chicago had changed since the time Jane Byrne first was recruited by Dick Daley; the machine, however, had stayed the same. It was essentially the same apparatus Daley had left behind, deeply rooted in the city, but with an increasingly tenuous tie to blacks, young people, and women. In 1975, Daley actually lost a majority of the black vote. The machine was a kind of affirmative action agency for the working class, a novel labor market, in which workers' job consciousness was expressed in support for the party on election day. But it became too exclusive, like a guild. A political machine should court new constituencies rather than reject them. The Chicago machine was suffering from political sclerosis.

In 1974, four of Daley's close associates were indicted and convicted of various crimes — in particular, accepting bribes. Daley portrayed these incidents as aberrations, and when he died there was no internal reform. His apotheosis followed his passing; any deviation from the past seemed like a desecration. The members of the machine disregarded reality as if time stood still. Bridgeport, the old neighborhood where almost all of Bilandic's entourage lived, remained to them the paradigm of Chicago. They were unwilling to retool the machine because they thought it unnecessary.

"It is a common fault of men not to reckon on storms in fair weather," wrote Niccolo Machiavelli in *The Prince*. In January 1979, the storm came — the biggest snowstorm in Chicago's history. Chicagoans reminisce about that winter as though they survived the battle of Stalingrad. They ran blockades down snow-clogged thoroughfares and were veterans of skirmishes with subzero temperatures on "L" platforms; they trekked over miles of ice and through enormous drifts to restock their food supplies. There was a camaraderie in living through a siege, but many citizens began to feel that winter wasn't the only enemy. They noticed that only certain neighborhoods had their streets cleared

— Bridgeport, for instance. Wards that hadn't returned overwhelming promachine pluralities in the last election, when the Democratic party slated unattractive candidates at the top of the ticket, were ignored altogether. The black wards, especially, were untouched. And, for the first time in anyone's memory, the trains stopped running on time, if they ran at all. Even when corruption charges were rife under Daley, services were always delivered. Chicago no longer was "The City That Works."

Bilandic belatedly attempted to respond. His efforts were far worse than doing nothing. He dumped the snow removal head and replaced him with an alleged Mafioso. Then, reporters discovered that millions of dollars in no-bid contracts, including the contract for the city's poorly prepared snow removal plan, were granted to large financial contributors to the machine. Bilandic claimed that the media were trying to crucify him. In a dramatic speech before the city council he compared himself to Jesus Christ and the victims of the Holocaust. Bilandic became a despised figure, seen as weak, indecisive, dispensing the favors of the machine only to those who were his unquestioning backers.

Daley's specter was always hauntingly present. Daley became the ghost in the machine. Qualities that enhanced Daley's reputation appeared as vices in Bilandic. When Daley was highhanded he seemed powerful; Bilandic seemed petty. When Daley defended a friend, however crooked, he seemed loyal; Bilandic seemed venal. When Daley undercut a rival he seemed astute; Bilandic seemed dishonorable. Bilandic couldn't compete with a force that existed only in Chicago's spirit world. Bilandic wanted desperately to be loved, as Daley was in death; but he wasn't feared, as Daley had been in life.

Even some of the precinct captains were disillusioned, neglecting to pass out campaign literature. What had once been manifestations of power — torch-light parades, precinct captains, rallies, leaflet distribution — had been reduced to empty ritual. With the passing of the old chieftain, the tribe began to lose the meaning of the old ways. The rituals were performed without feeling, like the customs of a dying religion. The traditional bonds had been loosened.

"When things stopped working it was everything people feared when Daley died," says Rose. "We capitalized on that anxiety." Bilandic's television campaign, which infuriated the public, played right into Rose's hands. "They made tragic mistakes in trying to generate their own media," Rose says. "They got a firm that was bush league, politically connected to city hall. It had a lot of city business, tourism as well as campaigns." (For the record, the firm was Weber, Cohen and Riley, scenarists for a disaster movie.) Rose provides commentary on the two ads the Bilandic campaign ran over and over again on Chicago television: "In the first ad they tried to make people think it was summertime. Bilandic was in a tee shirt. It read: 'I love you Chicago.' There were scenes of Summerfest (a city-sponsored summer festival). He was trying to fool Mother Nature, but only angered the public more. In the second ad, there's Heather — Bilandic's wife, heiress to the U.S. Gypsum fortune; you've seen what she looks like, Grace Kelly walking through the palace in Monaco. She looked superelegant, just not the image for Chicago. A dumb, fucking mistake. It's not what people look like. It's not what people's houses look like. Here was this lady with her Cuisinart asking snowbound working people to vote for her marvelous husband."

The commercials Don Rose created for Jane Byrne contrasted sharply with the Bilandic ads. Rose comments: "In the first shot, people are digging out of their houses. The second shot shows people frozen on an "L" platform. The camera pans down the tracks. It shows Jane standing in a snowbank. The voice-over says, 'No one could have stopped the snow. But good planning could have prevented the collapse of public transportation. I'm Jane Byrne.' Then there's a cutaway to Byrne talking to people on a streetcorner. 'It seems that nothing works the way it used to. I think we ought to get it working again for you.' And she points to the camera."

Rose worked closely with Byrne. Before Rose came on board, Byrne appeared brittle, shrill, and harsh. He toned her down. To begin with, he made her stop wearing bright red lipstick. It was through production of a radio ad that he gained her trust. "Before she went into the radio studio, I talked to her about the way to deliver her message. I explained how you talk on the radio, that it's an intimate medium. It's a personal thing. Radio is a friend who talks to you. When you're selling yourself on radio you're talking to a friend. Think of yourself as sitting next to someone in a car, or next to someone's bed. That made a great impression on her. She gave really good readings. When that happened she felt that I knew what I was talking about. She listened to and did anything I told her from then on. She demurred on very, very few things. She was a very good study. It gave her all the confidence she needed. She was the best candidate I ever worked with in the sense of taking direction."

Rose's commercials were Byrne's only instrument for reaching the voters. She didn't have an organization. All she had was purchased airtime. Scott Jacobs, a former *Sun-Times* reporter who worked with Rose in producing the Byrne ads, explains how the media worked for her. "Don Rose's genius," Jacobs says, "is in running cheap campaigns and in resource allocation. You can be outspent by an incumbent, but it equalizes your chances if you spend all your money on media. Byrne's ads gave her one-on-one credibility with Bilandic."

When the magnificent enterprise of the machine was a juggernaut, a media campaign was uncalled for. But with the bankruptcy of the organization under Bilandic, a media campaign became appropriate. Chicago was becoming more like the rest of the country. For Don Rose the media wasn't a sensibility, but a technique. He invoked the iconography of the old politics in a modern media campaign. In order to attain his goals, he had no choice. In the past, the machine's administrative functions coincided with its electoral functions. Now, however, only by resorting to media ploys could its traditional administrative capacity be perpetuated. Rose's media campaign didn't depict a fantasy land, but was a kind of salute to the old order. In doing that, Rose comprehended and therefore captured the transitional period Chicago was passing through, both in response to the changing world around it and the mortality of its political regime.

The next ad Rose devised was the most brilliant political spot ever used in a Chicago campaign. It was the show-stopper, and undoubtedly garnered thousands of votes for Byrne. Don Rose calls it Mayor Daley's "letter of reference" for Jane Byrne. He describes the commercial: "The voice-over says, 'If you want to know what kind of mayor Jane Byrne would make hear the words of the late Mayor Daley.' Then there's a picture of Daley wearing a hardhat. The camera pulls back to show Jane standing next to him, also wearing a hardhat. Then Daley praises her as 'one of the most competent women I've met.' The voice-over says, 'Jane Byrne learned about government and about leadership from Mayor Daley. Jane Byrne will get the city working again.' "

The ad had an electrifying effect on Chicagoans. Here was Daley's voice again, in the midst of their worst crisis, eerily commanding them from the grave. The godhead, speaking from the void, was laying hands on his true successor, a metaphysical transaction — beyond politics. "I felt devilish using Daley for Byrne," says Rose. "I didn't feel I was selling out. The man was dead. I was capitalizing on the good will he had. It was absolutely right for Jane. *The perfect metaphor.* It made her the logical heir. It harked back to better times and it capitalized on Daley's own theme that he made the city work." Studs Terkel, the nonpareil Chicago writer and broadcaster, wryly observes, "Don beat Daley using Daley."

Jane Byrne promised a return to more halcyon days. Implicitly, she pledged a return to first principles: equitable distribution of favors and services. On February 27, 1979 — election day — she won the Democratic primary. Even if she wanted to she could never restore the machine to the exact condition it was in when Dick Daley was in his prime. The coalition that carried her into office was very different. She swept two thirds of the black, female, and youth vote, putting her over the top. The *Chicago Reader*, the largest-circulation weekly in the city, conducted an informal sampling immediately after the primary to determine the attitudes of Byrne voters. The results were highly suggestive, if a bit unscientific. None of those polled mentioned being convinced by precinct captains, while nearly all said they relied on television and newspapers for their information, indicating the powerful role of the political consultant. Most of those surveyed claimed not to have seen a precinct captain since Daley died. They disliked Bilandic intensely, yet didn't want to dismantle the machine. They wanted it to work, but without abuses.

"Without Rose we might assume she would have lost," says Mike Royko, the *Chicago Sun-Times* columnist. "She needed every advantage. She turned to him because he's very effective. He produced damned good advertising. He's very influential among blacks and independents and liberals." Royko spells out what gave Rose the edge. "Most of the local top officeholders are members of the machine," he says. "There's no need to bring in some heavy consultant. Only someone on the outside trying to get in uses them. To be effective here you've got to have some entree with the Chicago press and television. They have to trust you. You don't come jetting in from New York City and do a good job walking in. It's not that easy to do that here. Rose knows people. He knows what will appeal to the press. It took someone who knows the territory. Garth couldn't have been as effective. But Rose was a factor."

"Before Rose came aboard, the campaign was scattered," says Basil Talbot, political editor of the *Sun-Times*. "It wasn't focused well. Rose focused it. Rose tutored Byrne, down to the color of her lipstick. He made her a different kind of commodity. But he did much more than the ads. He did the overall strategy. By Rose's joining the Byrne campaign he gave it credibility with the press. We're used to him. In the past, there was dependence on precinct workers to deliver. The media was the trim, the icing. You needed a little to make you look legitimate. But when a woman with $100,000, most of it borrowed, can beat a machine candidate with $1 million, they're going to have to reevaluate the role of the media."

For the general election, every machine hack in Chicago scrambled to ensure that Byrne's vote tally was immense. They weren't sure what she would do once in power, but they wanted to make a good impression while they could. In the finale she racked up 82 percent of the vote, more than Dick Daley had managed at his zenith.

But despite her stunning performance at the polls, Byrne is an edgy personality, lacking Daley's shrewd affability. She over-dramatizes and is often unpredictable. She's on her own, without Daley or Rose. When Jimmy Carter and Ted Kennedy courted her endorsement, her changing moods kept them attentive. Carter declared in early October 1979 that the March Illinois primary was the key to his victory. He came to Chicago in mid-October to extol Jane Byrne's virtues to a gigantic assemblage of 11,000 local Democratic retainers. He went back to the White House confident that he had her support. "It'll be great," she told him at the airport as he gave her a peck on the cheek. But while Carter was in town Byrne received a telegram at a small neighborhood church, where she was attending an informal political function. "Just remember that I have known you and loved you and Chicago longer," wired Ted Kennedy. Byrne remembered. When it appeared to her that Kennedy would run strong in Chicago even without her support, she acted quickly. Less than two weeks after Carter's visit she endorsed Senator Kennedy. Carter's people were livid. One of the Carter campaign coordinators in Illinois called Byrne a "lying bitch" behind closed doors. Kennedy phoned her and paid his respects: "The Washington Monument is shaking. The Lincoln and Jefferson memorials are shaking. The big wind came out of Chicago and they haven't stopped rocking since."

Jane Byrne is not, however, as omnipotent as Richard J. Daley once was. In late September 1979, a federal judge ruled that the Chicago patronage system was unconstitutional; the machine, of course, immediately appealed the ruling. Officeholders, Byrne contended, "should be able to select the people they want." This decision challenged a way of life that seemed eternal, perhaps the most elaborate institutionalization of the belief that the spoils belong to the victor.

Byrne's endorsement of Kennedy created even more serious trouble for the machine. Many people on the Democratic central committee opposed it. "We were just starting to milk Carter for federal money," explained one politician. Others viewed it as a ploy by Byrne to tighten her grip over them. They resisted her discipline. State Senator Richard Daley, Jr., the prince pretender, announced his intention to run for state's attorney, an office from which he could harass Byrne. She turned for support to "the cabal of evil men" she had excoriated during the campaign, selecting one of them as her candidate to run against Daley. "It couldn't happen to a better bunch of guys," says Don Rose. "Jane Byrne rules through paranoia. Nobody's safe. A guy is in one day and out the next. Somebody who's out is suddenly in. There's a pattern of confusion. Nobody knows what's going on. Byrne doesn't have organizational skills. And she doesn't have the emotional equipment. She's too personal, too fickle. She wants to see magic when you need development. She reacts personally to everything. She can't deliver like Daley. She's really wrecking things. Nobody will be able to put together a machine after she's done. I love it."

Don Rose, for his part, could have had a post in the new administration, but he didn't want one. "I don't have a compelling need for power," he says. "I have enough self-confidence not to need that. It's probably because I know I can have it when I want it. I'm not really a public person. I've always been a guy behind the scenes." He knows that he's changed Chicago, though. "We don't know what the machine will be. The nature of politics in Chicago is opening up. The machine will never be the same. As a result the consultants will become important because campaigns will become more important. Positioning candidates will be more important. Once the monolith is cracked vast new areas open up for consultants. It's not coincidental that these machines begin to wither away under the influence of television." But he's not sure whether the outcome will be ultimately beneficial. "Machine politics at its worst is manipulative and coercive. And television politics at its worst is manipulative. Neither politics is issue oriented." Rose prefers not to become part of the permanent campaign. His fame, however, is spreading. Campaign offers pour in as word of his participation in the Chicago victory makes the rounds of political circles. Rose, however, has his own agenda. He'll do what he wants, which includes time for restaurant reviewing. Before the campaign he thought of himself less as a consultant than as a local independent reformer. Now, to the world, Rose is a consultant, in spite of his diffidence about being categorized.

As Rose tells me his plans, a screenwriter and an assistant producer from ABC join us. They are in Chicago to gather material for a made-for-television movie on the life of Mayor Daley, based on Mike Royko's biography, *Boss*. They want Rose's impressions of Daley. The writer, a New Yorker looking for drama, inquires, "Were you witness to any confrontations between Daley and Martin Luther King?" Rose, nonplussed by these cosmopolitans' eager pursuit of the politically picturesque, replies, "There weren't any confrontations. Their meetings were as bland as could be." The assistant producer, dragging deeply on a cigarette, asks breathily, "I want to ask you about the Mobilization Committee!" They head for a bar to talk.

Rose leads them past the Wrigley Building and Tribune Tower, down a long flight of stairs to a street beneath Michigan Avenue, level with the water line of the Chicago River a block away, and into Riccardo's restaurant, a favorite watering hole of reporters. The specialty of the house is green noodles. Riccardo's has red tablecloths, amber lighting, and huge, garish paintings on the walls. A dwarf, wandering from table to table, plays an accordion. Mike Royko walks in and sits down. He orders a scotch. He wants a bit part as a crooked alderman in the television version of his book.

The writer begins his interview with Don Rose. "You've lived with all this for a long time," he notes. "You're a Chicagoan, aren't you?"

## CHAPTER SIX

# THE MEDIA PERSONALITY
# OF OUR TIMES

## TONY SCHWARTZ

In a nondescript gray converted Pentecostal church on West 56th Street in Manhattan lives the media personality of our times. Tony Schwartz has produced commercials for every Democratic presidential candidate since Lyndon Johnson, over 300 ads for Coca Cola, ads for Ford, American Airlines, Holiday Inns, and Johnson's Baby Powder, and has won two Academy Awards. He is a sworn enemy of Gerald Rafshoon, Jimmy Carter's media adviser, and the producer of Ted Kennedy's radio commercials for the 1980 campaign.

His home is his studio, and he rarely leaves it. He experiences the world through electronics; he perceives virtually everything as a sound or an image from radio or television. His studio resembles a radio station operated by a disc jockey for his own private amusement. Schwartz has created an artificial environment in which his sensibility seems natural, and because he's surrounded by a dense network of media he believes the public is surrounded too.

One political consultant recalls attending a seminar staged some years ago by the Democratic National Committee for candidates and their aides. "Tony doesn't go," says the consultant. "He has pimply faced teenaged electronic whiz kids with fourteen pens in each of their breast pockets set up huge loudspeakers in the room. Then the chairman announces, 'Ladies and gentlemen, Tony Schwartz!' Schwartz's voice booms out of the speakers. It's like science fiction. There's no explanation of where he is. It's Hal-the-computer's omnipresent voice from *2001.* It's eerie. This voice has got you under its control for fifteen or twenty minutes. When it's finished people dutifully applaud. Then the chairman says, 'It's always good to have Tony here. He's one of the true geniuses of political media.' "

"He's an egomaniac, but that doesn't bother me," says a political consultant who has worked on campaigns with and against Schwartz. "His reputation is that he's a controversial character and difficult to deal with. He's one of those guys who have to have things done their way." Schwartz's friends, however, regard him as warm and generous, and he doesn't dispel that notion when you meet him within his sanctum.

Schwartz's talent and shortcomings are closely related parts of his personality. He is media maestro who insists that every note be played according to his interpretation; when he's the conductor of a media campaign he tolerates no prima donnas other than himself. "He's not the easiest guy to get along with. He has firm ideas," says Joseph Napolitan, a political consultant who has worked with Schwartz on over 100 campaigns. "Tony sets down a lot of requirements," says Dick Dresner, a pollster who works with Schwartz on political races. "In his work, one person makes the decision."

Yet he has more troubling problems than merely being temperamental. Schwartz is agoraphobic. He will not travel above the fifth story of a building and rarely leaves Manhattan; when he does, he makes sure he's accompanied by a doctor. "Tony has made his problems work for him," says Dresner. "His awareness of sound has to do with his psychological problems. He manipulates sound as a way of getting the world to visit him. He's very efficient and effective in getting some of the most powerful people in the world to come by and talk."

"It's a psychological problem I've had since I was a kid," says Schwartz. As a child he was absorbed by radio. The idea of sound itself so enthralled him that he was determined to master it. He became a ham radio operator, but discovered that his fellow hams were interested mainly in talking about their rigs. Tony wanted to talk about folk songs or regional cuisine. In 1946, he hosted a weekly radio program on New York City station WNYC, airing tapes he received through the mail from hundreds of correspondents. A wealthy benefactor suddenly materialized, like a scene out of *Great Expectations*, and told Tony he could be paid to do whatever he wanted. The next day he quit his job and began recording the quotidian street noises in his postal zone, New York, 19, New York. He felt street vendors had to be recorded in their proper setting. Tony needed a recorder that didn't weigh much, one that he could carry with him unobtrusively as he roamed his little neighborhood. So he invented one of the first portable tape recorders. Eventually, Folkways Records produced seven Tony Schwartz records, "documentaries" of ordinary Manhattan sounds.

Soon, advertising firms were bidding for his services as a sound expert. His first breakthrough was an ad done in the mid-1950s for

Johnson's Baby Powder. Schwartz used real children's voices in the background instead of women mimicking children as had been done previously. It was, he says, "a sensation." He was a hot commodity, and in twenty years made over 4000 commercials.

His first political ad was for Lyndon Johnson in 1964. But his career as a political media consultant didn't really begin until he met Joseph Napolitan, who brought Schwartz into the 1968 Hubert Humphrey campaign. Schwartz always has been an independent, though. The advertisers have always come to him. And so have the politicians.

Even future presidents have made pilgrimages to the Schwartz compound when they wanted to be made appealing to the electorate. If you lean back on the couch in Schwartz's studio and tilt your head to the side you can see a picture of Jimmy Carter reclining on the very same sofa. Carter slept here! Carter turned to Schwartz during the 1976 campaign as his 32-point lead over Gerald Ford dwindled rapidly. The leisurely ads of Gerald Rafshoon were no longer working. A new approach was required.

Rafshoon had met Schwartz in the spring of 1976, when it was becoming clear that Carter would indeed be the Democratic nominee. They were introduced by Joseph Lelyveld, now deputy foreign editor of the *New York Times*. "I had written a magazine piece about Rafshoon," says Lelyveld. "I met Schwartz at the same time. I told Rafshoon about him. He said he'd like to meet him. Opportunistically, as a reporter, I said I'd like to be there. I had a hunch that they'd cross paths later in the campaign. Rafshoon looked him over cagily. Tony did his standard introductory lecture about the evocative powers of media. In a certain sense Schwartz was more sophisticated about the whole business than Rafshoon. But Rafshoon used Schwartz as a weapon. He got out of him what he needed. The ads Schwartz made were extremely effective. They were very well done."

"I'm Jimmy Carter," said the candidate looking directly into the camera. "The problem isn't six-and-one-half percent inflation.

That's just something written on a piece of paper. The problem is how can a family pay those grocery bills and keep up with the mortgage and the taxes and pay for a college education when the time comes . . ."

In the Schwartz productions, Carter stopped overpromising. He started showing sympathy for constituencies he had addressed previously in only general terms. The Schwartz ads weren't programmatic, but they did show the candidate to be more understanding and concerned. And the spots appeared to work; Carter's skid in the polls stopped. Rafshoon was angry and jealous.

CARTER TURNS TO NEW YORK STUDIO TO TAPE HIS REMAINING SPOTS read the headline in the *Times*. Lelyveld had gotten his scoop. "The headline really burned Rafshoon," says Schwartz. "Well, he turned vicious. Very frankly, he lied. He said I had no talent. He said all I wanted to do was negative spots. But *he* came to *me* and asked for negative spots. I did twenty-five spots that he used. He didn't use three. One he didn't use was about a job application for Jerry Ford for president, checking off his vetoes on a report card. It said: 'Well, Mr. Ford, you'll be hearing from us on November 2.' Rafshoon didn't go for that. You see, he doesn't understand. He's a very pleasant fellow. He's strong in his own ideas and very quiet. But his ideas of advertising are twenty-five years behind the times. He really comes out of the advertising school, not the communications school. When I wanted to see research, he said, 'Tell me what you want to know.' I said, 'I don't know what I want to know. I want to know what the research tells me.' He was really saying, 'I'll tell you anything you want to know.' "

Rafshoon, in Schwartz's view, was hopelessly anachronistic in his skills and comprehension of the medium in which he was working. "One," ticks off Schwartz, "he was behind the times in terms of technology. He was shocked, for instance, to discover the existence of a through-the-lens teleprompter. Two, he's basically a film maker. All his communication consisted of using the techniques of film. His idea was to photograph the general campaign going on and turn it into commercials. My approach was that if the candidate is sitting over there I want him to talk to me. All of Rafshoon's commercials had Carter talking to people standing to his side. I want him to look at me, the viewer. Here's the difference in understanding: Rafshoon thought that unemployment wasn't an important issue because only 7.9 percent of the people were unemployed. I said, 'You know, there's no such thing as 7.9-percent unemployed. When you're unemployed you're 100-percent unemployed.' The real question is to do ads on unemployment and run them where unemployment is high. But he didn't understand."

Schwartz had another suggestion for the campaign that Rafshoon nixed as well. "One of the most important things is to have instant information. I suggested that in the last two weeks of the campaign, wherever Carter was, he should have a television studio ready that day. Have Carter comment on something if it was important and have a spot on the air that night. It might cost him $1000 a day. It'd be well worth it. But Rafshoon said, 'It's too expensive.'"

Then Lelyveld published his story in the *Times*. The tension between the two media consultants became nasty. "If they want to hate each other that's their business," says Lelyveld. Both men called Lelyveld to tell him their side of the fight. But he wasn't interested in reporting what he regarded as a petty dispute.

Rafshoon had the key advantage in the struggle with Schwartz — control of the purse strings. "He didn't pay me," Tony says. "I had to threaten suit to get paid, finally, in 1977. I haven't been in touch with him and he hasn't called me."

"I can tell you the truth about that story," says Barry Jagoda, a former Carter media adviser. "I'm a partisan of Tony and I've had my differences with Jerry so bear that in mind. But the reason Jerry went to Tony in the first place is that Ham Jordan, Jody Powell, myself and a few others were saying that the Rafshoon stuff wasn't any good. Jerry decided to reach out to others. But he didn't want anyone else to take credit for inventing Jimmy Carter. There was professional jealousy. Tony passionately believes he knows more about reaching people than anyone else. He may be right, but who knows? And he probably should be more modest about his accomplishments. Tony was proud of the fact that the Democratic nominee was coming to him, while Jerry saw it as himself seeking a little help. What really happened then was that a reporter wrote a story. And there it was — Rafshoon was no longer solely responsible for the image of Jimmy Carter. One of the characteristics of presidential campaign advisers is that if someone in the entourage seems to be grandstanding, not calling complete attention to the candidate, you can take a shot at them. So Rafshoon took a shot at Schwartz. As long as Rafshoon did Carter, just following him around in a peanut field, that was fine. But if you go to Tony Schwartz then you're manipulating the American people. It was a necessity to reduce the influence of this consultant because Carter would be seen as being in trouble . They had to downplay this new entry. That's why Tony got beaten up. Jerry treated him very poorly. It was an example of Carter's problem with his subordinates acting in a shabby way with people trying to help."

Interviewed in his Washington office, which he shares with presidential pollster Pat Caddell, Rafshoon had only this pithy comment: "Tony Schwartz is a bad-ass."

Schwartz's basic suspicions about advertising people were borne out by Rafshoon, further confirming his theories. "I think," he observes, "the worst people in politics are advertising people. You could go into an advertising agency today and tell them you want to run for Congress. What's today, Tuesday? Friday they could come back to you with a whole campaign. They wouldn't think of doing research. They might test their commercials to see if the public remembered the ad. But remembering the ad doesn't tell you the effect it will have. People sell you candidates the way they sell soap. I say, I wouldn't even sell soap the way they sell soap."

Unlike most media consultants Tony Schwartz is guided by a theory. The theory, however, is solely about technique, not about politics, although Schwartz's ads are often so affecting that they supplant politics, at least in its familiar variations. He tries to turn politicians away from making a simple pitch. He doesn't want to show how charismatic, strong, or virtuous they are. He wants them to represent the feelings of the voters, which is not necessarily the same thing as representing the voters on the issues. Emotion suffices.

In his book, *The Responsive Chord*, Schwartz criticizes consultants who concentrate on framing a candidate's image as if magnetism on television will attract voters. To Schwartz, this is a fundamental misunderstanding of the medium. He doesn't want to package candidates; he wants to package voters. This is not only the goal of a campaign, but a natural act. "The voter," he writes, "is surrounded by media and dependent on it in everyday functioning. The stimuli a candidate uses on the media thus surround voters. They are part of his environment, his packaging."

It follows then that the consultant's role is not to sell the candidate at all. Instead, he's selling the voters their preconceived notions; in voting for the politician who can mouth their notions in an evocative manner, the voters reaffirm themselves. Schwartz wants voters to "feel a candidate." It's not so important even to see him; most pols, to Schwartz, look dishonest because they don't know how to look into a camera. It makes sense to him that television is the ideal medium for "surfacing feelings voters already have" rather than using it as a vehicle for projecting visual images. "Indeed," he writes, "the best political commercials are similar to Rorschach patterns. They do not tell the viewer anything. They surface his feelings and provide a context for him to express his feelings." Schwartz dismisses what he terms "the newsreel commercial" as ineffective and inappropriate.

Television, to him, is not meant for politicians to convey information; television spots are "electronic posters."

He conceives of television essentially as radio; sound is his specialty. His theory on media is not so much an extension of Marshall McLuhan's insights as it is a personal self-justification. For Tony Schwartz, though, the theory works admirably. Campaigns illustrate his precepts.

The most notorious political ad Schwartz ever produced — quite possibly the most notorious ad ever produced by anyone — was shown only once. It caused such a furor that it was yanked off the air almost the instant after it appeared. Yet it was so devastatingly effective that it defined the entire 1964 presidential campaign. The spot depicted a pretty blond-haired little girl in a field pulling petals off a daisy, counting them as she dropped them to the ground. When her count reached ten, the frame was frozen. An announcer quickly counted down from ten. At zero the viewer saw a billowing mushroom cloud from an atomic bomb explosion. President Johnson then spoke: "These are the stakes, to make a world in which all God's children can live, or to go into the darkness. Either we must love each other or we must die."

The spot vaporized Barry Goldwater's presidential campaign. After it aired Goldwater was constantly on the defensive. "When I went to bed," said Denison Kitchel, a Goldwater campaign manager, "if ever I could have just a few hours sleep, I would lie awake asking myself at night, how do you get at the bomb issue? My candidate had been branded a bomb dropper — and I couldn't figure out how to lick it. And the advertising people, people who could sell anything, toothpaste or soap or automobiles — when it came to a political question like this, they couldn't offer anything either."

Actually, the ad never branded Goldwater a bomb dropper. It never even mentioned Goldwater's name. What the "Daisy Girl" spot played on was the feeling among voters that Goldwater might be trigger happy and press the atomic button. The meaning of the ad was supplied by the viewers themselves. This feeling was so overwhelming that eight years after the ad appeared, the *New York Times* offered this description of it: "In 1964, the Democrats demolished Goldwater with a simple one-shot television spot. A little girl picking daisies moved happily across an open field. Suddenly, a mushroom cloud filled the air and the announcer asked sternly, 'Whose finger do you want on the trigger?' " This recollection was fantasy, accurate only in its summary of voters' emotions.

Some of Schwartz's best ads were never aired because they were too inflammatory or satirical. During his campaign for Hubert Humphrey in 1968, his most clever spots weren't exhibited outside his studio. Schwartz narrates these forbidden gems: "I did one against George Wallace and General LeMay [Wallace's running mate]. A guy is very anxious to get into the voting booth. He says, 'Where is it? Wallace and General LeMay.' And he pulls the lever and the whole world explodes. An atomic bomb. Boom! Then I did a commercial that was a takeoff on an Excedrin headache commercial. I had a soundtrack, a thirty-track tape I did with Moondog, a street musician. I've recorded him since 1943. I used this music of Moondog, which sounds like a headache. A crawl comes across the screen: 'Excedrin Headache Number Two.' Then I flash the words: 'Spiro T. Agnew.' Then, 'Excedrin Headache Number One. Richard Nixon.' "

An ad Schwartz did for the Humphrey campaign was perhaps the most succinct fear spot ever aired. All that is seen on the television are two names — Edmund Muskie and Spiro Agnew. In the background is the sound of a thumping heart. "Who," ominously asks an announcer, "is your choice to be a heartbeat away from the presidency?" Although the Humphrey campaign afforded Tony Schwartz another chance to test his theories, the candidate flunked.

The next Democrat who ran against Richard Nixon didn't do nearly as well. George McGovern — victim of his own political imprudence, his own party's hostile bosses, Nixon's dirty tricks, and Tom Eagleton — turned to Schwartz for a bit of magic in the waning days of the 1972 campaign. Nothing, of course, could resuscitate McGovern, but Schwartz applied emergency procedures. Once again he used the gimmick of the man talking to himself in the voting booth. This time it was no joke. Schwartz saw his task as stopping the wholesale defection of Democratic voters to Nixon. How could he engage their feelings? "Well," says an obviously working-class man in a voting booth, his hand wavering back and forth between the levers. "Either way it won't be a disaster. What am I looking for? I mean, so I'll vote for Nixon. Why rock the boat? I'm not crazy about him, never was. I gotta decide, though, I gotta make up my mind. I don't have that much time, I can't keep people waiting. The fellas are voting Nixon. They expect me to vote for him too. Me vote for Nixon! My father'd roll over in his grave. The fellas say they are. Maybe they're not. Crime? I don't feel safer. Prices up. Gotta feeling: Don't vote for Nixon. I'm confused. Who am I measuring McGovern against? My gut feeling: McGovern. This hand [raises hand] voted for Kennedy. I mean, it's just possible McGovern's straight. Maybe he can . . . [The man pulls the Democratic lever] That's the way!"

Schwartz's best spot about Nixon was never intended to be aired. He produced it after the hopeless McGovern campaign, when Nixon was slowly twisting in the Watergate wind. Late one night Tony was putting the final touches on a new Coke ad. Nixon's visage on television interrupted his work. It gave him an inspiration. Tony spliced the Coke soundtrack into Nixon's speech, blending the commercial and the political in a contrapuntal message in which distinctions were blurred.

Schwartz sits at the controls, commander of the tape deck. "Are you ready?" he asks. The familiar music begins.

*It's the real thing.*

"Good evening," intones a grave Richard Nixon. "I want to talk to you tonight from my heart on a subject come to be known as the Watergate affair. How could it have happened?"

*It's the real thing.*

"The easiest course would be for me to blame those to whom I delegated the responsibility."

*What the world wants to see. It's the real thing.*

"That would be a cowardly thing to do. I will not place the blame on subordinates."

*People want to buy life's good things.*

"In any organization the man at the top must bear the responsibility."

*You want to feel free.*

"That responsibility belongs here in this office. I accept it."

*That's the way it is.*

"There can be no whitewash."

*The way it will stay.*

"At the White House. God bless America." And then a reprise of Nixon: "How could it have happened?"


Good question. In Schwartz's spot there's no clue. That's not his style. "Voters can only identify with things they've had experience with," he says. "And no one has had experience with the answers. But they've had experience with the problems. I don't think the real question is differences on the issues. The issues in a campaign are the candidates, not the things they refer to as the issues. The question is which candidate will feel more like you do in relation to an issue." Schwartz's logic may seem attenuated, but the nuances in his argument make for a special emphasis in his spots. His ads aren't all in the same mold. Yet his trademark is apparent in the visceral way he deals with the issues.

"When I was doing Gaylord Nelson's campaign, Abe Ribicoff's campaign, Mike Gravel's campaign," he says about a passel of Senate races, "inflation was a concern of people in the research. I asked each one what they would do about it. No one had a clear answer. I wasn't impressed. So if I wasn't impressed, I'm not going to use their answers. What I did was ask them how they felt about inflation. I did spots with Ribicoff and Gravel with their wives. I had them talk about the high cost of groceries. I had slides of them walking through a store. I had them say they would fight against it. They weren't giving answers of what they would do, but how they felt about it. And this did impress me."

Schwartz works for candidates he likes and who like him. "Much as he'd hate to be called a liberal," says Dick Dresner, "he's a liberal." If he's a liberal, he's an aging one. He has a neoconservative streak although he hasn't memorized Irving Kristol's *Wall Street Journal* catechism. His politics are his feelings.

"He's not a political strategist," notes Dick Dresner. "He's a creative genius." Barry Jagoda says, "When I go to see him I feel like I'm traveling to India to see a guru. He's an applied McLuhanite. I never could understand McLuhan until I met Schwartz. He's going to look better and better in the 1980s and 1990s. We're going to have more and more electronic images."

When Schwartz's political clients visit his studio, they are given special treatment, bathed and massaged in media. "He surrounds you in a good atmosphere. You relax," says Percy Sutton, whose media material in his 1977 New York mayoral race was prepared by Schwartz. In Schwartz's realm a session starts with casual banter. Then the candidate reads the copy Schwartz has composed for him. Schwartz listens intently to the candidate's voice inflections, offering advice. If the candidate wants changes in the script they are made to put him at ease. At last, the candidate tapes the spot. But he doesn't leave the studio after that. Schwartz reviews the ad and they may try again. "He selects the best," says Sutton. "And he has very reasonable fees, a lot less than he has the capacity to command. When I made money available to him he took me far in the polls."

A client Schwartz holds in especially high esteem is Daniel Patrick Moynihan, who is a U.S. senator from New York partly because of Tony Schwartz's efforts. His spots for Moynihan were some of the clearest examples of his use of television as radio, a fully realized exercise of his theory. "Some of the most effective ads I've done have been stills of candidates' faces," Schwartz says. "I'll freeze the frame. That's when I want you to hear what I'm saying. The listening increases. I did Moynihan's campaign that way. When I was speaking about him I'd use a still of him. I used, as a symbol, his walk down the aisle to the speaker's platform at the United Nations when he was ambassador. My slogan: 'He fought for us in the UN and he'll fight for us in the Senate.' Another ad had him talking about himself. He's an exquisite Irish poet, probably one of the best candidates to work with. He can just improvise artfully. Another symbolic thing I did was to take just his name and put that on the screen. The color would change every time a different person was speaking about him. I wanted people to be familiar with that name because they were going to have to try to find it on a crowded ballot." This ad is known within the cult of political consultants as his "tutti-frutti" spot.

"Moynihan has a tremendous background," Schwartz says. "You could talk about the road tax and he could get into a discussion of the highway system and how it developed in this country and what happened with highways in New York in relation to the Erie Canal. He really knows. He's astute."

Schwartz isn't as upbeat about all his campaigns as he is about Moynihan's. In 1978, he found himself in the meanest campaign of his career — the U.S. Senate race in Illinois. This contest pitted incumbent Republican Charles Percy against lawyer Alex Seith, the Chicago machine's man and Tony Schwartz's client. The trouble began when Percy incautiously bleated his nostalgia for former secretary of agriculture Earl Butz, dismissed in disgrace in

1976 after muttering a racist joke to stool pigeon John Dean who promptly reported the remarks to *Rolling Stone.* "Remember Secretary of Agriculture Butz and the slanderous remarks he made against black people?" began a Schwartz ad aired on black radio stations in Chicago. "Well, Senator Percy says, and we quote Percy exactly, 'I wish he were in office today.' With friends like this you don't need enemies."

Percy understood his opening. He cast Tony Schwartz as his opponent, an ideal foil. Interviewed on CBS Evening News, Percy declared that his "real opponent" was Schwartz, "a shrewd, brilliant political strategist from New York."

"He called me a 'New York recluse,'" says an outraged Schwartz. There could be no better enemy for a Midwestern candidate than a New York media manipulator with strange personal quirks, who had invaded the heartland with commercials to mislead the innocent folks about a man they knew and trusted. Tony Schwartz was made for Charles Percy.

But Percy's campaign, which should have been easy once he had the image of Tony Schwartz to play against, was complicated by his own mudslinging. He accused his challenger of having Mafia connections. Unfortunately, he couldn't prove his claims. Seith regained momentum. The combatants met in a television studio. When confronted by the aggrieved Seith, Percy, out of fatigue, ill-health or prescient political instinct, fainted in range of the cameras. He was carried off by his aides and with him he took victory. Here was a man who knew how to wrap up the sympathy vote.

Schwartz does not have kind words for Percy. "Frankly, he's a goddamned liar. He's a shrewd, shrewd, cheap politician." Schwartz only wishes he knew then what he knows now about Percy. "Do you know that when Percy fainted they took him to the Chicago Athletic Club? That's where he lives when he's in Chicago. If I knew that before, I would have done this spot: 'Do you know where Senator Percy lives when he's in Chicago? He lives in a place that is restricted — no Jews, no blacks, no Catholics. That's where this senator lives.' "

Tony Schwartz toys with the idea of employing that commercial in a future contest in Illinois. In the meantime, he entertains new campaigns and lectures visitors on his theory of media politics. Behind his studio door, which is decorated with a huge plaster ear with a brass nameplate affixed about the lobes, he is abuzz with projects. In Ted Kennedy's last campaign for senator, Schwartz did his radio spots. "He's very capable," he says. "You can discuss a subject with him, he thinks about it and then he knows what to say. You don't have to write something down for him. Kennedy is very good to work with because he can keep to a discipline. I happen to like Kennedy. I'd love to see him be president."

Schwartz didn't know in advance what kind of advertising campaign he would conceive for Kennedy. "You don't know these things in advance. They're so temporal," he says. "It's a tough problem. The people who are for him are for him and they don't care why. And the people who are against him are against him and don't care why. I have to look at the research."

For the campaign in the Iowa caucuses Schwartz produced an ad attempting to provide a rationale for the Kennedy candidacy. "Replacing a sitting president may not be pleasant," intoned the narrator. "But sometimes when you make a change you're not rocking the boat — you're stabilizing it." After Iowa, however, Schwartz decided to abandon ship. The Kennedy organization failed to link research to media, the basic condition for a successful effort. The Kennedy campaign was simply not the kind of modern media politics Tony Schwartz understands.

CHAPTER SEVEN

# THE CAPTAIN OF INDUSTRY

## JOE NAPOLITAN

Valéry Giscard d'Estaing, president of the Republic of France, dressed elegantly in his country tweeds, left the presidential palace, stepped into his chauffeured limousine, protected by his security guards, and motored to his rustic estate to relax before beginning the final frenetic push in the 1975 campaign. At least, that is what the French press was dutifully told by the president's press secretary. Actually, Giscard was driven to a Parisian hotel, ushered quickly upstairs before any reporters might spot him, and taken into a room where he was introduced to the man who would secretly advise him on campaign strategy in the tight race against Francois Mitterand, Socialist candidate of the insurgent Union of the Left. Giscard listened intently as a cigar-smoking American, Joseph Napolitan, laid out the game plan. Napolitan had taken polls, conducted survey research, figured out the themes, and written a campaign plan, just as he would for an American politician. But his work for Giscard was kept as closely guarded as if it were a state secret. In fact, if his role had become known, he would have been a major issue in the campaign, certainly targeted by the Left as a murky foreign influence. He was never uncovered, though, and like a good American candidate, Giscard followed the outline of the political consultant's strategy. And he won.

Who was that political jet setter, faster than a mimeograph machine and more powerful than a giant party rally? He was none other than the captain of industry himself, the first political consultant to understand the new technological politics and to work on an American presidential campaign, and the founding father of the International and American Associations of Political Consultants. When Valéry Giscard d'Estaing hired a consultant he chose ne plus ultra.

Like all captains of industry, Joe Napolitan's origins were modest. He was an American boy, living in a medium-sized Massachusetts town, with a fierce ambition to succeed. He didn't know what he wanted to do, he had no scholarly interests, but he was willing to work hard to reach the top, wherever that might be. At the age of seventeen he was a cub reporter for his hometown paper, the *Springfield Union*. Two years later he was sitting in the press box at Fenway Park covering the Boston Red Sox, perhaps the most sought after assignment on the newspaper. "But after a while," he says, "everyone sliding into third base began to look the same, so I decided to go on to other things." Although the Fenway press box was an enviable perch, he could see that there was nowhere to go from there. Like many newspapermen eager for a break in the fifties, he rented an office and had his name painted on the door above the title Public Relations Counsel.

One day, in 1957, a friend walked into the office and wondered if

Joe would be interested in running his campaign for mayor. "Sure, why not?" he replied. Napolitan produced his first political television commercial, a ten-second spot showing a round black bomb with a long fuse exploding into the words "New Leadership — Tom O'Connor." It was a dynamite campaign for its time, and O'Connor won. Four years later, however, Napolitan managed O'Connor's opponent, and won again. Without any patronage he had made two successive mayors. He was the new boss, only nobody really knew it.

Like all good Massachusetts political talent at that time, he was signed on to the Kennedy roster, where he worked for Jack for senator and president and Ted for senator. Joe worked as an assistant to top campaign operative Lawrence O'Brien, another Springfield product whom he had known since childhood. Napolitan says he was just "a spear carrier" in the Kennedy army, but the experience provided new contacts for him. He was able to set himself up as a political consultant, one of the first who understood the implications of media politics and its impact on the political party.

The same year Ted Kennedy first ran for the Senate, Napolitan was hired to run an important Massachusetts campaign. As campaign manager for the Democratic candidate for governor, Endicott Peabody, he turned for advice to the man he considers "the pioneer," Edward L. Bernays. He telephoned Bernays and asked him what suggestions he might have for the campaign. "Well," said Bernays, "I would make as your number-one issue the idea that Massachusetts ought to have offices in Chicago, St. Louis, New Orleans, and so on, to attract business to the Bay State." "Thank you very much," Joe replied. Bernays's nostrum made a paragraph in a Peabody speech.

Napolitan was making a reputation for himself within mainstream Democratic circles, but the significance of his media work was not really apprehended. He was regarded as an operative who happened to possess some specialized skills, but his skills were not thought of as different from the other operatives .

In 1968, his big test arrived. Larry O'Brien, then chairman of the Democratic party, called on his old friend to salvage the campaign of the Democratic candidate for president, Hubert Humphrey. "The Joe Napolitan I know is a one-man band," says O'Brien, now the commissioner of the National Basketball Association. "He takes on assignments, campaigns, but he's never a fellow who moved to some big Madison Avenue operation. He operates on his own. The challenge of the 1968 campaign was greater than in any other campaign. The convention was a disaster. You had a candidate who wasn't wildly accepted. We were limited on money. We had to cut our media time-buys in half. We had to maximize dollars. Joe did an outstanding job. He took over coordination of media. He hand-picked the various experts. He had a great sense of the media side. He's always able to spot the best radio man, the best half-hour documentary film maker, the best guy to do a half-minute spot. He can put it together as a coherent unit."

Napolitan did not have an adman's view of campaigning. One of the first things he did as Humphrey's media adviser was to fire the Madison Avenue advertising firm Doyle Dane Bernbach, which had been producing spots for the race. The company relied on a computer to judge the value of repeating ads in given cities on given topics. A Doyle Dane Bernbach representative gave Napolitan a presentation of a major ad they wished to produce for Humphrey at the cost of a quarter of a million dollars. In the ad an elephant with the letters GOP marked on his head would walk backward and then the name Humphrey would be flashed on the screen. Joe reviewed the spot, reviewed the price, and dismissed the hucksters. In addition to charging astronomical fees they did not understand political media. Napolitan promptly hired Tony Schwartz.

Humphrey, like DDB, did not understand the strategic uses of media. He was a very traditional politician whose relationship with television was best captured the night he was nominated, when his wife's face appeared on a screen in his hotel suite, and he rushed up to kiss her image.

Napolitan's general political instincts in that campaign were more advanced than Humphrey's. He was discouraged that Humphrey did not, like George McGovern and Eugene McCarthy, go bravely into the streets of Chicago to speak to the crowds that had been bludgeoned during the police riots. Instead, Humphrey proclaimed in his acceptance speech "the politics of joy." When Napolitan pleaded with Humphrey to challenge Nixon to a debate, the candidate balked. He did not really understand the power of television. And he did not take Napolitan's best advice, which was about the Vietnam War. In retrospect, it is clear that if he had, he, not Richard Nixon, would have been president. A month and a half before the election Napolitan sent a memo to Larry O'Brien spelling out his plan. "It is my strong belief that if this campaign continues as it has started we will lose," he wrote. "The tragedy is that we have it within our means to win! We have nothing to lose — and the presidency to gain— by being bold." He urged "a sharp break with Lyndon Johnson" and the articulation by the candidate of "an independent Vietnam policy that will win back votes that should be Humphrey's but which now are wavering." Humphrey, however, rejected the proposal. Then, a week before the election, in a speech delivered in Salt Lake City, Humphrey weakly took a small step away from Johnson on the war; his ratings in the polls climbed so fast that the election became too close to call. "That dramatically changed public attitudes," says Larry O'Brien. "But it was too little and too late."

"Humphrey suffered from a tragic disease, uncommon, very rare, called loyalty," says Napolitan. "Hubert was such a nice guy that being loyal meant more to him than being president. He knew that if he had done some of the things I had suggested he would have made it. If I had been Humphrey I would have gone into Johnson and said, Look I have a shot at winning this thing. I can win it if I can break with you on the war. The alternative is I don't break with you and we get Richard Nixon. Lyndon wasn't stupid. He would have yelled and screamed but he would have said, 'You do what you want.' But I admire Humphrey. He almost won it the way it was." And the way it was was that Humphrey lost by .7 percent of the vote.

In 1968, the focus of media politics was on the sterile Madison Avenue style of the Nixon campaign, in which the candidate was quizzed by prescreened panelists and questioned by a soothing moderator hired by the ad agency. The new Nixon, as Joe McGinniss pointed out in *The Selling of the President 1968*, was a facade. The Nixon campaign was less innovative in employing the new stratagems of media politics than Joe Napolitan. Nixon's people were essentially admen, while Napolitan was a political consultant.

From 1966 to 1968 Napolitan ran a race — which he calls "the textbook campaign" — that elucidated the new politics more blatantly than perhaps any previous effort. It occurred in Alaska. In 1966, he was contacted by another Springfield native, Mike Gravel, who had moved to Alaska and become Speaker of the House of Representatives. Gravel wanted to be a senator. In order to accomplish that end he would have to run against Ernest Gruening, the grand old man of Alaskan politics, who had led the state into the union. For two years, Napolitan orchestrated a careful media campaign. His biggest problem was that Alaska did not have many media outlets. So, to compensate for that drawback, Napolitan created the media. Gravel had an image as an abrasive figure; this had to be softened. "Capitol Comments," a fifteen-minute television show about state problems, was launched with Gravel as the host. He smiled and urged calm while his guests argued. Then the Gravel camp started a monthly newspaper and magazine insert called "Today in Alaska," a full-color publication that ran many articles about that up-and-coming young man, Mike Gravel. Soon, "Today in Alaska" became the biggest-circulation publication in the state. Then with the assistance of a ghost writer Gravel penned a book, *Jobs and More Jobs*. It was not a best seller, but it was prominently displayed in local drugstores, newsstands, and supermarkets, and it was serialized in Alaskan newspapers. A week and a half before the election Napolitan put on television a half-hour campaign documentary — "Man from Alaska" — about Mike Gravel. Alaskans had never seen a political commercial like this. The day before it was shown Gravel was losing by a two to one margin; the day after it aired Gravel was ahead 55 to 45 percent. He won. It was campaigns like this that Napolitan had in mind when he said, "Few experiences I know, save perhaps having an orgasm, equal the feeling on election night when the vote reports start coming in and it looks as though you are going to spring an upset."

The next year, 1969, Napolitan formed a partnership in a political consulting firm, Public Affairs Analysts, with an unlikely partner, F. Clifton White, Barry Goldwater's campaign manager in 1964. Superficially, the alliance of the Humphrey media man and the Goldwater manager might have seemed wildly absurd. But Napolitan says, "We are diametrically opposed politically, but we share the same techniques."

Clif White began his career as a liberal, but swiftly turned conservative in the post–World War II period. He became a party operative in great demand. "I had ten or fifteen titles in the Republican party," he says. His first position of responsibility was to lead the Youth for Dewey demonstration at the 1948 convention. In 1957, he set himself up as a "public affairs counselor," a hybrid profession of the mid-1950s that trained businessmen in the political fine arts. "It's the same thing the political action committees do today," says White. He specialized in training junior executives. His clients included General Electric and U.S. Steel. Relying upon his corporate and party contacts White took over the

Young Republicans in the 1950s and worked as an operative in the 1960 Nixon campaign. In 1964 he was taken by the ideological fervor of Barry Goldwater and was determined to make him the next nominee of the party. He drew upon his contacts for the National Draft Goldwater Committee. He was an expert in primary politics, recognizing that you had to elect your own delegates to the convention, not influence delegates once they had been elected. So when the convention opened, the issue of who would get the nomination was already settled. Once Goldwater had won, however, he and his aides reduced White and his forces to a subsidiary role and ran a truly miserable campaign. Nevertheless, the historic transformation of the party had taken place and Clif White could claim credit as the catalyst.

Clif White's mechanical skills were used to realign the Republican party. Acting as an independent operative he forced the critical transformation of the party and displayed the impact a single-minded consultant might have. "I think consulting has changed politics," says White. "Historically, the function of the consultant was performed by the party leader. There is no doubt that the rise of the consultant and the decline of the party have been running neck and neck for the last decade."

With Napolitan, White continued his public affairs work for corporations. "We do a dog and pony show," says Napolitan. "There was a need for bipartisan public affairs consulting for business," says White. "We run seminars for executives on how government functions and how you can have your employees become effective in political campaigns."

Although the partners do not join hands in domestic campaigns they have worked together overseas, handling, among other clients, President Ferdinand Marcos of the Philippines and former president Carlos Andres Perez of Venezuela. Abroad, the differences between the Democrat and the Republican blur and they appear only as practitioners of the latest American techniques. "I don't have any feeling of intervention," says White. "All we're doing is exploring methods of politics. They won't be effective if they are in total conflict with the society you're working in. In any case, the consultant should not have anything to do with the substance of issues."

Larry O'Brien secured the 1969 Marcos contract for Public Affairs Analysts. "I went over to visit with Marcos," says O'Brien. "As a result of that visit Joe was committed to the campaign." Through some elementary survey research Napolitan learned that in the Philippines only 20 percent of the population owns television sets. Radio is the mass medium there. Still, the night before the election, Napolitan staged a telethon for the candidate reminiscent of the Humphrey telethon. "No president of the Philippines had ever been reelected," says Napolitan. "The guy Marcos was running against had been convicted of treason, of collaborating with the Japanese during the war. As far as I could tell Marcos seemed like a decent guy. He was a war hero. He didn't give any indication he would change the system. However, he suspended the democratic process [near the end of his term]. I'm disappointed. Preserving the process is more important than preserving yourself in office. In 1973 I did a campaign for Carlos Andres Perez [of Venezuela] and he was elected. In 1978 I did a campaign for a guy who was not anywhere near as good a candidate. We lost. Our guy acted as though the campaign was something to be endured en route to the coronation. He felt he couldn't lose. The important thing was not that we lost, but that the democratic process was maintained."

Because of his world travels, Napolitan thought that there ought to be an association of international political consultants. He began to meet his counterparts in distant lands, who agreed with the idea. He was the initiator of the first convention in 1968. A year later Napolitan and White founded the American Association of Political Consultants. "The number of consultants in Europe who work as we work is very few," says Napolitan. "The techniques are different. In many European countries television is controlled by the state. There's a lot more reliance on print and posters. Most of the consultants tend to be linked with a party. Most of them tend to be on a party payroll." Because parties exercise tight control over politics in Europe the consultants do not act as agents of nonalignment. The parties there are more clearly class based, with definite programs and ideological perspectives; consultants are rarely more than mere operatives. They cannot rise above the party to create currents that batter it.

"Here," says Napolitan, "consultants are extra-party. The parties are obsolete here. Before television, in order to get your message across, you had to filter it through the party. Now you don't need the party. I work in lots of campaigns in lots of states where I don't even know who the Democratic party chairmen are. It doesn't matter to me or my candidates. I was early in my perception that the party was on the decline. The party didn't do much, it didn't mean much, it never had much money. And it was often staffed by guys who couldn't find real jobs. I didn't need them. I got in the habit of never consulting them."

Napolitan has become the captain of industry. He has earned his esteemed rank three times over: first, as an innovator in strategic media politics; second, as a political consultant to corporate interests; and third, as the founder of the industry's trade association, the formation of which was an event heralding the unmistakable ascension of political consultants.

The captain of industry as a social archetype was first drawn by the estimable early-twentieth-century social critic, Thorstein Veblen. According to Veblen, the captain of industry begins as a socially useful adventurer, a free enterpriser, a master builder, who organizes new technological forces and tests new processes. But as business expands and becomes more complex the adventurer gradually becomes removed from the industrial process. He becomes an absentee owner of "the price system," Veblen's euphemism for capitalism. Day-to-day operation falls to the technicians, engineers who could run the technology, and therefore the society, on a scientific basis as master craftsmen, but they are stymied by the absentee owners. Veblen urged the technicians to supplant the captains of industry and run society as "a Soviet of technicians," a technocratic utopia. He did not foresee that there would be engineers who could engineer consent, a craft that would develop into an industry. Joe Napolitan has turned Veblen on his head, bridging the categories Veblen believed were in opposition. Napolitan is the technocrat as captain of industry.

## CHAPTER EIGHT

# CALIFORNIA DREAMS

### STUART SPENCER

"Who are you voting for, Mother?" asked an inquiring reporter of a little old lady knitting in a rocking chair.

"I'm voting for the Republican, Frank Merriam," she answered, "because this little home may not be much, but it is all I have in this world. I love my home and I want to protect it."

Next, the reporter approached a bedraggled, bearded man in a mangy overcoat. "I am voting for Seen-clair," he replied in a stilted foreign accent. "His system vorked vell in Russia, so vy can't it vork here?"

This political spot, produced in 1934, was part of an elaborate smear campaign against socialist writer Upton Sinclair, who was running for governor of California as a Democrat. It was also part of the most sophisticated multimedia campaign of its day, a landmark in the development of the political consultant.

The roving reporter advertisement was a newsreel produced by the MGM studio at the behest of Louis B. Mayer, statewide chairman of the Republican party. Theater owners were obliged to exhibit these ads if they wanted to receive MGM features. In another of this series of newsreels an army of hoboes is depicted hopping off a freight train and whooping it up upon arrival in the Golden State. "Sinclair says he'll take the property of the working people and give it to us," says one of the bums.

The anti-Sinclair forces rented 2000 billboards across the state, plastering them with the following message: "If I am elected governor, half the unemployed in the country will hop the first freight to California — Upton Sinclair." Much of the public believed that Sinclair himself had put up the billboards. In still another assault on Sinclair, newspapers printed lurid cartoons about him. One showed a ghoul labeled "Communism" standing behind Sinclair as he lambasted an innocent but voluptuous Miss California. Statements of Sinclair's, taken out of context from his books, surrounded by splotches of black ink, were reprinted in pamphlets and newspapers. All of these were the products of the husband and wife team of Clem Whitaker and Leone Baxter, the first political consulting firm in the nation.

"Upton was beaten," Whitaker said, "because he had written books." In 1933, the prolific Sinclair published a tome entitled *I, Governor of California and How I Ended Poverty: A True Story of the Future*, in which he described his plan to combine the New Deal with socialism in order to end the Depression. He called his program End Poverty in California (EPIC). His book was an incredible best seller. EPIC clubs were organized widely and the EPIC *News* was distributed to nearly a million subscribers. In the Democratic primary for governor, Sinclair, who was dismissed as a quixotic visionary, rolled up a vote total greater than all his opponents combined, so impressive a victory that it was the largest primary vote total in California history. Needless to say, business interests and the Republican party viewed Sinclair with alarm. They gathered an unprecedented campaign fund to defeat him, estimated by historians to be in the vicinity of $10 million. "We felt we had to do a fast job," said Whitaker. "We had to make a drastic change in public opinion." They succeeded, handily beating Sinclair in the final election by 12 points.

The Whitaker and Baxter alliance had been forged only a year before, in 1933. Clem was a veteran newsman — city editor of the *Sacramento Union* at age nineteen — turned public relations agent, a more comfortable way to earn a living. His roots were deep in evangelism. His father and uncle were Baptist preachers (his uncle was a socialist as well). Exhortation and a tone of moral uplift came naturally to Clem. Leone was manager of the chamber of commerce of Redding, California, when they met. That year the legislature passed a bill authorizing the Central Valley Project, an irrigation and flood control development. Pacific Gas and Electric construed the measure as an attack on private enterprise; the company launched a ballot initiative to defeat it. Proponents urged Whitaker and Baxter to take on PG&E. Through skillful use of contacts with radio stations and small-town newspapers the new PR team easily beat the power company. The surprised power company promptly put the couple on a lucrative annual retainer. When the anti-Sinclair campaign came along, they were awarded that plum, too.

Whitaker and Baxter incorporated themselves as Campaigns, Inc., bringing what was then a novel approach to politics. They were no ordinary press agents. Instead they offered full campaign management — strategy, organization, and advertising.

It was almost inevitable that the modern campaign management concept would emerge in California. Its development was an indirect outcome of earlier reforms that intended to abolish special privileges. But like so many reforms of the Progressive Era there wasn't a linear effect: the reforms were distorted over time.

From the 1870s to 1910 California politics were a wholly owned subsidiary of the Southern Pacific Railroad. It ran the governors, the legislature, and the judges on a timetable that best suited the corporation. In 1910, Hiram Johnson, a Bullmoose Republican, led a citizens' revolt against the Southern Pacific's imperious dominance of state affairs. The revolt succeeded and Johnson was elected governor. Once in office he enacted popular democratic measures — the rights of initiative, referendum, and the recall of public officials. Moreover, Johnson's good government campaign eliminated patronage in state government, making all jobs civil service appointments and rendering political machines inoperable. In a coup de grâce to the corrupt party system, a Progressive proposal allowing candidates to list their names under any party label was passed. From then until the saturation of the state by a politics based on television, politicians were permitted to crossfile as both Democrats and Republicans. The political parties lost their coherence. More than elsewhere, politicians became dependent on the mass media and media managers. California politics became subject to elite political management firms and a parade of ephemeral social movements that were never absorbed by the weak political parties.

Whitaker and Baxter, in the meantime, were propelled to the center of California politics. From that vantage point, Clem surveyed the scene and issued his report. Californians had come a long way since the Progressive Era. "The average American," Whitaker said, "doesn't want to be educated; he doesn't want to improve his mind; he doesn't even want to work, consciously, at being a good citizen. "But," he observed hopefully, "there are two ways you can interest him in a campaign, and only two that we have ever found successful. Most every American loves a contest. He likes a good hot battle, with no punches pulled. So you can interest him if you put on a fight! Then, too, most every American likes to be entertained. He likes the movies; he likes mysteries; he likes fireworks and parades. So if you can't fight, put on a show!"

Whitaker and Baxter confirmed these dictums to themselves and their clients in countless campaigns. In 1946, in a notable effort, they campaigned to prevent the recall of San Francisco mayor Roger Lapham. Unfortunately, in a recall, there is no adversary; only the officeholder's record is in question. Whitaker remedied the situation by inventing a dastardly opponent for his client. On a restaurant tablecloth he doodled a picture of a sinister man with a derby hat tilted so that a shadow obscured his face. This was the man trying to steal Lapham's job — "The Faceless Man." On billboards and in newspaper ads he became "The Undercover Candidate for Mayor." Why was he hiding? What were his motives? Was he part of a nefarious conspiracy? Lapham's campaign suddenly had a focus. He was no longer on the defensive. This bit of fantasy worked admirably, and the recall attempt failed. The campaign was a primitive but seminal example of creative imagery, foreshadowing later events. If a politician could invent his enemy why couldn't the politician be invented as well?

Whitaker and Baxter had many achievements after their campaign against "The Faceless Man." The most significant was a successful effort spanning three and a half years on behalf of the American Medical Association to prevent national health care. The AMA supplied the firm with a budget of $4,678,000 and forty employees to mount the campaign, which, for decades afterward, stigmatized any government health program as "socialized medicine" even though such a system had been enacted in Germany in the 1880s by the Iron Chancellor, Otto von Bismarck.

By the mid-1950s, Whitaker and Baxter no longer held a monopoly on political consulting in California. There were other firms springing up, some led by graduates of the Whitaker and Baxter shop. Still, the couple, with more political experience than any politician in the state, kept at their work, although it appeared that they were losing their touch. In 1967, Whitaker and Baxter handled the congressional campaign of Shirley Temple, and their Good Ship Lollipop sank. The firm stopped dealing with candidates altogether. When Clem died, Clem Junior decided to concentrate on nonpolitical advertising and the fertile field of initiatives; Leone turned to international advertising. Whitaker and Baxter had had their day.

The new wave of politics that superseded Whitaker and Baxter was based on expert use of computers, statistical survey research, and television. During the 1964 Republican presidential primaries, California became the testing ground for these techniques. On one side was Barry Goldwater, precursor of the New Right, and his ideological managers — mainly youthful operatives, highly skilled in the new methods of organizing. Facing Goldwater and his minions were Nelson Rockefeller, grand seigneur of moderate conservatism, and his managers, including some of the best new operatives money could buy. Goldwater, who started with a big advantage in the polls, hired Whitaker and Baxter to assist his campaign. They were, after all, synonymous with California GOP politics. Rockefeller, for his part, hired Stuart Spencer and Bill Roberts, new boys in the game. Spencer and Roberts's main accomplishment before running Rocky's primary drive was managing the campaign of Congressman John Rousselot, an avowed John Birch Society member. Spencer and Roberts, therefore, knew the nature of their opposition when they worked for Rocky; they had helped create it. Goldwater beat Rocky in the California primary by just one half of a percentage point, a victory guaranteed only when Happy Rockefeller gave birth to Nelson Junior a few days before the election, a timely reminder to the conservative Republican electorate of Rocky's marital troubles. The campaign, however, was a moral victory for Spencer and Roberts.

"I would position Stu Spencer as the dean of political consultants — the man who started it all," says Malcolm MacDougall, who was advertising director for President Ford's 1976 campaign. "Before Stu Spencer, the consultants had big cigars in the smoke-filled rooms. Then he came along. He was good at knowing where the voters were and how to pull them out. He combined communications with precinct savvy. Ad agencies don't bring precinct savvy to the candidate. That's still his forte. Spencer is not the David Garth type, really putting most of his weight into television. Stu is much more of a pure consultant. He works out the political strategy."

Spencer began his career as recreation director for the town of Alhambra, California. He was active in the Young Republicans, and through that connection was drawn into the larger world of politics. He understood, before almost everyone else, the application of computers to political analysis. His firm founded its own computer division, Datamatics, devoted to the analysis of election districts. Once the data was programmed, the results could be forecast more scientifically. Spencer modernized ancient necessities of politics: identifying voters, reaching them with the message, and bringing them to the polls. In California, a state without political machines, Spencer's use of software machines was a signal advance, later copied everywhere, as the old ways disappeared. Spencer calls his method "prioritizing precincts." It is an old game, by a different name, by a different means.

When Ronald Reagan's wealthy friends, interested in promoting his candidacy for governor, wanted professional advice, Barry Goldwater suggested Spencer and Roberts, confiding that he wouldn't run another California race without them. The firm was sounded out. After the Goldwater debacle, Spencer and Roberts didn't believe that an extreme right-wing candidate could win the governorship. If Reagan wanted them as his managers he would have to agree to moderate his tone and work with liberal Republicans. Reagan agreed; immediately he lowered his decibel level. Roberts noted that he was "a reasonable guy with a sense of humor who didn't take himself too seriously."

Without Spencer and Roberts, Reagan might never have become a serious politician. He understood what he had to do in order to be a contender. His willingness to be cast as a player in a script showed his professionalism. He knew that mass entertainment was a collaboration of technicians. More, Ronald Reagan longed throughout his career for the image of a leading man. Politics offered what the movies had denied him.

Reagan's first job was to fabricate baseball games. As a sportscaster for WHO radio in Des Moines, Iowa, in the mid-1930's, Reagan had to translate terse, telegraphed descriptions of Chicago Cubs and White Sox games into exciting play-by-play action. Reagan would be wired only that a batter got a hit, with no mention of balls or strikes or bobbled catches. It was his job to fill in these details and to create a sense of live coverage. Reagan perfected his speaking voice. Then, through a series of fortuitous circumstances, he was signed to a movie contract with Warner Brothers.

As an actor he had a certain kind of self-consciousness that manifested itself in external physical control. "It has taken me many years to get used to seeing myself as others see me," he wrote in his autobiography, *Where's the Rest of Me?*, which is titled after his most famous movie line, uttered when he woke up from an operation in which his legs had been amputated by a villainous doctor. "Very few of us ever see ourselves except as we look directly at ourselves in a mirror. Thus we don't know how we look from behind, from the side, walking, standing, moving normally through a room. It is quite a jolt."

Reagan presents the growth of his political views as a process of enlightenment. Originally a "bleeding heart liberal," by his own account, he saw the light and became a conservative. Actually, Reagan had never been much of a liberal, although he had been a Democrat and president of the Screen Actors Guild, in which capacity he testified as a friendly witness before the House Un-American Activities Committee (HUAC) during its 1947 hunt for Communists supposedly subverting Hollywood. When ten screenwriters and directors — the Hollywood 10 — refused to testify before HUAC and were cited for contempt and sentenced to prison terms, Reagan publicly supported their blacklisting by the industry. His position wasn't on the far right, however. There were others — like dapper Adolph Menjou who proudly declared himself a "red baiter" and "witch hunter" — who claimed that honor. Given the spectrum of opinion, Reagan was just a trifle right of center.

His patriotism, however, didn't compensate for his lackluster image. He was no longer drawing good roles from the studios. He had to move on. While many actors refused to leave the movies for television, which was considered lacking in prestige and demeaning, Reagan had no such compunctions. To him, film was never an art form anyway — it was "the picture business." He gladly signed a $125,000-a-year contract with General Electric to host the weekly "GE Theater" and serve as a company spokesman, visiting factories to improve employee morale and generally enhance the corporation's image. When "GE Theater" was canceled (knocked off in the ratings by a western called "Bonanza"), Reagan found, through his advertising executive brother, a new vehicle to host — "Death Valley Days." He exchanged a business suit for cowboy duds.

His off-camera chores for GE were instrumental in the development of his political outlook. He was engaged in a campaign on behalf of corporate imagery, traveling constantly, visiting 125 plants, giving speeches to hundreds of thousands of workers, and assimilating the world view of the business executives he spent most of his time with. At age forty-five, when he began with GE, he had no defined perspective. "I told him," said Ralph Cordiner, GE president, " 'You'd better get yourself a philosophy, something you can stand for and something you think this country stands for.' I think this is when he really started to change."

Reagan finally became a political activist during the Goldwater campaign. At a televised fundraiser he delivered an electrifying speech similar to his GE banquet talks, but much more portentous. He freely borrowed lines that had worked well before. "You and I," he said, "have a rendezvous with destiny. We will preserve for our children this, the last best hope for man on earth, or we will sentence them to take the last step into a thousand years of darkness." After the 1964 election, Reagan instantly appeared as a potential candidate for governor of California, a new hero for the crestfallen Republicans. The California Republicans had found their champion.

The Golden State had changed a great deal since the campaign of "The Faceless Man." Southern California, especially, had boomed. In 1953, Anaheim, for example, had a population of 20,000; within a few years it blossomed into a city of 200,000. The suburban spread out of L.A. seemed infinite. Many of the suburbanites in Orange County, next to L.A., were homeowners for the first time, and many were heirs to a Depression legacy of conservative social values, economic insecurity, and a desire to reestablish a golden past they imagined existed before the New Deal. Although much of their new-found stability and affluence was based upon the largesse the federal government dispensed to the aircraft and aerospace companies that employed them, many Orange County residents were suspicious and resentful of the government's role in aiding the poor. They ascribed their comfortable survival to hard work and free will. In the early 1960s, the John Birch Society became firmly entrenched there as a respectable political group.

The representative thinker of Southern California was Walt Disney, as important to that region's history of ideas as Henry David Thoreau or Bronson Alcott were to New England. Disney's paradise was the Walden, the Fruitlands, of Orange County. Disneyland was a totalitarian utopia for Middle Americans, a total environment efficiently organized in every aspect of its operation, offering itself as an idealization of the laissez faire myth. It provided a nostalgic, painless trip back to Main Street and a visit into an immaculately clean, chrome future — a vivid contrast to the littered world of rioting blacks and unkempt youths. Orange County contained the essential constituency longing for Ronald Reagan — the man who would abolish the present and usher in the past.

Astride this base of alienated suburbanites was a new ruling class of oilmen, real estate entrepreneurs, drugstore tycoons, and wildly successful automobile dealers, the nouveaux riches of L.A. They were neither old money, represented by the Chandler family, which owns the *Los Angeles Times*, nor movie money, which is partly Jewish. These newly rich became flush virtually overnight. The suddenness of their elevation gave them no time to adjust their social outlook; their money exaggerated their individualism and conservatism. Ronald Reagan was their man to oppose traditional Democrat Pat Brown, running for a third term. Reagan articulated what they all believed without question to be true, and he was one of them. All he lacked was political experience and knowledge. He was ready for the political consultant.

Stuart Spencer's office is located atop the Security Pacific Bank Building in Newport Beach, where the nouveaux riches dock their yachts. Pictures of his most famous clients — Ronald Reagan and Gerald Ford — adorn his walls. Spencer wears an open-collared shirt and a Lacoste sweater to work, formal wear for this resort town. Despite his creased face and his slicked-back gray hair he has a youthful, jaunty air about him. "I wanted to be a football coach," he said. Instead, he coached the man who played the Gipper.

"Style is so important in these things," Spencer says. "I always felt, I think correctly, that Ronnie Reagan didn't say a damn thing Barry Goldwater didn't say in 1964 — the same things, but he said them softer. It was style that carried the day for Reagan, more than the issues themselves. He was a trained actor. I'm not so sure Ronnie was politically perceptive. But Ronnie knew the medium of television, and what he was saying hit a chord among Republicans. He knew about timing, the physical aspects of looking at cameras, and he had a presence. Most candidates don't understand any of that." Reagan, however, had deficiencies. "He did not have a real feel for the political world. But he was a very good student.

From our point of view he was an excellent candidate to work with. Reagan is the best media candidate I have ever seen."

The media, for their part, handled Reagan gently. "The press was extremely kind to Reagan," says Spencer. "They were almost in awe of him. He was a new breed. They couldn't figure out where he was coming from, so they were cautious."

This passivity by journalists and editors gave Reagan time to paper over his political ignorance. Spencer hired two behavioral psychologists as campaign consultants. The academics prepared facts on and answers to a wide range of state problems, framing responses in ways that would be most compelling to the voters. Reagan studied the file. He carried the index cards with him wherever he went. If asked a question he couldn't answer, all he had to do was consult his file, demonstrating his knowledge of social issues and dispelling the notion that because he had never been elected to any public office he was ill-equipped to be governor. This liability was turned into an asset by billing Reagan as a "citizen politician." His inexperience was projected as positive: Reagan was better than a professional politician.

A theme emerged early in the campaign. In 1966, when Reagan first ran for governor, Lyndon Johnson's Great Society was still riding high. Reagan suggested a Republican alternative — the Creative Society. The idea for the Creative Society was hatched by fundamentalist right-wing radio preacher, the Reverend W. S. Birnie, a pal of Reagan's. (After the election, Birnie arranged for Reagan to be given a gift of a baby elephant by the pretender to the throne of Albania.) "We built everything around the Creative Society," says Spencer. "Whatever Reagan wanted to do, it was creative. Shut down Berkeley? It was creative. Every program he came up with we touted as the Creative Society."

Reagan's campaign, of course, relied heavily on television. Spencer cut out many needless personal appearances at shopping malls and banquets, partly because Reagan tired and got irritable under a stressful schedule. Spencer also recognized that television could replace shaking voters' hands. Yet there was another problem, a key question of image. Having no political experience could be dealt with by the "citizen politician" gambit, but how could Reagan effectively confront his image as an actor, a trained performer?

Reagan's television spots were deliberately awkward and artless. The candidate was positioned in front of a camera, a talking head lecturing viewers on assorted issues; fancy sets were avoided. This was an improvement on slickness: it seemed to exhibit Reagan as real.

His ads portrayed him as honest, hard-working, nonintellectual, trustworthy, and all-American. Yet, this was precisely the persona Reagan had developed in the movies. Consider some of his archetypal roles: Shirley Temple's adult boy friend, no threat to her virginity, in *That Hagen Girl;* a soldier who refuses to share a room with Eleanor Parker when they're forced to spend a night in her apartment during a storm, in *Voice of the Turtle;* and, memorably, a scientist who raises chimpanzees as a way to convince his girl friend's father that his own father's criminal background is not hereditary, in *Bedtime for Bonzo.* In countering his actor image, Reagan was typecast as the same character.

In 1970, after Reagan's reelection campaign, Spencer and Reagan had a falling out. Spencer was pushed aside by two courtiers, Mike Deaver and Peter Hannaford, public relations men who were more ideological and less critical. Reagan's wife, Nancy, encouraged the coup of the palace guard. "Nancy," says Spencer, "can be tough as hell at times. She hates my guts now, I hear. In some ways she is smarter politically than Ron. He tended to be naive. In politics people always whisper in your ear, saying nice things. He believed they meant it. Nancy didn't. She's a lot tougher than the image America has of her. The image America has of Nancy isn't correct. The image America has of Betty Ford is totally correct. She's no different in public than she is in private, a very open person. Nancy is very ambitious, very ambitious."

By then, however, Spencer was not the most advanced consultant in the business. A plethora of consultants, mostly Republican oriented, followed his example. Dick Woodward and Jack McDowell managed Spencer's San Francisco office until 1971 when they struck out on their own. Their first big splash was the campaign of S. I. Hayakawa for the Senate. Its focus was entirely negative, featuring a television spot in which John Tunney's record was represented by a mud-splattered windshield. In 1978, Woodward and McDowell hit the jackpot with the initiative process. When a Clean Indoor Air Initiative was put on the California ballot to ban smoking in public places, tobacco companies amassed a $6.2 million fund to fight it. At the consultants' suggestion, the tobacco group called itself the Common Sense Committee; it was not inspired by Tom Paine. Woodward and McDowell carefully observed a sample group of voters assembled to discuss the issue — a focus group, as it's called in the trade. As a result of what they learned from the focus group they ran an anti–big government campaign — by prohibiting public smoking, bureaucracy was again impinging on God-given freedoms. The pitch went over.

Another consulting firm, Butcher-Forde, was largely responsible for Proposition 13, the anti–property tax initiative. First, through a direct mail campaign, they raised the money to sell the issue. Then, the firm ran the ad campaign. "The one thing we weren't sure we had in the campaign was credibility," said Arnold Forde. "So to get it, we asked Milton Friedman to do a spot for us. It was just him standing there for thirty seconds." The Nobel Prize–winning conservative economist is a short, bald man with an unexciting, drab speaking style. He was perfect. He gave authority and respectability to the cause.

Butcher-Forde, however, was fined by California's Fair Political Practices Commission (FPPC) in 1978 for violating campaign regulations. To wit: The firm recruited a third candidate for a race to increase their own client's chances of winning; they even paid the spoiler's filing fee. And the scheme worked. "Almost everyone in this business has had fines levied against them," said Bill Butcher. "We could have defended ourselves and won, but the FPPC just took its pound of flesh. It was no big event."

In the meantime, Stu Spencer, the Rockefeller consultant who became the Reagan consultant, became the anti–Reagan consultant. He had once convinced California to take Reagan seriously; now he would convince the country that Reagan was a joke. He was hired to run President Gerald Ford's campaign in 1976, an opportunity to use his intimate knowledge of Reagan's foibles. He sought to catch Reagan, Ford's opponent for the nomination, when, he said, his "blood sugar's low."

"We tried to get Reagan to make mistakes," he says. "The early primaries made Ford. If we hadn't won New Hampshire, we'd have been dead. Just forget it. So we did a lot of research. We discovered that back in September 1975 Reagan advocated cutting $90 billion from the federal budget. It was reported in the *Washington Post* and buried on page 23. I was out in Chicago and I met with the *Post* reporter who picked that up. He kept badgering me about it, kept asking me if I had seen it. He was madder than hell at the *Post* because they had buried it. Typical reporter. I looked it up. We started analyzing it. I said, 'If we look at the state of New Hampshire, it has no income tax; it receives a lot of federal funding. If we could figure this out we could do Reagan a lot of harm.' We had a researcher put some numbers next to the $90 billion figure and it showed that Reagan would have wiped New Hampshire out. So we prepared a good background piece on it and gave it to the key press people. The first day Reagan hit New Hampshire to start his campaign we nailed him on it. We had a New Hampshire legislator ask him the question about the $90 billion. He staggered around, fumbled around, it caught him off guard. He wasn't ready for it. Every place he went for five days he got nailed with it. It did him irreparable damage. The perception of how he handled it was what hurt him. Our polls showed that Republicans split 50-50 on the issue. There wasn't any strong feeling on it. But Reagan came in and didn't handle it well. We put him on the defensive."

Taking advantage of Reagan's mistakes was one part of Spencer's strategy; preventing Ford from making mistakes was the other part. "The big strategy in the Ford campaign," says Spencer, "was to keep as low a profile as we could and use the presidency." Gerald Ford did not have a presidential image; he fell down or bumped his head too often. "We had data after data after data that indicated that every time he went out on the road he shot himself in the foot. I say that with kindness. But there was a direct correlation between his swings around the country and his polling data. Every time he was inactive he'd go up. That's where the Rose Garden Strategy came in. That was to stay in the White House and do the presidential thing. Just be president."

Unfortunately, Ford had lapses, like when he claimed in a televised debate with Jimmy Carter that Eastern Europe was not dominated by the Soviet Union. Spencer couldn't control Ford completely; he couldn't stop the president from occasionally being himself. And so Ford lost.

During the campaign, one of Reagan's operatives, Bob Hope's nephew Tom Malatesta, asked John Wayne for an endorsement of Reagan. Wayne, who lived a mile from Stu Spencer in Newport Beach, didn't care as much about supporting Reagan as attacking Spencer. He made his own radio ad assailing the consultant, which the Reagan campaign never used. Eventually, Wayne did make spots for Reagan, but he kept hollering wildly about Spencer, making charges nobody really understood.

"Folks, John Wayne," said the Duke in his homemade tape against Spencer. "California had a governor who in eight years took it from a bankrupt state to a four-billion-dollar surplus: Ronald Reagan. His proven administrative abilities are certainly now needed in our country. Not that I don't think the president is trying. What I worry about is his political camp. It's not a team. They're not his followers. They're manipulators. They have forced him into a position of vacillation many times. Two of the men in high places and prominent on his team are the same who allowed their names to be used to insinuate the lie against Goldwater in 1964.* The prejudiced press has been forced to admit the lie about Goldwater, and these men, in his own party, knew that to be a fact, but still allowed ads in the *Los Angeles Times*, in the California primary, to insinuate the lie as a truth . . ."

When Malatesta asked Wayne the identity of the second Ford manipulator, besides Spencer, Wayne's memory failed him.

"Duke had a problem with me. I'll tell you why," says Spencer. "Years ago Wayne was pretty close to Reagan. Wayne wanted to appoint a certain person to the horseracing board. He did not check out. If you were a drinking buddy, a card playing buddy of Wayne's, you were a buddy. But this guy just would have been an embarrassment. He had a habit of blowing a lot of money in Vegas. He was a gambler, a high-liver. The governor wouldn't appoint him, and I had to carry the message. Duke was madder than hell. I will not repeat what he said when I told him. Duke didn't like politicians basically. He was always dumping on them. He just felt anytime they wanted something he did it for them and they never did anything for him. He was that kind of guy. Sometimes his requests were a little outrageous. He was an honest man, don't misunderstand me. But he did impulsive things."

In Orange County, after Wayne's death, the airport was re-named the John Wayne Airport. Luggage tags now read DUK. "He was an American institution," muses Spencer. John Wayne, like Ronald Reagan, the actor, was created by Hollywood. Ronald Reagan, the actor, without another kind of production system behind him, would never have been transformed into a successful

---

*Wayne obliquely refers here to the 1964 California primary in which Spencer worked for Rockefeller against Goldwater. To Wayne, this is somehow "the lie."

politician. "Duke has become a legend, now, hasn't he?" says Spencer, marveling at the process.

## CHAPTER NINE

# HIS OWN BEST OPERATIVE

### JERRY BROWN

To older journalists California governor Jerry Brown is a man-bites-dog story. He does everything wrong. He's unpredictable. He sleeps on a mattress on the floor. He travels to Africa with rock star Linda Ronstadt without apology or discretion. He breaks old rules without penalty. He feeds off this old-fashioned perception of what a politician can or cannot do to project himself as original. Gray Davis, Brown's chief of staff and alter ego, says, "Jerry is like the mirrored ball hanging above a dance floor." He has many images and shines brightly.

What kind of rare plumed bird is Jerry Brown in the American political aviary? He is a politician in the ultimate media state who flutters above definition. He knows how to manipulate conventional media well. To him, media is merely part of his nervous system. He is Homo Californius — the California Man.

Brown could never employ a Gerald Rafshoon, Jimmy Carter's

media adviser, someone who designs his public actions. The Rafshoon type of consultant shapes events around the politician and tries to make very sure he knows what the events mean. He creates a world in which the politician looks best. Since Brown considers himself an event, he is always in place and doesn't need to be positioned. For Brown, the permanent campaign isn't something he has tried to create and sustain; instead it's merely reality, which is embodied in himself.

Those who have educated opinions about Jerry Brown fall into three categories: (1) those who dislike him; (2) those who respect his political acumen but don't understand or trust him; and (3) those who work for him. All think he's mysterious, that his character is unfathomable in some way, that his intent cannot easily be charted, and that he acts intuitively.

To some, Brown represents the leitmotifs of Los Angeles and San Francisco, the movie star and the bohemian. The traditional bohemian from San Francisco is a special sort — laid back, erratic, lulled by the pleasant amenities of Bay Area life, his edge artificially sharpened by Orientalism. On the other hand, the L.A. star is opportunistic to a fault, without discretion, eager to be buffeted by movie or TV offers, glitzy, cunning, glib, and, above all, understands the value of an appearance on the "Tonight Show."

Is Jerry Brown the offspring of mingled L.A. and San Francisco chromosomes? Max Palevsky takes this view. Years ago Palevsky founded his own computer company and built it into a multimillion-dollar enterprise, which he sold to Xerox; he's now a major Xerox stockholder. He was a major financial supporter of George McGovern's 1972 presidential campaign. He backs many liberal candidates and is considered a leading light among liberals in L.A., a loose grouping known as the Malibu Mafia. Jerry Brown was the beneficiary of his largesse when Brown first ran for governor. Palevsky has few kind words for Brown now. "Have you ever read anything about Hitler?" he asked me. "I'm not saying Jerry Brown is Hitler, but Hitler led a really bohemian life, keeping strange hours, doing what he wanted when he wanted. Jerry leads a completely chaotic life. He has a short attention span. It's ad hoc totally. You can't get him to organize to get at the problem. Movie stars, when they're hot, become awful. They become Barbra Streisand. Everyone has to suffer every kind of childish behavior. Jerry is essentially bored. That's one of the real wellsprings of his behavior. He's on a permanent campaign. There's action when there's a campaign. He's not interested in running the government. Brown is someone with no center. When you spend time with him you see that. He doesn't care about anything. It's the disease of someone who doesn't have any ties to sex, money, family, scholarship. Jerry has no ties to society. All that's left is celebrity. And that doesn't fill your stomach very much. He doesn't get much satisfaction out of it because there isn't anything he really wants. He's always looking."

Stanley Scheinbaum, another Malibu Mafioso, isn't as certain about Brown. I paid Scheinbaum a visit at his Bel Air mansion on Bentley Drive, which isn't visible from the road. He doesn't have a front lawn; he has a sculpture garden. Through the large plate-glass windows in his home you are presented with a panoramic vista of Westwood, the site of UCLA, and several movie studios. Scheinbaum has been appointed a regent of the University of California by Brown; his wife is an heiress to a movie fortune, old money from Beverly Hills. In the mid-sixties Scheinbaum wrote in *Ramparts* magazine one of the first exposés revealing the training of South Vietnamese police at CIA expense on the Michigan State campus.

"I have gone through a period of figuring out what to do about Jerry Brown," he reflects. "He came over to my house in late February [1979]. 'Why don't you guys support me?' he asked. I told him, 'We're not fronting for anybody.' I was once with Jerry when he suffered four major defeats in one day. That didn't faze him. He seems to have some vision of where and how he's going.

Setbacks don't seem to affect him. He has something on his mind. When he ran for president in 1976 he had a cocktail party in Beverly Hills. He said that a campaign is like a cake of ice that rides on its own melt. As it rides along it develops its own momentum. Jerry doesn't need an organization. All he needs are money and media." Scheinbaum has stopped giving money.

Few professional politicians in California like Brown. "The legislature hates his guts, to say the least," says a liberal lobbyist for a labor group at the state capitol. "They're trying to do him in. He's not respected. His legislative support is terrible. He doesn't pay enough attention to other Democrats. He's a very cold fish." Ed Salzman, editor of the widely read *California Journal*, which is devoted to state politics, observes, "He's doing nothing in this state. The professional pols have always been against Jerry Brown. But people who write him off are crazy."

The alienation of the professionals is not necessarily impolitic in California. In fact, it serves Brown's purpose of casting himself as beyond traditional politics. The consequences of this disdain aren't really great because party loyalty and the party structure are virtually nonexistent. The battle between the regulars and Brown takes place primarily on the symbolic level. The pros may rail against Brown, but they have no army of patronage employees to order into the breach. The reason for their weakness lies deep in California history, a history that Brown is highly conscious of.

The first genuine television candidate swept California in 1952. He was Estes Kefauver, a populist-leaning U.S. senator who gained national prominence with the first televised Senate hearings, captivating the public in a way that had never happened before. Kefauver challenged Harry Truman, a sitting president who was low in the polls, by going above the heads of the party bosses, appealing to the voters through the new medium. He picked the ideal state in which to stage a show of strength. His victory in the California primary pushed Truman into retirement and demonstrated that on the basis of television alone a candidate could win delegates to a national convention. One result of Kefauver's campaign was the nomination by the Democratic party of Adlai Stevenson, a highbrow candidate backed by the bosses who wanted to thwart Kefauver. Stevenson, however, dismissed television as a lowbrow medium. He would never deign to manipulate it. Meanwhile, his opponent, Dwight Eisenhower, permitted his campaign to hire a Madison Avenue advertising firm to produce television spots for him, an indirect outcome of Kefauver's California victory.

From Kefauver, an antipolitician politician, it was not very far to the antipolitician outsider. Ronald Reagan was a celluloid figure, a manufactured construct, created by a production studio. Becoming governor was the logical fulfillment of his career — leading man in B-grade films; host of "Death Valley Days"; corporate spokesman for his benefactor, General Electric; governor. His rise to the top, without having been elected to any previous public office, was the final blow against traditional politics. Yet he was not in control. He was subsumed in the process. His persona, not his person, triumphed. It was a triumph of political consulting, of the firm Spencer-Roberts, which ran his campaign. When Jerry Brown arrived he did more than succeed Reagan; he transcended him. He doesn't have to act. He is. Tom Quinn, Brown's media adviser, says, "Jerry is his own director of politics." Brown isn't an actor in somebody else's screenplay. He is the auteur, the culmination of California political history. To understand him is to understand his state.

For instance, Brown is an archetypal Californian in his belief that he represents the future. To speak of an alternative culture in California is a tautology. California has always posited itself as America's alternative culture, a crucible of new values and ways of living. Brown is not so much the alternative as he is the Californian. Since the Gold Rush, California has been the alternative culture in the American scheme — more flamboyant, public, and self-serving. In California, American character traits are magnified. Mere greed, for example, becomes the Gold Rush mentality; an attempt to seek a calmer state of mind becomes Esalen. Brown would prefer that we not see it that way. Gray Davis says, "I don't see Jerry riding with California banners against the rest of the country." Regardless of his explicit desires, however, his position is inescapable. He is, after all, the governor of California, a state so large that it feels no need for the rest of the country. No one else seems necessary. California is roughly the same physical size as Japan. It has the seventh largest economy in the world. The state is hermetically sealed like a separate nation, bounded by the Rockies, the Sierras, the ocean, and the desert.

For that reason, Jerry Brown, more than any other politician, carries the burden of a nation fragmenting into regional rivalries. In the sixties, among those of the postwar generation, there was an illusion of a national counterculture, represented by Fillmore East and Fillmore West, Cambridge and Berkeley. Now the illusion has dissolved, leaving California with sun and New England with winter. One can almost believe in the validity of Montesquieu's theory of geographical determinism. In *The Spirit of the Laws*, he wrote, "In temperate climates we find the inhabitants inconstant in their manners, as well as in their vices and virtues: the climate has not a quality determinate enough to fix them."

In his presidential campaign, Brown is implicitly attempting to revive the golden fable of California as progressive and forward looking by proving that he is indeed the future. This effort comes at a time when the counterfable of California seems in ascendancy. In looking for a quick route to utopia one may discover in the Golden State its opposite: dystopia. The mass suicides of a California congregation at Jonestown, Guyana, had the shocking effect of a modern Donner Party, an incident in the last century in which settlers trapped in a snowbound mountain pass ran out of food and devoured their dead companions. The Manson Family murders and the assassinations of San Francisco mayor George Moscone and city supervisor Harvey Milk by disgruntled right-wing supervisor Dan White (who was subsequently convicted only of manslaughter because the jurors in his trial sympathized with his plight) are taken by many Easterners as signs of California's pathology. For Brown, a question in his presidential bid must be to dispel California's negative image. His quest, which may last until the turn of the century, is the winning of the East, a reverse manifest destiny.

The Far East is something Brown strives to understand. The American East is a mystery to him; it is a different coast. Unlike California it was the beginning; it was the first chance, not the last. A relatively settled class system frees the East from wild expectations. One knows what to expect; grandiose fantasies are uncalled for, and acting them out is unseemly. Robert Frost wrote: "I met a Californian who would/Talk California — a state so blessed,/ He said, in climate none had ever died there/A natural death." Jerry Brown, in staging a presidential campaign, seeks to overcome regional differences. In his bid he confronts for the first time those who live on the cutting edge of the era of limits.

"Why should we talk about the era of limits and lowered expectations in California? We're riding an unparalleled wave of prosperity out here," says Gray Davis. "If our interests were strictly parochial, why would we advance those ideas? We don't have to temper our appetite in this state. We have bountiful resources, much of which, like agriculture, we export. But Jerry's politics aren't grounded in parochialism." What then is the basis of Brown's politics? Gray Davis interprets Jerry Brown to the outside world in terms it understands. He describes Brown's physical properties and empirical plans, not his abstract motivation. When you're listening to Davis you're getting a more lucid but removed version of Jerry Brown's intentions. He is a key Brown political aide as well as his chief of staff, controlling his appointments and the flow of his administrative tasks. He helps Brown govern by helping him keep a high standing with the public, which is maintained not through any party channels but through television, the most direct link. "I remember meeting New Hampshire governor Hugh Gallen's campaign manager," recalls Davis. "He told me the key to his campaign was television. That's like telling me the key to life is the sun. We've long since accepted that. Television is the glue that binds California together. It's the institution that homogenizes and synthesizes the state's experience. There are very few settled institutions that have a hold on people or their imaginations like there are in the East. Television is an anchor people can hold on to. Virtually nothing is fixed in California. The benefits to that lie in our receptivity to new ideas. Many of those ideas, for better or worse, are exported to the East."

With Brown's presidential aspirations in mind, Davis asked all sorts of questions about local political conditions in Massachusetts, especially details about the Boston media. Finally, I suggested that if he really wanted to plumb the mysteries of the East he had only to understand the Boston Red Sox–New York Yankees rivalry, and then understand why the Red Sox fans rooted for the Yankees against the Dodgers in the 1978 World Series.

Davis is a Dodgers fan. He started complaining about Graig Nettles's brilliant fielding in that Series. "I watched the Series over at Pat Brown's," he said, referring to Jerry's father, the former governor.

"Was Jerry there?" I inquired.

"Yeah," Davis said. "But he was sitting in a corner reading something on Zen."

This was a revealing anecdote, encapsulating Jerry Brown's studied indifference to his father, Brown's political keenness, and his devotion to systematic thought. Jerry Brown is Edmund G. "Pat" Brown Sr.'s eldest son, but not his eldest child. Pat Brown is an effusive, warm public personality. If he was scheduled to give a speech to a group holding a meeting in a hotel, he would purposely arrive early and wander into another group's meeting. When he was recognized, as he would be inevitably, he would say, "Why, I must have stumbled into the wrong room." Of course, he would be invited to give a speech. "Oh, I can't," he would say, and then give a speech. He courted public affection avidly. But, to his son, by all accounts, he never seemed more intimate than he was when he was clapping fellow politicians on the back; his affection for Jerry didn't seem special. This caused a reaction. Instead of adhering to his father's New Deal liberalism, which was mostly instinctive and didn't require much rigor, Jerry was attracted to more disciplined systems of thought. His years of training at a Jesuit seminary may partially be interpreted in this light. When Jerry left the seminary, he entered Yale Law School, where another discipline of thought, complete in itself, was taught. In becoming a politician Jerry didn't exactly follow in the footsteps of his famous father. He used his father's contacts and, of course, his name, but made a point of neglecting his father personally. During one of Jerry's early campaigns for public office, Pat Brown met his son at a Japanese restaurant where he was dining with friends. "What are you doing eating this food? Why don't you eat real food?" Pat demanded. Then he asked Jerry what role an operative named Pete had in the campaign.

"What's Pete's role? Pete's a Tootsie Roll. Pete's a Tootsie Roll," Jerry mocked.

Pat Brown's defeat at the hands of Ronald Reagan completed the political trinity of the Brown family. If Pat was the father and Jerry was the son, then the holy ghost must be television. What lesson did Jerry learn from his father's defeat by a media candidate? "Just that," says Gray Davis. "Media was king in California and you couldn't wish it away. It's part of life and politics. I don't know if Pat tried to build an organization, but I'm convinced you can't. You can't build a machine in California. There is no machine in the arts or finance or anything else in this state. There's no real patronage available."

Jerry Brown learned the indispensability of using television.

But what should one fill it with? This part came naturally to him. "There are no institutions that have any claims on people's allegiances in California," says Gray Davis. "Jerry understands that the thing that pulls people together in California is an idea. There is no substitute for a compelling attractive idea."

"What about images?" I asked.

"*An idea is an image,*" says Davis. "Jerry's success in the way he's reached people is not by developing a cult of personality but through ideas that in and of themselves are attractive. The only way to organize people in California is around an idea. Jerry is his own best political and media adviser. And the best organizing tool is an idea."

Spinning out ideas has enormous political value in California. "Because ideas have the power to organize human behavior, their efficacy can be radical," wrote Walter Lippmann in *The Public Philosophy*. "The images matter very much." These ideas don't always have to be grounded programmatically to be effective. It is policy, not ideas, which is suggestive and sketchy; the ideas are more elaborate, more captivating, and more appealing. Small-is-beautiful and the era-of-limits, two ideas closely associated with Brown, aren't ruses. He believes in them; he also knows their practical utility. They are cosmic conceptions of what his programs only hint at.

Sometimes, though, it's necessary for Brown to cease playing with ideas and just play rough. Hardball politics isn't a backroom affair in California; it's a media event, too. During the last gubernatorial election, Brown, dangerously down in the polls, turned the tables on his opponent, Evelle Younger. He made Younger the issue and deflected criticism from himself. Tom Quinn, Brown's media man, handled the attack. Quinn was born to California politics. Quinn's father started the City News Service in L.A., a major local agency, and also served as deputy mayor to L.A. mayor Sam Yorty. After the Democratic and Republican primaries Brown was riding low and Younger riding high in the ratings. Proposition 13, which Brown had opposed, passed by an overwhelming margin. It looked good for Younger, who was exhausted by the grind and decided to prepare for the final race by vacationing in Hawaii. It was perhaps his worst political mistake. A Jerry Brown radio spot blanketed the state; it was merciless. An authoritative newsreel-style voice opened the spot, announcing the passage of Proposition 13. Jerry Brown, informed the narrator, went back to work to make sure the bill was really enacted. Jerry Brown became Jerry Jarvis, leader of the taxpayers' revolt. Suddenly, the ad's narrator was interrupted by ukuleles strumming Hawaiian melodies. "Meanwhile," the heavy voice said, "Evelle Younger went to Hawaii." "Everyone remembers that spot," says Ed Salzman, *California Journal* editor. "It helped turn the campaign around. It was pivotal. Jerry won the battle."

Sacramento, the capital of California, located on the northern plain of the fertile San Joaquin Valley, is clean, quiet, and boring. It is overwhelmingly white, middle-class Protestant, the kind of town where white bread is served with dinner. The most exciting section of town is called Old Sacramento, a Western street reconstructed for tourists who appreciate California's myriad attractions. The capitol dome rises above the city, catching the first sunlight. The sun is blinding and temperatures in mid-summer often rise past 100 degrees. On an especially blistering day when I was there, the local television news opened with a story about the increased numbers of people taking bus tours of the city. As it turned out, these "tourists" were actually residents seeking relief in the air-conditioned buses. There is no Sacramento of the mind.

I had a long wait before meeting Jerry Brown. Apparently he runs late as a rule. This gave me time to meet others passing in and out of the office, such as Walter Maguire, associate dean of the Hastings Law School in San Francisco, who organized Brown's write-in campaign in the Oregon primary in 1976 and also did advance work for President Carter in Korea and Jerusalem, the only man freely admitted into both camps. "Brown's perception of a leader is less of leading the bureaucracy than of leading public opinion," says Maguire. "We have a political system that aids that tremendously. The state is larger than most countries. There are seven major media markets. Running a campaign here is like running a national campaign. There are no parties here. The Democratic party has very little power. There's no reason to have a party. Campaigns are organized around issues and individuals. To the extent California is perceived as fresh, that's an advantage." Still, Maguire isn't quite sure about the effect of Jerry Brown's pronouncements. He thinks he knows what they mean, but not certain how they translate into policy. "I'm not sure," he says, "that lowered expectations refers to the economy. Brown is talking about something more philosophical."

Throwing off ideas is Brown's way of experimenting and campaigning. It's a biologic process. You can never attack him by attacking his ideas. By helping him winnow out the weaker ideas you are helping him survive. No single idea is crucial to his survival. That's why he's so supple. This is his method of polling. The only kind of polling that truly makes sense to him is personal, not statistical. Impersonal polls are helpful to him in perfunctory ways. His private pollings generate the feedback he really needs, especially when he talks with journalists, who use and discard symbols as readily as he does. Other pols cultivate journalists for obvious reasons — good press and influence. But they're afraid of testing ideas on journalists; they're too close to their ideas, maybe because they have so few of them. Brown, however, is uninhibited. His sense of personal boundaries is very different from that of the typical politician. It's hard to discern where he's vulnerable. He has little fear of the inevitable distortion ideas undergo in the press. He understands that any organism that absorbs new information transforms it into something of its own, even if only to broadcast it. That's just another step in the process.

It is this process of everything in flux, constant evolution, that made waiting for Jerry Brown different from waiting for other pols.

Once inside his office, I found that Brown was thinner and more intense than I had anticipated, like a high-strung greyhound. On Brown's desk, amidst a shuffle of papers was a book entitled *Muddling Toward Frugality.* Hidden behind a curtain was a framed picture of Jimmy Carter and Jerry Brown, inscribed "Best wishes to my friend Governor Brown." The photo, propped on top of an air-conditioning vent, was being continually cooled. As he sat at his desk, his legs jiggled constantly as if he were running a race; his pace never slackened. He didn't really answer many of my questions directly; he didn't answer them elliptically either. In my interview with him, he offered an epistemological analysis: he answered questions by explaining how he thinks. We ran through a wide range of subjects, in no particular order. He began by explicating a metaphor, currently making the rounds, in which his politics are compared to his canoeing style: he paddles on the left and paddles on the right and moves straight ahead. "I can tell you about the canoe metaphor," he said. "It's from Gregory Bateson, one of the most thoughtful men alive today in the world." Bateson is the first husband of Margaret Mead, the first man to attempt to decipher the language of dolphins, now a gray eminence among California philosophers, appointed to the University of California's board of regents by Brown.

"If you're on a canoe," said Brown, "and you stand up in it, you shift your weight in relationship to the canoe itself. The more rigidly positioned you are, by putting all your weight on one foot or the other, you will fall into the water. If you maintain a relationship with the canoe, you can achieve a balance, a form of stability. If you want to call it the canoe image, it is the image of the way life is. Some of the critics don't understand that. Has anyone ever canoed on one side of a canoe? They haven't. So you can say canoeing is different from other parts of life. But I think that if you examine everything, whether it's a relationship to your own mind or body or nation, there is a movement, a balance, a rhythm that endures. It's not just a rigidity, which is the characteristic of something dead, something that's not evolving, not open to the processes of life. Life is inhaling, exhaling, growing, blossoming, and the leaves coming off in the winter. If we look at the way life is, it's different than the dead thinking we see in much of politics."

Brown clearly bears an animosity toward traditional politics. But what of the new politics of symbolism and media of which he is a leader? "Everything is a symbol at some level of analysis," he argued. "People are making fun of symbols. But language is a symbolic undertaking. In fact, the difference between higher orders of animals and lower orders is the ability to symbolize, to deal with symbols. Now, somehow, symbolism has become a pejorative undertaking. Why is that? *Symbols are the only way we communicate.* Communications is the handling and processing of symbols. It's interesting to me that some symbols are called empty and are said not to stand for anything, that they're a false lead of what someone is really up to. I've talked about planetary realism, and someone said those were buzzwords. And I said, 'What about the New Deal? The New Deal, is that a buzzword?' Buzzword is a buzzword. You have to analyze what people mean. I guess you could say I use symbols, but you couldn't say I'm not following a course of substance."

Brown paused, thought for a moment and continued. "In a technical biological sense, what is an idea? An idea is some kind of image in your mind that is moved by some kind of electric circuitry. But obviously patterns in the mind stand for other things. There's no communication without that. That's a truism. You have to say, what are you aiming at? The question is not, are symbols appropriate, but are the symbols employed consistently and accurately and do you agree with the message. We live in nets of message material, transmitted at high rates of speed. That's a cybernetic truth."

I asked Brown about his feelings about his father's defeat by Reagan. He seemed to resist the straightforward answer that Gray Davis gave. Once again Brown moved through his response until he could explain more about how he knows things. "There was no difference in the amount of television they bought. Reagan had an appealing package of political ideas. The fascination with the technology is a misplaced emphasis, because Reagan has a message. He stands for a certain organization of America and a certain relationship between the public and private sector. And that's what he stands for. The fact that he may say it in a way that makes it more interesting to people does not negate the content of his message. I think it's a very superficial analysis to say that he doesn't stand for something. What does a media candidate mean? What is a nonmedia candidate? There aren't all those traditional networks out there. There's not a lot of patronage."

I interrupted Brown here to remind him I came from Massachusetts, where there are still some nonmedia candidates, relying on party and patronage. "What can we say about that?" asked Brown rhetorically. "One has to take the world as you find it." He continued on the track he had been heading: "Who's a media candidate? Was McGovern a media candidate? I don't think that question gives you a lot of useful information. You might say that someone is so devoid of content and full of slogans that they're not saying anything. Well, I think that's saying something. I find that most journalists are media personalities. They always have a pen in their hands, or a microphone. They're too self-conscious about it. It just is. It's like your vocal chords. Media is just an extension of our vocal chords."

I wanted to go back to the apparent contradictions between the reality of Massachusetts and Brown's projection of California as the national paradigm. But Brown dismissed this notion. "I think the East/West schism is a journalistic device to give more definition to stories," he said. "I think you'll find people at Harvard are not different from people at Berkeley. You'll find the suburbs of New

York City are very much like Orange County. Decaying cities, deteriorating infrastructure, that's all a problem obviously. There are some conflicts. In new cities, newer infrastructure, warmer weather, it's easier, and investment is flowing in that direction. I think there's something in the differences, but they're overplayed."

He wanted to get across his program more than anything else. So he eagerly asked himself the next question. "The next question," he posed, "is what do I stand for?" Then he answered: "We're living off our capital. We're borrowing, we're consuming, and we're not building. I'm not saying that all private investment should be turned over to the marketplace. I'm saying that government ought to be doing some of the investing, government ought to be laying down some of the rules. There's a difference between saying seventeen different kinds of toothpaste is the goal or saying the goal is to generate enough capital to have public transit, to have more efficient energy, to have conservation. People with money right now, what do they do? They collect antiques, silver, and paintings. If people don't have faith in the future or they put their money in some risk investment, then you run down your capital stock. When I say investment, I don't just mean private investment. I mean public investment in what I consider the key areas, namely energy-related technology, transportation, rebuilding the cities, and then our environmental investment. America has its back to the wall. I'm sure we're going to plan more. There's no way to reorder priorities without some degree of planning. The difficulty is that we're not used to that. We ought to be a little wary of too much government running of things. I'd like to see some examples of where it works well."

I pushed Brown on this, asking him what he felt about nationalizing the oil companies. "I don't think it's a matter of an absolute," he replied. "Mere public ownership is not going to solve a lot of the tough societal conflicts. It's so easy to say let the public own it and turn it over to whomever the politicians appoint to run it. I have my doubts about that. I'm not saying that can't work. Certainly, with the big oil companies that's the direction a lot of people want to move us in. I would like to think about it."

Clearly, Brown has a long-range view of how the country ought to cope with its problems. Despite his eclecticism, he has given much thought to it. He has a coherent world view. "Obviously I campaign by presenting my ideas," said Brown. "My strategy is to do what I'm doing and find out what's going on. We'll just let the future take care of itself." Nothing he said states his position more clearly: Brown believes that as the future unfolds he will always be there.

After the interview, a state policeman, a member of the governor's personal security detail, drove me to the airport. The trooper asked me where I was from and I told him Boston. Immediately, he began inquiring about the Red Sox. "They're my favorite team," he confided. To him major league baseball in California is somehow an ersatz experience. "I watch the Red Sox on television," he said. "I imagine that when I'm at a ballgame I'm at Fenway Park." To him baseball is real, and baseball is real in Fenway Park.

Gregory Bateson is neither San Francisco nor L.A. He is the Santa Cruz Connection. At the University of California at Santa Cruz, where he teaches, there is a graduate department in the history of consciousness. Ecology is never an issue there, but the fundamental shared assumption of belief. The question at Santa Cruz is which philosophical school you follow. Bateson is one of the deans of consciousness.

Bateson's method isn't as tenacious as that of the Jesuits or the Yale Law School faculty, but it forms a complete, intricate system, based on a genetic metaphor in which society is portrayed as a series of DNA molecules. To Bateson, the linear world of Newton and Locke is "obsolete." Bateson seeks to reconcile mind and matter in his evolutionary theory. He believes that social forces like "power" are a "myth." "There is no objective experience. All experience is subjective," he writes. This experience consists entirely of images, which are created unconsciously. Western thought, in which objectivity is held to exist, is itself spurious. "Our civilization is deeply based on this illusion," he notes. In Bateson's view change comes from mutations that have assimilated new information from a seemingly random gene pool. In order to create what he calls "a new order," randomness, unpredictability, and the utter differentiation of individuals are necessary. "Logic is a poor model of cause and effect," he says.

It makes perfect sense that Jerry Brown applies Bateson's concepts in a political way. Brown grew up in a totally political milieu; it was the natural world to him, and still is. Brown has the modern biologist's sense of the interplay between environment and organism. He's concerned about the texture of that relationship. He believes that the way he thinks is exactly analogous to the way the political system works. Both involve exchanges of energy, circuitry, and an indefinable chemistry.

Brown accepts the continuing adaptability of human character, which Jimmy Carter, who stresses perseverance, fortitude, and will, would never accept. Brown accepts the fact that we present ourselves differently in different environments. We are constantly engaged in a dialogue with nature because we're part of it. It's inevitable therefore that media will affect your message. When he's upset at being accused of being a media candidate, he's rebelling against the notion that he's a mechanical object, even a willing puppet who's hired the puppeteer.

In many ways, Jerry Brown and Jimmy Carter are reverse images of each other. While Carter wants to have faith, Brown wants to know. Carter's presidential campaign in 1976 insisted he was real, not manufactured. The proof he was real was his virtuous consistency as an emotional person. He knew that we wanted "a government as good as its people." We could get it by recognizing in him our own worthiness. Brown insists that he's real as well. But his reality is that of inconsistency, of Bateson's randomness. He doesn't pretend to Christian steadfastness, among other things. Brown considers himself an event. He is always happening, and unlike most of us he is happening in public and in the media. For Jimmy Carter to regard himself as an event would be hubris. It would break his covenant with the congregation for he would be guilty of the sin of pride. And only through public penance could he absolve himself. In Jerry Brown's world there's no hope of total absolution. Brown never apologizes. All his errors are on the model of genetic experiments, and nature never apologizes. Nature just is.

For Brown, protest is information; for Carter protest is denial. Carter believes as a Christian that all people can feel the same, that everyone can love Jesus as their Savior and accept Jimmy as their president. Brown accepts that you can replicate emotion, but that people don't really feel the same emotions. This doesn't upset him. It's part of an ecological universe where you get feedback to help you survive.

Brown thinks of himself as a manipulator of symbols, as he believes we all are. Carter, on the other hand, never wants to appear as a manipulator of symbols because it places him above the congregation. It is the congregation that maintains the power of the symbol. To manipulate a symbol is to violate the trust of the community that sustains it and the fundamental premise that all decide and are equal before Jesus. Carter feels qualms about manipulating; therefore, he has to rationalize why he manipulates. Since he believes that he understands our emotions better than we do, he sees himself as our vehicle for expressing our situation. He's not really manipulating symbols then; he's identifying our feelings for us so that we can awaken to our latest consensus.

The old politics maintained the illusion of consensus, which Carter attempts to maintain through his person. This is anathema to Brown. He doesn't believe in final goals. To do so denigrates the process. Brown wants to be elected as Jerry Brown, not as a symbol or figurehead of a coalition. Reaching a final goal would mean the end of change; it would deny the validity of his experience as a subjective individual.

Jerry Brown believes everyone is different. For Brown, consensus has nothing to do with the moral equivalent of war. Consensus can't provide him with information, and without information he can't survive. For the old pols consensus was an act of political balance, uniting coalitions around vaguely common concerns and forging broad programs; consensus was a pragmatic goal. Brown rejects the need for an illusion of consensus. He believes he has to override consensus, particularly in its New Deal manifestation, to treat the body politic. This is the most realistic alternative — "planetary realism." He knows he's not going to get planetary consensus. Carter doesn't know that because it's part of his faith to believe in a shared universal vision. Brown believes we can be saved, but not by any appeal to our moral sense. With his hands on the left and right throttles he can set up a dialectical rhythm, providing a tempo to regulate change.

Unfortunately, there is a material world where power and social forces are not mere metaphors, but truly objective conditions, like Democratic party leaders. Acknowledging them simply as metaphors without engaging them — although they are a vanishing species — might be politically precarious. Treating an upstate New York Democratic boss as a metaphor means there is no relationship between them, and that means Brown isn't getting information. In the Bateson/Brown system, information is essential in order to evolve and adapt.

In California, party bosses have virtually no leverage and treating them with disrespect bears no consequences. But the antiquated East has not yet progressed as far. Brown prefers to see that East/West schism as a "device," a symbol used by journalists. What does he do if the East turns out to be the reality principle? As that obsolete thinker Freud once pointed out, sometimes a cigar is just a cigar.

By denying the realities of such social facts Brown has corrupted his vision with the enduring idea that California is the forerunner of the nation, a notion so arrogant that Brown and Californians generally feel no arrogance about it whatsoever. In its weak political parties, California does indeed provide a glimpse into the future, but Californians' unshakable belief that they represent the future in all matters, temporal and spiritual, is a conceit hindering them from facing themselves in the present. By constantly thinking about the future, Californians are never quite here; they are literally absent-minded. But that's why they're Californians in the first place: they want to escape, unsettle and remake themselves. They need the future desperately. And since the future has no physical shape it must first exist in the mind. The future is something all Californians share, and this abstraction is one of their few common denominators. Brown believes in the power of the abstract, which is a reasonable and practical political deduction in California. Politics — the working out of collective interests — is ideas in California. Few of these ideas, or the movements that promote them, last longer than a half hour television show in the program guide of history. If they lasted longer the future would be fixed, and that's something Californians don't want. They need to keep moving, to campaign forever.

Yet Jerry Brown is not an opportunist, as often charged. He is an idealist in the pure Hegelian sense: he seeks to become a world-historical figure who expresses an idea striving to be realized. For him the material world reflects developments on a more abstract plane; he is trying to free himself from its limits while advocating a philosophical era of limits. He wants the triumph of his own consciousness. Jerry Brown casts himself as the subject, not the object, of history.

When I left California I took a taxi to the airport, traveling a road almost close enough to the surf to be sprayed by white foam. The route veered suddenly away from the far edge of the continent. The cab driver, a working-class surfer with stringy blond hair, wearing sandals and a San Diego Padres cap, asked where I was going. "Boston," I said.

"Is Boston mellow?" he asked.

"No," I replied.

The cabbie liked Jerry Brown. Brown was mellow. But then the cabbie started asking me about the Red Sox. "With Thurman Munson dead and Carlton Fisk injured, the New York–Boston rivalry isn't what it once was, is it?" We talked baseball for a while and then we fell silent. He flicked on a large transistor radio he kept on his front seat. There was a drum roll and the loud, plaintive voice of the Girl of the Golden West, Linda Ronstadt, speaking for her governor: "When Will I Be Loved?"

CHAPTER TEN

# THE REPUBLICAN CADRE

## DOUG BAILEY AND JOHN DEARDOURFF, DAVID KEENE, EDDIE MAHE, JOHN SEARS

The Republican party is the party of lost opportunities. It is a venerable institution that always appears too entangled in its roots to grow. It is the party that rejected Theodore Roosevelt for William Howard Taft, allowing the Democrats to steal the Progressive mantle. It is a party that in the 1920s was so mesmerized by its own Yankee image as the advance agent of prosperity that it ignored its own restive constituencies — farmers, blacks, craft unionists — who defected to the New Deal coalition. The Eisenhower administration of the 1950s was a maintenance operation, bereft of new ideas. By passing up Nelson Rockefeller for Richard Nixon the GOP lost a major victory in the 1960 election, permitting the civil rights revolution to occur under the Democrats, who solidified their black support. If it had happened under Rockefeller, the black vote might have been split between the two parties forever. In 1968 the Republicans were presented with what was perhaps their greatest opportunity. If Richard Nixon had ended the Vietnam War, which during the campaign he hinted he might do (picking up the surprising support of liberals like the *New York Times's* Tom Wicker), he would have stamped the GOP as the party of peace and the Democrats the party of war, defused the radical movement, and suffused the Republicans with an aura of righteousness. Nixon, of course, preferred war.

Even before Watergate the GOP's base of faithful followers had drastically diminished. It now confronts the 1980s as a more compact party than ever before, more ideological than the Democrats, more homogenous in composition, and, superficially, less divisive because intraparty debates are seemingly a thing of the past. With the figures of Nixon, Rockefeller, and Goldwater more or less removed from the scene, it ought to be entering a new era. Yet the GOP is still the party of memory. When faced with a dilemma, its leaders invariably call up an answer from the past. And its separate factions never let each other forget their errors. Many Republicans would rather be right than win.

The GOP, however, is not as fractious as the Democratic party. The Democrats represent diverse constituencies comprising a polyglot majority party. But as it fragments under the stress of social problems unanswered by New Deal formulas it too shrinks. More voters, their needs unfulfilled, become alienated. They register as independent. Nonalignment becomes the order of the day. This trend has only provided short-term succor to the Republicans. They have appealed to the alienated voters on the basis of single issues or vague themes, not with a new inclusive approach. "Nonalignment has helped Republicans to win elections, but it hasn't helped them to gain adherents to the party," explains the preeminent Republican pollster, Robert Teeter of Market Opinion Research.

Republicans, for the most part, fail to understand that they are presented with an opportunity greater than a chance to win an election. The reason may be that the Republican party has been through a wrenching internal realignment that may render it incapable of taking advantage of the debilitating effects of non-alignment on the Democrats. Republicans are experts in defeat. The most overwhelming recent GOP presidential defeat occurred in 1964 after Barry Goldwater and his minions captured the party. Despite the disaster of that campaign, it forged a critical realignment within the GOP. The party itself was transformed: it lost its traditional support in the Northeast and gained a new base in the Sunbelt. It became more ideologically and aggressively conservative. In many ways the effect of the 1964 election is analogous to the change the 1928 election brought to the Democrats. The losing campaign of Al Smith, the first Catholic candidate for president, won majorities of Democrats in the urban centers for the first time; the campaign was a harbinger of the New Deal coalition. The Goldwater campaign, on the other hand, realigned the party on a new minority basis. The GOP was altered but not broadened.

As the party was changing, the Republicans increasingly relied on the new political consultants who employed sophisticated polling, computerized survey research, and television to win elections. Republicans came to the consultants in a different way from the Democrats. Because the Republicans had far less patronage to dispense to secure followers, they were more willing to try new techniques. They had seen some of these techniques used in the private sector to good effect. "The Republican party over the last ten years," says Robert Teeter, "has been a little ahead of the Democratic party technically and mechanically — phone banks, polling, advertising. Republicans are more familiar with marketing from business. When you're a minority, you have to learn to work the edge better." Republicans always believe that politics and public policy should be managed in a more businesslike manner, so it was natural for them to transfer the new techniques of business to politics. They had no qualms.

Consultants have not replaced the Republican party, although to some degree consultants have supplanted the old party bosses as power brokers. Each major GOP presidential campaign has a consultant running it; they have chosen each other because of shared perspectives. The campaigns are like separate parties in themselves, indicating the atrophy of the central party organization and the effect of consultants.

"We are one of the centers of moderate Republicanism," says John Deardourff, partner with Doug Bailey in Campaign Coordinators, Inc., the leading GOP consulting firm, which is handling the 1980 presidential campaign of Senator Howard Baker. "We serve as a clearinghouse and broker among moderate Republican interests. The successful political consultant has become an independent operation. He has a life of his own. He is a separate power center. It's a replacement party for the decline of the parties. The day of the political party boss is over."

Bailey and Deardourff have been responsible for the election of eleven of the eighteen Republican governors; numerous senators, including Percy, Danforth, Chafee, Mathias, and Schweiker; and the 1976 campaign of President Gerald Ford. "They have a talent for translating a campaign strategy onto film," says Robert Teeter, who has worked with the team on many campaigns. "They have a good sense of nuance and tone. But their greatest strength is a broad background in politics."

During the 1964 presidential campaign of Nelson Rockefeller, Bailey and Deardourff had parallel responsibilities. Bailey, who had been Henry Kissinger's assistant at Harvard, was deputy director of foreign policy research in the vast Rockefeller operation; Deardourff was deputy director of domestic policy research. He understood, in the early 1960s, that the Rockefeller effort was somehow a behemoth that was about to become extinct. "Bailey and I talked about how television and sophisticated use of computer technology and the increasing sophistication of survey research were changing the nature of political campaigns. They made it much more difficult for amateurs. And party leaders were less equipped to cope with that technology. The precomputer politician was beginning to be a burden."

Lacking venture capital, Bailey and Deardourff were not able to realize their vision of how politics ought to be managed. Deardourff left the Rockefeller organization after the candidate failed to win the Republican nomination and joined the John Lindsay campaign for mayor of New York City. This effort taught Deardourff the subtleties of big-city politics and the uses of television in that setting, experiences denied to most Republicans. "That campaign," he says, "put heavy stress on local issues and then publicized them. No issue was too small. It was the first major campaign to focus television news coverage on the media event. That became critical because there was a big newspaper strike."

In the meantime, Bailey established himself in Washington as a policy consultant to an emerging group of moderate Republican congressmen known as the Wednesday Group. At the end of 1966, Bailey and Deardourff incorporated themselves in Boston as Campaign Coordinators, Inc. They were hired to run the 1968 presidential campaign of Rockefeller. "If anything, the Rockefeller campaign suffered from an overabundance of resources," says Deardourff. "The problem was organizing them." To Deardourff, Rockefeller was an inspirational figure. "I thought he was the most exciting politician in the country from 1962 to 1968. He loved to wrestle with conflicting ideas. He really was fascinated by ideas. But you were always part of a larger operation. It cemented my notion that I wanted to make a career of politics."

When Rockefeller lost the nomination again, Bailey and Deardourff moved their operation to Washington. "In that ten years it has been a rapid expansion of business," says Deardourff. "We have changed our focus since 1969 somewhat in that we've been much more involved in the advertising side of campaigns. We expanded that side of the business as a political decision. It became clear that if you didn't control the advertising of a major campaign you didn't really exercise control period. If someone else was responsible for what the audience was hearing, they exerted influence and you didn't. That's dictated by television. Campaign advisers like us suggested that politicians needed to move in that direction. That's where we moved them. I don't know of a campaign anywhere where at least half the budget is not spent on broadcast media. I can think of one campaign we did in which 90 percent of the budget went to media: James Rhodes for governor of Ohio. He had four people on his campaign staff."

Political advertising differs from commercial advertising in many ways. "In a political campaign," says Deardourff, "all of the sales take place on the same day. The timing is important. You deliver on election day or it doesn't make a difference. In political advertising you are not interested in small market shares. The political advertiser can't be satisfied until he has 51 percent of the market. The political salesman — I l.ate that term — has got to find ways to communicate with all kinds of people. The commercial advertiser knows how much money he will spend. But in a political campaign you almost never know. You improvise."

There's another crucial difference: political advertising is employed in the service of larger political goals. Bailey and Deardourff understand that idea and they use advertising as an implement in their own permanent campaign. "We see our work as a way of having major impact on those kinds of Republicans we want to see in public life," says Deardourff. "It is true that the spectrum has moved to the right; as the Republican party has shrunk, the residue tends to be more conservative. But it's a mistake to believe that moderate Republicanism is on its way out. We go out and look for those candidates. We can offer our services to the people we want and the rest we can forget."

With the death of Rockefeller, Bailey and Deardourff, more than anyone else, represent the moderate wing of the GOP. Liberal Republicanism, in a sense, has been reduced to the campaigns of a political consulting firm. And that is why Howard Baker hired Bailey and Deardourff to run his presidential campaign. Who else could the most moderate major candidate turn to? "Baker needed them," says John Topping, president of the Ripon Society, a liberal Republican organization. "One of the roles consultants play is validating the seriousness of a candidacy which, in turn, enables a candidate to raise money for a media campaign. And Bailey and Deardourff are probably more important than the Republican Governor's Conference.

Howard Baker, all things considered, was the logical Bailey and Deardourff man in the 1980 race. More than any other candidate he hails from the historic center of the Republican party. He is not a product of Richard Nixon's "Southern strategy," although he comes from Tennessee. The section of Tennessee he comes from has been Republican since the birth of the party, under very trying circumstances. It was unionist during the Civil War and has returned heavy Republican pluralities all along. Baker's Republicanism is not the blush of Sunbelt conservatism; it has deep roots. In internal Republican battles, Baker, as a border-state Republican, is set apart from the old New York/Ohio and newer East/South rivalries. Baker's position is independent of faction and therefore acceptable to all sides. Yet he has inherited the liberal Eastern position within the party because there is no one else to claim it.

The death of Rockefeller affected the Baker campaign perhaps more than it did any other. Rockefeller's political and financial prowess allowed him to control the Eastern wing of the party, which consisted mainly of upper-crust and middle-class Yankees. As a party leader, Rockefeller never allowed anyone else to share his factional power. With Rockefeller's death, Baker attached himself to the Rockefeller replacement, Bailey and Deardourff, in an attempt to gain the moderate wing of the party.

A political consultant, unlike the old party boss, cannot deliver votes. But he can grant access to his other clients. And this is one of the greatest resources that Bailey and Deardourff provide Baker. They have the best client list in the business. "It is quite possible to grant access," says Deardourff. "In addition to the professional service we perform, we do two other things for Baker. We provide an alternative access to major party figures with whom we've worked. Because we have an independent reputation we provide him with some visibility; we have a reputation for success. That signals something. I don't have any qualms about calling up ten governors and telling them why Baker is the best choice. The relationship that exists between us and our clients is a close, trusting relationship. We have been through some tense times together. Their futures rode on our decisions. There's a bond there. If I came to them to tell them what I think about Howard Baker, that has some influence. That's an influence I enjoy having."

In a party that is becoming more narrowly ideological, discussions about liberal Republicanism may be entirely academic. "There's no one taking over the liberal wing of the party," suggests Robert Teeter. "If you define moderate as being in the middle, there are not great ideological differences between the candidates. They are moderate in the sense of being in the middle. If you take the range from John Anderson to Ronald Reagan neither of the ends are as far out as ten years ago. In 1980 you don't have two candidates who are at polar extremes like Rockefeller and Goldwater. There isn't a great deal of difference between them."

If the moderate wing is disappearing, leaving only a middle, then George Bush is working effectively to hold that ground. His raiment is that of moderation, but his talk is fashionably conservative. Bush is the crossover candidate, embodying more than any other the shift within the party from East to West, from dominance by moderates to dominance by outspoken conservatives. Bush is attempting to recreate the way Eisenhower ran the country in the 1950s: as a New York–Texas alliance; this time, however, Texas will take the lead.

The son of Senator Prescott Bush of Connecticut, graduate of

Andover and Yale, Congressman, CIA director, ambassador, George Bush is a folk hero to the old business elite because he fulfilled the ideal of free enterprise, planting himself in Texas and making it on his own as a successful oil entrepreneur. It's hard to beat the image of a Texas freebooter who was also chairman of a $250 million alumni fundraising drive for Yale. In Texas, Bush ran unsuccessfully for senator as a right-winger. Through his posture, he ceded minority and liberal votes to his conservative opponent. "If anyone is to the right of me they'll fall off the end of the world," he told some Republicans during that campaign.

Within the party Bush has been reliant on Eastern establishment support, which comes through his family and the old school tie, his enthusiastic conservatism, and his organizational connections. He was, after all, chairman of the Republican National Committee (RNC) during the sordid Watergate affair. "A lot of party people feel Bush carried our water when it was most painful," says John Topping of the Ripon Society. Many of the RNC operatives who worked under him have become Bush campaigners. The old RNC provided the Bush operation with a natural network of experienced, skilled workers.

It was hardly surprising then that Bush employed an ideological political consultant as his campaign manager. "I'm a conservative. I'm ideological on a lot of the issues," says David Keene. In his own right, Keene is a new breed Republican. He emanated from a new political network within the party. In 1969, Keene was national chairman of the Young Americans for Freedom (YAF), founded by conservative columnist and Yalie, William F. Buckley, Jr. "When I went to work for Bush I checked to what extent he was acceptable to the people I worked with," says Keene. "He's acceptable."

Upon graduating from YAF Keene became Vice President Spiro Agnew's political aide. For three turbulent years, from 1970 to 1973, when Agnew ignominiously left office pleading no contest, Keene was his political point man. "Agnew has a sense of history," says Keene. "He was able to take himself out of things and look at them. The system is such that by the time you get to the top you lose sight of what you wanted to do."

Keene was heavily involved in the 1970 Republican midterm campaign, coordinated by Richard Nixon as a law-and-order campaign to stigmatize the Democrats as being soft on crime and radicalism. "It was what the White House viewed as a conservative campaign," Keene says contemptuously. "You had people who came out of nonideological politics who had decided they needed a conservative campaign. But it was a caricature of a conservative campaign. The law-and-order issue was used without substance. And calling old-line Democrats radical-liberals was foolish."

In 1972, Keene was Agnew's liaison to the Committee to Reelect the President, CREEP. Despite CREEP's perversity it was the model for the modern presidential campaign, separate from the party, emulated in most respects by all succeeding campaigns. "It was the first centralized campaign," notes Keene. "Everything was computerized. If you're running a national campaign you have to look at your resources. The places where party can deliver are limited. In large measure, the party is a paper structure not up to the responsibility of the campaign. As the result of the party's atomization the candidate has to build his own organization. CREEP did it to a greater extent than in the past."

After Agnew's demise, Keene went to work as executive assistant to Senator James Buckley of New York, brother of the YAF founding father. When Buckley lost his seat, Keene joined the Reagan campaign as a coordinator in the South, a key region for the insurgent candidate. When Reagan lost, Keene remained part of his apparatus, preparing for the 1980 run, although Keene contemplated setting up his own consulting firm. But before he had time to establish himself as an entrepreneur of politics, he quit the Reagan camp to manage the Bush effort. "There were problems with the Reagan campaign," he says. "It's too old. It's been around too long. It has too many chiefs and not enough soldiers. It's a hydra-headed monster." He did not view his jump as an abandonment of principle. Bush, to him, was just as conservative as Reagan.

"I think moderates are a lot different than they once were," he says. "By 1976, we had Ford and Carter taking positions more like Goldwater than McGovern. The old disputes within the GOP are old. They took place in 1960 or 1964. The power has shifted away from the Northeast. Who is making decisions now? The old Republican party was basically the business establishment. You could sit down in a Wall Street boardroom in the 1940s and make your guy the nominee. Now it has shifted over to the party activists. The older guys are gone. The new leadership came up under a new system. The new people are basically conservative. There is more homogeneity of philosophy; you don't have emotional divisions. It's a different world."

Within this world, George Bush is a paradigmatic character, positioned in the middle but not a moderate, which succinctly summarizes his campaign strategy as well. "The function of all the campaigns," says Keene, "is to be the alternative to Reagan without driving away the other campaigns. We take pains that our candidate is not attacking the other candidates. Reagan not only has to say he's right, but that he can handle the job. That can wipe him out on a nonideological basis."

Although the Bush campaign professed no enmity toward the other campaigns, Bush himself must have hard feelings toward fellow Texan John Connally, who as a Democrat contributed to his defeat in his senatorial bid. In that race, the Connally faction of the Texas Democratic party placed a liquor-by-the-drink initiative on the ballot in order to get the prohibitionist-minded east Texas Baptists to the polls, where they inevitably vote Democratic. The increased turnout helped beat Bush.

If this were H. L. Hunt's utopia where every dollar had a vote, John Connally would be president. In the 1980 campaign, he is the

Fortune 500 candidate, which is both his greatest strength and his greatest weakness. Corporate executives seem dazed by Connally's brash articulation of a will to power they share. He tells them that the country is theirs if they are only willing to act. But these businessmen are not for Republicans or Democrats so much as they are for business. "I was a Republican in Republican districts and a Democrat in Democratic districts. But everywhere I was for Erie," said Jay Gould, a notable railroad robber baron. While corporate money fills Connally's coffers, many of the Republican rank-and-file do not truly accept him as one of their own. Some regard him suspiciously as the big government candidate, differing from the Democrats only in that he would use the state apparatus to ensure welfare for the wealthy not the indigent. Connally, to these diehard Republicans, is Lyndon Johnson without a heart. Connally's strength with the financial elite masks his party weakness. There is, after all, no real Connally faction within the GOP. He is a newcomer. He has never run for anything as a Republican. Because of that he has no means of retribution within the party against those who undercut him. It is dangerous to project a belligerent attitude when you are not feared. Connally steams into the close quarters of combat like a magnificently outfitted battleship with a wooden hull.

If the perfect campaign manager were to be invented for Connally it would be a character with strong organizational ties within the party, and a Westerner who could empathize with Connally's sensibility and who understands the imperatives of corporate political action. In short, you would have Eddie Mahe. "A lot of people felt it was a logical combination," says Mahe. "He understands what power is and how to use it. You sense it from listening to him." Connally sees politics without any illusions as a struggle for power. He told one small private group of Republicans, "I'll tell you what motivates people in politics — power." Then he paused and added, "And one more thing, pride." Eddie Mahe says, "There's an inherent understanding that goes beyond the business community — that it takes a strong man to run the country. There's nothing wrong with the system if we get the leadership we need. The trouble is at the top." This statement, apparently a routine boost for his candidate, reveals a great deal about Eddie Mahe's own motivations in politics. When he talks about a change in leadership he means overthrowing the East. He is for a Western coup through the electoral process.

In 1962, Eddie Mahe was a real estate agent in Colorado. He volunteered to work for the local Republican party. The next year he moved to New Mexico, where he resumed his real estate practice and his political interest. "My thinking hasn't changed since then," he says. "I just think the government screwed up and something needs to be done to fix it. The question is whether the individual is going to control the government or the government is going to control the individual." His first political job came in 1965 when he was named executive director of the Albuquerque county Republican organization, as part of the Goldwater upsurge. He worked himself up through the organization, without any spectacular breaks. When George Bush was RNC chairman, Mahe became political director. Through his post he built up and was integrated into a national political network, one he hopes to draw on for Connally. But after four years at the RNC he decided to leave and become an independent political consultant. "It seemed to be the only logical alternative if one was going to stay in the business," he says. "I didn't want to stay in the committee structure anymore. You lose your creativity. I knew I could have more freedom."

He took political and corporate clients. He had established a reputation as a tough-minded mechanic in the trade, and they came to him for help. In 1978 he was politically ambidextrous, working for the New Rightist Gordon Humphrey from New Hampshire for the Senate, and for liberal Richard Thornburgh for Pennsylvania governor. Both candidates won. Although he plays key roles in campaigns, he does a substantial amount of work with corporate political action committees (PACs). Because of new campaign financing laws — limiting contributions from big givers — the special interest PACs have multiplied at a geometric rate. There may be more than 1500 groups pooling resources within a corporation or industry to funnel money into campaigns. Mahe is the organizer behind the American Medical Association PAC, the Realtors Association PAC, and the government affairs division of Standard Oil of Indiana. "Most of the work has to do with training seminars," he says. He travels around the country teaching management personnel the techniques of precinct organization and fundraising to further their immediate goals within politics.

This proliferating new force is viewed by Mahe as weak, not the vital corporate expression of self-interest he would like to see. His complaints about the limits of PACs barely conceal a right-wing populist grievance against labor unions and a lower-middle-class resentment against the old rich. "Organized labor has had a lock on this thing for twenty years. Hell, we're just catching up," he says. "The corporate money has been divided in such a way that they've added more dollars to the system, but they've not greatly impacted the system. They split their money between Democrats and Republicans. They tend to perpetuate the system rather than change it. The only force they have is financial."

He doesn't believe that when money talks, everybody listens. The reason is that money fails to understand. Money is too indiscriminate. Money spreads its affections around too loosely. Money lacks common sense. "In the West," Eddie Mahe says, "you're dealing with a different mindset because of land and space. We would think nothing of driving 100 miles to see a movie. Two hundred miles doesn't represent that big a problem. You just have a people and a lifestyle that is more oriented toward the individual because there are not so many people pressured around you all the time, constantly jostling for your space." The urban culture of subways and newsstands, of Wall Street and Harlem, of skyscrapers and tenements — they are the nub of the problem, Mahe thinks. "In the West," he says, "you've got your space and you can live a little bit. It creates an attitude. The government intervenes in that more and more. Government is basically run by Easterners, not by Westerners. The government is in the East. Many people in government have no understanding of the West at all. They pass a rule or regulation or make an utterance that makes a whole lot of sense in New York City but doesn't make a whole lot of sense in Idaho. Even in California you don't see the crowds you see in downtown New York. John Connally feels very strongly about the role of the individual. This country was built by people, not by government."

Since the Goldwater campaign, many conservatives have harbored a desire to set the eastern seaboard adrift in the Atlantic. Goldwater even said as much once. But Ronald Reagan's campaign has none of that rhetoric. His campaign manager, John Sears, wants to win the Wild West, the New South, *and* the Northeast. Reagan's announcement of his candidacy from New York City was itself a statement that the campaign would not be that of a sunbelt favorite son. It would contend nationally. And in order to do that it would not be a rigid, ideological campaign, but one that attempted to occupy the center of the GOP. Reagan was malleable to the shape Sears was giving to his race.

John Sears is by all accounts the best political operative the Republicans have. He has a crisp mind, appealing wit, decisive nature, and genial relations with the press corps, a rare feat among Republicans who have been quick to attack the media for supposed liberal bias. "Sears is the class of the Reagan organization," says John Topping. "John Sears is the best strategist in the party. The best thing about working for Reagan was working for Sears," admits David Keene. "John Sears is smart. That's his illuminating quality. He understands how things interrelate. I don't know where Reagan would have been without him," says Robert Teeter.

In the late 1960s, Sears was a bright young lawyer working for a

Manhattan law firm, Mudge, Rose, Guthrie, Alexander and Mitchell, when a new partner named Richard Nixon joined the firm. It was from this office that Nixon resurrected himself, and John Sears assisted in the reconstruction. He was a key political operative, unusually perceptive in spotting quick-moving trends. He acted as Nixon's specialist on Eastern parties, attempting to counter the strategy of Nixon's nemesis, Nelson Rockefeller. Rockefeller sought to stop Nixon on the first ballot in 1968 by lining up delegations behind favorite son candidacies. Just before the balloting began, the Rockefeller operatives unwisely let it be known that they had halted Nixon fifteen votes shy of nomination. Sears maneuvered with great speed. With the aid of New Jersey's Nelson Gross, the Bergen County party boss, Sears took five votes from favorite son Clifford Case's column and moved them to Nixon's. He broke open the convention and a stampede to Nixon resulted. This gave Sears a reputation as an expert in locating weak points in the Eastern faction of the party.

In the White House, Sears served as Nixon's liaison to the Republican National Committee. Sears belonged to a faction of experienced party politicos. In the internecine warfare of Nixon's White House, however, Sears lost to the likes of Haldeman, Ehrlichman, and Mitchell. He left quietly. "You never felt in great awe of Nixon," he reflects. "His strengths were obvious; his weaknesses were, too. His strengths were determination and work; he worked himself to death. He had difficulty relaxing because he felt it was a waste of time. Most of us have a capability of looking at ourselves to some degree. Whether we admit it to anyone else, we know what we do well and what our insecurities are. This creates a middle ground allowing you to go out and grapple with the rest of the world. Nixon had never done that. There was no middle ground. A lot of people were around him for years and they never really knew him. They felt that if he fulfilled his quest it might give him some self-assurance. But it didn't work that way."

Out of the White House, in private law practice, Sears handled a variety of clients, including Sony, the electronics company. Soon after the Senate Watergate hearings revealed Nixon's taping system in the Oval Office, Sony executives expressed their distress to their attorney. The system in question was a Sony and Nixon had denigrated it as a cheap one that couldn't pick up sound well. "They wanted to go right out there and deny that there was something wrong with their products," says Sears. "I convinced them that it wouldn't be a good idea to drop into the middle of Watergate. Obviously, their products were good products as everyone would see once they got their hands on those tapes. Sony didn't have cause to take any undue umbrage."

In 1974, after a long fishing trip in the wilds of the Adirondacks, Sears returned to civilization, bought a copy of the *New York Times*, and saw his picture on the front page. He read a story about how he was among seventeen White House aides wiretapped between May 1969 and February 1971 by Nixon's Plumbers. "You had to suspect," he says, "that that was not beyond the realm of possibility because of the nature of the system."

After a sabbatical at the Kennedy Institute of Politics and resumption of his law practice, he was contacted by the Reagan organization. "I got to know him," says Sears. "I discovered him to be a different person than I imagined. I don't know how I quite imagined him. He seemed very facile, a fellow who was a good person, manageable in the sense of being able to communicate ideas and accept advice, which are important things for someone like me, all good qualities. So we hit 1975 and I decided to go ahead with the Reagan campaign."

Reagan ran a strong race against an incumbent president, but his campaign effectively had reached its limit before the convention. John Sears kept the candidacy alive through a startling ploy. He had Reagan name his vice-presidential running mate *before* the convention, a gesture that broke the traditions of political etiquette. The Reagan choice was Senator Richard Schweiker of Pennsylvania, a liberal. It was a gamble on Sears's part to capture an Eastern delegation, breaking up the bloc against Reagan. "What we wanted to happen happened: we held the thing open until we could get to the convention," says Sears. "There was a good chance we would have been counted out of the race before that." Sears's move created the appearance of uncertainty because it was so dramatic and unorthodox, but changed no votes. Schweiker could not deliver and Reagan went down in a prompt defeat.

In the intervening four years, the Republicans have moved farther to the right and John Sears has moved Ronald Reagan a bit to the center. "The vast majority of what Reagan has had to say over his public life is far more popular today than when he first said it," says Sears. "He has not changed his position. What society wants out of the presidency is what is nakedly called leadership. But it is more than that. The voter feels he is not going to figure this all out anymore. He wants to find someone who can run this place, even if he disagrees with some of the things he says. But if he believes the candidate can run it better than anyone else, he'll vote for him."

The disarray of the Democratic party presented the Republicans once again with a historic opportunity. John Sears was willing to temper the conservative tone with pragmatism so that he could seize the chance. "I believe very strongly that you would be hard put to prove that this country has ever been a very philosophical entity," he says. "This country was born in a spirit of principled pragmatism. What is true is that those who have stayed on the activist side of the issues have done pretty well in politics. The activists have always carried the country. Over the years the Democratic party has had strong positioning on the activist side of the issues. Right now, the Democrats, in the main, are saying the future will be terrible: we will be getting a lot less; we've got to stretch it; you ought to trust us; you know us to be fair people.

Now, that is a very bitter pill. This position is presented partly because of the internal strains within the Democratic party. As Democrats go around to all these little constituencies, what they have to do these days is say that they've got their list of eighty-five demands and that they're with every one of them. So, for the first time in a long time, there's an opportunity for the Republicans to be on the activist side of the issues. The Democratic party used to be a very powerful institution because it had great disparity. But it worked because it had great discipline. What you have now is a party without discipline. Since the Republicans are a smaller, less representative group, we don't have those problems. If anything, if the party can conduct itself better than in the past, and that's not a sure thing, it has a good future."

## CHAPTER ELEVEN

# LIBERALS
# AT THE CROSSROADS

## JOHN MARTTILA    DAN PAYNE
## TOM KILEY    DAVID THORNE

John Marttila had a bad year in 1978. He and his partners in the political consulting firm of Marttila, Payne, Kiley and Thorne (MPKT) managed some of the most widely publicized liberal losers of the season. Founded as an instrument to reform American politics, the company disbanded.

MPKT was no ordinary political consulting enterprise. If the average consultant was viewed as a gunslinger, equipped with computer, mailing lists, and polls instead of a sidearm, then MPKT was *The Magnificent Seven* of consultants — gunslingers with a sense of justice. With many liberal Democrats preferring images to issues, MPKT faced a quandary. *They* hadn't changed, but the object of their reforming impulse had. The authors of the campaigns of Robert Drinan, Morris Udall, Coleman Young, and numerous U.S. senators, congressmen, and mayors, they always knew there was much more to consulting than projecting an image. They were commanders in the cause of reforming the Democratic party and electing liberals, although they were often better than the politicians they represented: smarter, shrewder, and more progressive.

"The firm was always having an identity crisis," remarks Ralph Whitehead, an unofficial member of the MPKT gang. He served as press secretary to Boston mayor Kevin White in the 1975 campaign and taught at the University of Massachusetts at Amherst. "They saw political consulting as an avenue to promote their political principles. They took risks. MPKT wasn't only a firm with a professional service. It was an idea. It urged a state of mind. At a distance they looked like characters in a medieval morality play. But when it got dark and the lights went on in the city they were romantics."

The partners discussed the break-up of their firm when it occurred in early 1979. Tom Kiley said: "We worked for the Democratic good guys. That gets cloudier as time goes by. The Democratic party embraces everything. It goes way beyond my criteria for progressive politics. These new Democrats in Congress are jokes. The way to win is to stand as a Democrat and run as a Republican. Everything is negative, hiding from the major issues. Nobody is talking about the redistribution of wealth. In the early 1970s, when I became involved, the meaning of the causes was more evident. Liberalism needs a new definition. Either Ted Kennedy or someone else is going to have to reshape the agenda. But it isn't happening in the campaigns I'm involved in. They're all hiding for political reasons.

"It's instructive to make a list of progressive Democrats. A whole list of egomaniacs. They haven't said or done anything. It's really depressing. There is no longer a meaningful two-party system. There's a New Right, all the action's there. What's the difference between candidates? It's not the same as five years ago. There is no meaning today. It's all personality. We're like people who speak a foreign language when we ask candidates why they're running. Candidates as a class exist in a void today. They won't define themselves out of it. They're in a big black hole. I guess we need a good war or some moral purpose to define them. I don't look forward to doing this business with any enthusiasm unless I can find something to give it meaning again. I've been in a position to do mainly what I've wanted for the social welfare. And I liked it. But I've lost the spirit."

Dan Payne said: "I'm frustrated. The public is so cynical and the press is feeding it. And the politicians give them back what they want. There's pack politics. The pols have boxed themselves in. And the public tells them they're incompetent and that they shouldn't do anything. It's spiraling downward."

David Thorne said: "The soul isn't there. It's a great problem. We all approach this thing from an ideological commitment. We'd like to use the tools we have to change priorities in the country. We thought we could do it through the system. The early 1970s seem remote today. All of us are trying to understand. Politics may not be the way to do it anymore. I'd be disappointed if I were running campaigns four years from now. Issues aren't clear-cut anymore. It's been a disillusioning experience. There's all kinds of money to be made in political consulting. But we haven't been a business. We've fettered ourselves with principles. We haven't built a monolith because it doesn't work unless you throw principles aside. It's not like making Coke bottles."

John Marttila said: "One of our great strengths is that we don't like to lose."

But when the losses came, they were devastating. The race for the Democratic nomination to the U.S. Senate by Don Fraser of Minnesota was among the most crucial that Marttila and his associates undertook in 1978. When Fraser lost to a right-wing millionaire, Bob Short, it was a stunning blow to the state's Democratic Farmer-Labor party, a bitter aftermath to happier days of Hubert Humphrey. The defeat was reviewed in the press as evidence of the liberal rollback. Conservatives were supposedly reinvigorated, and liberals traumatized by the mere call to battle. Fraser's defeat was offered as an instructive case study. Yet Marttila dissented. He believed that Fraser lost because 100,000 Republicans crossed over into the Democratic primary to vote for Short and because Fraser misspent his media money. Marttila also blamed himself. "I really might have lost the Fraser effort," he said. When the Fraser campaign disagreed with Marttila on how media money ought to be allocated he didn't argue because of very favorable polls, which didn't assess potential crossovers. "Do you have to be a raging dictator with other people?" Marttila wondered. "It's not right for us to run his campaign. I don't buy that approach. But I kick myself once a day for that campaign. I was just shocked when Don lost. That moment was as painful as I've ever been through in the business. Then, after going through a crushing week, I was confronted with a moral obligation to work for Frank Hatch. I was tempted to say, leave me alone, let's end the year right now."

When liberal incumbent governor Michael Dukakis was unexpectedly beaten in the Massachusetts primary by aggressively conservative challenger Edward King, Frank Hatch, a moderate Republican, appeared as a viable alternative. Taking on the Hatch campaign was partly an attempt at redemption for MPKT. "The issues were so compelling," said Marttila. "To work for a Republican was a tough decision. Part of our success is the knowledge that people have that we're Democrats. We're inside Democratic politics in an untraditional way. We're very active. People were pissed off about us working for Hatch."

Hatch was a patrician gentleman who was reluctant to adopt the advice of his consultants to press the attack on Ed King. There were technical problems as well. The polls the Hatch campaign relied on showed him 10 points higher than any other polls; the error skewed his campaign strategy. The firm's decision to supply its expertise to a moderate Republican who called himself a "fiscal conservative" was a strained effort to maintain the continuity of liberalism in Massachusetts. Many liberals felt the same way about the election, but none took as long a leap as MPKT, which was trying desperately to reanimate the early seventies paradigm of liberal success. When Hatch was defeated, MPKT dissolved itself.

The first campaign of MPKT was a seminal political event for Massachusetts liberalism. Their candidate was a Jesuit priest, Robert Drinan, running as a progressive against a long-entrenched traditional machine politician, supported by every hack in the state. Drinan's victory was a dramatic upset. It was not only one of the harbingers of the state's lonely 1972 presidential vote for George McGovern, but the crucible for the quintessential liberal political consulting firm. When the election ended, Marttila, Payne, Kiley, and Thorne decided to keep campaigning.

"If you were trapped in a Nazi prison camp you'd want John Marttila as your cellmate," says Whitehead. "He'd crawl through barbed wire and smash through walls to get out. He's will personified. He's a Big Ten Maoist, all volition." Jack Flannery, political columnist for the *Boston Herald American* and former Frank Hatch speechwriter, says, "Marttila's a very authoritative guy. He could walk in and say it's Saturday and you wouldn't disagree. Of course, he might be wrong."

John Marttila is a long-distance runner. During the final weeks of the Hatch campaign, when he was working twenty-hour days, he and Tom Kiley impulsively hopped a shuttle to New York City to run in the marathon. Marttila ran only eight miles. It was too hot. He's a cold-weather runner. He has run the Boston Marathon in three and a half hours. "It's not hard if you train right," he says.

Marttila's father was an automobile worker at the mammoth

Ford River Rouge plant in Detroit. "He was part of the initial UAW organizing effort," Marttila says. "There weren't any discussions of politics in my house, but a lot of talk on the virtues of taking care of working people. I grew up with all the biases of a progressive UAW household. That shaped my political views so much that last year I asked him again what happened." He needed to be refreshed with stories of union men picketing in pitch darkness, battling cops and company goons. "My values," he says, "in certain ways are uniquely Midwestern and not of Massachusetts. The Midwest is more open, and race is a much more powerful part of society. Here it's much more intricate. Institutions and politics are overdeveloped." Marttila attended a mostly black public high school in Detroit. After college he went to Wayne State law school where he met Dan Payne. Both of them were discontented and dropped out. Payne went to work for the Urban League. Marttila was hired by the Republican party. "I don't know fully how it happened," he recalls. "I was unhappy with law school and they gave me a free ride for two years to organize. I was the house liberal." At the time, the GOP in Michigan was controlled by moderates trying to recruit blacks, a major constituency there. Marttila was paid to attract blacks through community action projects. "It was a strange move. I had no business being in the Republican party. I wanted to get away."

Two days before Marttila moved to Boston, Dan Payne accepted a job with the Michigan Civil Rights Commission. Marttila asked him if he wanted to come along; Payne packed his bags. "I came out here not sure I was going to stay," Payne says. "I knew next to nothing about political campaigns." He became Drinan's press secretary. During the campaign Payne and Marttila (whom Drinan calls "the dropout twins") met Tom Kiley, a Jesuit seminarian who had left Detroit to work for Drinan; the candidate had a commitment to social justice that Kiley shared. "I had four years of Jesuit training," Kiley says. "It's a good education. The Jesuits are very structured, very rational. As a Jesuit I came to work for

Drinan. I thought Jesuits like myself ought to be involved in moral questions."

With the election over and Drinan in office, Marttila, Payne, and Kiley journeyed to Philadelphia to work for Bill Green — heir to that city's mainstream Democratic tradition — who was running for mayor against the law-and-order police chief Frank Rizzo. Green lost. In the Green campaign the division of labor began; Payne handled communications and Marttila took care of strategy. The lines weren't rigid; they never were. All the MPKT operatives were good generalists, although Payne excelled at advertising, Kiley at polling, and Thorne at fundraising. While Marttila was in Philadelphia he was visited by an aide of Kevin White. White had heard stories about Marttila's effectiveness. The mayor wanted him to run his 1971 reelection campaign. Marttila met White and agreed. A romance developed, as it had with many progressives who worked for Kevin White and who eventually left disillusioned. "Kevin's record was as liberal as any mayor in the United States," Marttila says. "His first years were wonderful." White's 1971 victory over Louise Day Hicks was a resounding triumph for urban liberalism, a force that Marttila regarded as so vital that he thought it ought to dominate the 1972 Democratic presidential primaries.

The candidate he initially picked to carry the presidential torch was New York mayor John Lindsay. This affair was a brief infatuation, terminated as soon as the initial blush faded. "We were trying to create an urban candidacy," says Tom Kiley. "We blew it. We didn't know what we got ourselves into. Lindsay was just a media hype. He was exposed for what he was."

In 1972, Drinan ran again and won. In another Massachusetts congressional district John Kerry, a leader of Vietnam Veterans Against the War (VVAW), was defeated, in part, by a dirty tricks campaign coordinated by the Nixon White House. Kerry's campaign manager was his brother-in-law, David Thorne, who had become close to Marttila and eventually joined the firm as a partner. Thorne first met Marttila at a caucus in Concord in 1970, where Kerry challenged Drinan for the Democratic nomination for Congress.

Thorne's background is the opposite of Marttila's. He's blue blood instead of blue collar in origin. Thorne's father was an executive with the Bankers Trust, a high-ranking diplomat, and publisher of the Rome *Daily American*, a newspaper covertly funded for years by the CIA. Thorne attended Yale where he belonged to its most exclusive club, Skull and Bones. "I came from a conservative background," he says modestly. After Yale, though, he spent two wrenching years with the navy in Vietnam and his attitudes were transformed; he helped organize the Vietnam Veterans Against the War. Then he went to the Columbia School of Journalism, wrote some pieces for the *Village Voice*, and coedited a book, entitled *The New Soldier*, on the dramatic VVAW march on Washington in 1971 where disgusted veterans threw their medals on the Capitol steps. By the time he met Marttila he was ready to focus his anger and energy on the political process.

Even though the war raged on in the early 1970s, it seemed to have less urgency for the electorate. Nixon's illusory Vietnamization and trips to Moscow and Peking confused public perception. When Watergate occupied center stage, the public could play only a reactive role. There was no plebiscite scheduled on Richard Nixon.

But Nixon created a test situation when he named Gerald Ford as his vice president. In order to take the post, Ford had to vacate his congressional seat, which had to be filled by special election. The contest became a forum on the Nixon presidency, and MPKT ran the campaign of the Democratic candidate, Richard Vander-Veen. The firm recruited one of its friends, Tommy Vallely, to join the fray. Vallely, son of a local judge, a Marine Vietnam veteran who had turned against the war, started his political career as Robert Drinan's driver and worked his way up. One day he encountered Tom Kiley in an ice skate shop. "He asked me if I wanted to go to Michigan for the VanderVeen campaign. 'Sure,' I said, 'I want one more whack at Nixon.' " Marttila and friends applied every device they had mastered in that race. They knew from the beginning that the stakes were higher than just an election. "We knew we were going to shake the presidency," says Vallely. "And we did." VanderVeen dominated the media without spending any money to get the time — a technique that was a novelty for Grand Rapids but a stock-in-trade for MPKT. "Election night was one of the most moving experiences I can remember," says Vallely. "We were sitting in a dumpy office and we realized we'd won." The victory party took place in a small building that literally swayed from the uproar. Vallely says he felt the earth move.

The following year, in 1975, Marttila again went to work for Boston mayor White. They conferred occasionally, perhaps once a month, during Marttila's tenure. This time out, the fight with State Senator Joe Timilty was a grueling fifteen-round decision in which the combatants landed punishing blows but no knock-out punches. Unknown to the public, White was at odds with his own political consultant. Marttila advised White to clean up his act. "I confronted him on many occasions on the issue of using public employees in the campaign," says Marttila. White had no use for the suggestion; he greeted it derisively. After the election, which White won, he and Marttila parted ways, not on congenial terms.

Three years later, during a referendum campaign on taxes, White again called Marttila for advice. The referendum was being used by White as an occasion for flexing the muscles of his political machine. Marttila pointed out that the machine was superfluous in mobilizing for a tax issue that was in the interests of virtually all Bostonians. Only media advertising was required to constantly remind voters of the stakes involved. White vehemently disagreed. All you guys understand is media, he shouted. Marttila believed his relationship with the mayor was finally finished. But in 1979, when White ran for an unprecedented fourth term, counting on his machine to deliver the vote, he privately asked Marttila to serve him one more time. Marttila, however, didn't want to be on White's payroll. Still, he offered some advice and spent election night with the mayor.

In 1976, a presidential year, the company took on the campaign of liberal standard-bearer Morris Udall. When MPKT entered the race Udall was spinning his wheels. He had been trounced in the Iowa caucus by Jimmy Carter and political columnists were sneering at his chances. But MPKT ran a good race with the Udall campaign. They discovered that Archibald Cox, famous Watergate martyr, had endorsed Udall; nobody in the campaign had bothered to play it up. Soon, however, MPKT featured Cox's picture in full-page ads in major newspapers in primary states, emphasizing the key endorsement. The consultants also pushed Udall to stress the powerful issue of concentration of economic power. Udall's standing in the polls shot up; he was now finishing second to Carter in key primaries, good but not good enough. In Wisconsin, MPKT believed they could make a breakthrough. Thorne informed the campaign that through his fundraising effort $350,000 was coming into the campaign coffers. Ten days before the Wisconsin vote, however, $250,000 of the expected money hadn't materialized; Udall panicked. Two days before the primary Udall canceled all his television spots, as well as much newspaper advertising. He lost the primary to Carter by 1 percent. Shortly afterward, the money made its appearance as predicted. Udall was a perfect MPKT candidate on the issues. He lacked, however, the will to power that the consultants themselves possessed. While they were in overdrive, Udall was satisfied with second gear.

Things have changed in the American political scene since Marttila and his colleagues brought their technical know-how to the aid of liberal Democratic candidates. Now, the techniques are common and the candidates are not often as ideologically exciting as before. Marttila depended as much on finesse, political knowledge, and the coherence of his efforts as on refined media technique in the service of electing liberal Democratic candidates to office.

"There's so much mysticism about what we do," Marttila lamented. "The trick is to get campaigns to execute. The elements of a political campaign are classic." He has an Aristotelian sensibility. John Marttila is a playwright of contemporary liberal campaigns. He understands their measured drama. It is almost a literary exercise. The play must appeal to a variety of audiences, make do with the props on hand, and not force the protagonist to act out of character, for he would then be unbelievable. How to script this drama can be partly learned; but much of it depends upon native talent and instinct. Not all playwrights have the same sense of structure, plotting, and characterization. It helps to see the craft as more than automatic writing.

With the reduction of many campaigns to media events, consultants emerge as the only active political philosophers able to test their theories in practice. Almost everyone else is engaged in weaving ideas from a distance. Yet not all consultants recognize their status. Too often they sell know-how, not knowledge. They routinize politics, computerizing its nuances. Consulting is a scientific way of reaching constituencies. But as traditional constituencies disintegrate, the new consultants intensify their polling to certify momentary shifts of mood. Politicians respond to these freeze-frame opinions, although they aren't the whole picture. This attempt to dominate the process becomes the process itself. And firms like MPKT, which have a definite commitment to a certain brand of politics and are not trapped or entranced by technology, are forced to respond to the new circumstances. The consultants become captives.

"Two or three years ago I thought consulting wasn't necessarily a growth industry," said Marttila. "Now it's going to explode because of public apathy. Constituencies per se have broken down. There is a distressing single-issue trend. There are two forces at work. One, modern politicians have mastered contemporary communications and survey research technique. The worst will use this to play upon people's fears. Two, there has been a change in society. There has been a disintegration of public purpose, which occurred in the 1960s. There is no need for politicians to act like gentlemen on issues like civil rights anymore. Because of polling, politicians know with more certainty what they can and cannot say. Those who benefit most are those who are most negative. The country remains Democratic. But there's an ambivalence. I'm not going to say the country has gone conservative. I'm not a Pollyanna either. But if this is what American politics is to be like — see you later. I have no interest."

Although they closed up shop in 1979 the partners didn't stop campaigning. They rented a new office, in which they all had rooms (except Thorne, who was busy on real estate business most of the time), and took occasional races on their own. They also freelanced for environmental and consumer groups needing professional advice.

In Dan Payne's case he picked up assorted campaigns and odd jobs until an opportunity for a windfall presented itself. The campaign of John Y. Brown, Kentucky Fried Chicken tycoon, who had prepared himself for a run for governor of Kentucky by scuttling two professional basketball teams and marrying television broadcaster and former Miss America Phyllis George, approached Payne about preparing a campaign brochure. Much to Payne's pleasure the deal fell through; it got him off the hook of supporting a patently vacuous candidate. He wondered why he had ever considered it. Brown, however, went on to stage a razzle-dazzle media campaign, running as an antipolitician in a state that had never before been subject to a total television blitz. Phyllis George spelled out the character of the campaign. "Basically," she said, "show business is like politics. If you work for a network, as I did, it's who-you-know that counts. And politics, with its media blitz, is very much show biz. What matters is whether a candidate is handsome and articulate and has a good smile. The big difference is that politics is real, very real, and that show business is a fantasy world."

Payne said: "That's where she's wrong. For a lot of people politics is about as participatory as the National Football League halftime show Phyllis used to host. The worst of show business has been visited upon politics. I'm not disillusioned, though. It's just tougher to be a principled liberal consultant. The field has been whittled down. The great moral issues are not as apparent. I say that with ambivalent feelings. The issues that made liberalism exciting in the late 1960s and early 1970s were terrible things to live through, like Vietnam. While Nixon provided fuel for liberal fires the fact he's no longer with us is good. It's just as well those issues aren't there. The real challenge is identifying those issues which advance the liberal cause, if you will, making them the substance of campaigns, and using techniques which may seem foreign to liberals. Their visions of running campaigns are romantic. Even a campaign like Drinan's still required modern means of communications and organization. People entering politics from the left just want to meet the people, meet the issues. They're losers. They have prejudice against technique. The New Right and the business community, meanwhile, use sophisticated resources and have the disposition to use them.

"Without liberal issues the liberal candidate has to rely upon people where he finds them — watching television and alienated from the traditional political apparatus. So the candidate goes where they are. He polls them because he doesn't have any way to know what they think. They don't have leaders. He uses computers to generate mailings. The candidates aren't pushing out beyond the narrow confines of survey data. That magnifies Kennedy's difference. He looks much more exciting. Ted Kennedy may temporarily remove the liberal malaise. I don't think he'll unleash the left in the sense of making it public. Kennedy has been waiting like unseated royalty outside the presidency. What happens? If he's shattered in this campaign maybe we have no more heroes. Maybe that's good, or maybe something is irretrievably lost."

When Jerry Brown came to Boston in late 1979, Thorne hosted a reception in his Beacon Hill home for the candidate to meet some of the key Bay State operatives. Thorne was friendly with Brown but told him that his campaign would be best served if he stayed out of Massachusetts. Thorne said: "I feel ambivalent about politics right now. I think there's a major change taking place, a transition. Liberalism as we've known it is dead. I don't know what the answer is. I only know I'm dissatisfied with most people in public life. We're running out of the old formulas. I learned all the techniques, but it just doesn't have much meaning anymore. I know you can't take a walk on society, but politics per se is not a meaningful forum right now."

Tom Kiley said: "I'm inclined to believe that there's a realignment of competing ideologies moving into a corporate/anticorporate division. If we're on the frontiers of a new epoch based on energy scarcity, I don't think the Kennedy campaign will promote that development. It's a throwback. His candidacy is one of older concepts. I say all this as a firm supporter of Kennedy, although I'm not enamored. I think that what he talks about is part of a discussion that took place years ago. But really the basis of my support for Kennedy is that I think the potential for realignment through him exists. I don't know if it'll happen. On the partisan level his message and appeal are directed at the classic Democratic constituencies which have broken down recently. His campaign may be a minor detour to complete fragmentation."

Marttila said: "You can describe me as old-fashioned. My political values have been unchanged in twenty years. On race and economics I'm discussing the same things I discussed since high school. I'm not a programmatic liberal so much as a spiritual liberal. I'm also convinced of the American people's generosity and compassion. And I'm committed to the intensive use of survey research. Unquestionably it's a difficult political time and clearly the conservatives have the upper hand. Liberals have to use all the weapons of campaigning to guard their situation."

## CHAPTER TWELVE

# THE POSTMASTER GENERAL
# OF THE RIGHT

## RICHARD VIGUERIE

Just as Hollywood producers once found starlets sipping sodas at Schwab's Drugstore, the New Right now discovers candidates at meetings in motel function rooms called to protest issues like the Panama Canal Treaty or Salt II. The rise to power of U.S. Senator Gordon Humphrey (R-New Hampshire) is a case in point. Humphrey, a thirty-eight-year-old commercial airline pilot, got his start when he was invited to a gathering against the canal treaty. Nine people showed up, and Humphrey volunteered to serve as chairman of a "Keep Our Canal" rally. This time, 500 people attended. From that group, Humphrey built up the Conservative Caucus in New Hampshire to 1500 members, providing a network of support for his candidacy. When Humphrey won the GOP nomination, the New Right summoned its considerable resources. Huge sums of money were raised, enough to buy into the Boston television market, which blankets southern New Hampshire, and to hire expensive political consultants. The result: Humphrey unseated the popular sixteen-year Democratic incumbent, Thomas McIntyre.

Was Humphrey's victory a lucky accident? Not quite. His name originally surfaced on the mailing list of political entrepreneur and generalissimo of the New Right, Richard A. Viguerie. "Things don't happen by accident," he says. "They're planned. They're organized. We don't have a notebook with the whole thing carefully mapped out, although that's not a bad idea. But we have plans."

Forty-six-year-old Viguerie has become a very powerful man in a short span of time. He's the publisher of a flotilla of publications ranging from the mass circulation *Conservative Digest* to the insider's newsletter *New Right Report*. Several political action committees are run by his associates, providing modern consulting methods to specially selected candidates. Several U.S. senators owe their seats to Viguerie in some way. Senator Jesse Helms (R-North Carolina) was dubbed the Six-Million-Dollar man last year when he ran for reelection, a reference to the amount Viguerie raised for him as a result of direct mail solicitations. (Viguerie, incidentally, keeps a hefty chunk of the loot; in some cases more than 75 percent of what he raises goes to him and his subsidiaries.)

Viguerie's IBM tape decks and high-speed printers work twenty-four hours a day, with time off only on Christmas, Thanksgiving, and Easter. In the vault of his computer room, to which entry is permitted only by a security guard, is his treasure of 11 million names on tape. This is the core of the New Right.

Viguerie is ready for the presidential election year, another milestone, he hopes, in the progress of the New Right. At first,

Viguerie's candidate was Congressman Philip Crane of Illinois. In the eleven months after his announcement in August 1978, Crane raised $2,490,276 in funds through direct mail. But he paid out $1,191,847 to five companies of which Viguerie is an owner, officer, or director. Crane disagreed with Viguerie about the direct mail strategy. He wanted to resolicit those on the "house list." Viguerie wanted to keep "prospecting" for new supporters. Eventually, Crane and Viguerie had a falling out.

Meanwhile, Viguerie approached another presidential contender, John Connally. "He was interested and we got married," says Viguerie. "Connally and I agree on 75 percent of the issues. And he has the best chance of beating Ted Kennedy." This factor is paramount to Viguerie. He is terror stricken by the thought of a Kennedy presidency. He believes Kennedy will attempt to put the New Right out of business by promulgating campaign contribution reforms and by political use of the Justice Department. If Kennedy is the candidate for the Democrats, Viguerie sees the election as a life-and-death struggle.

"It's a sign of our strength that there is no candidate in the Republican party who is going to run a left of center campaign for president," says Viguerie. "I think the new vitality of the conservative movement definitely is responsible for that. This will be the first time in our lifetime that no one who is a serious candidate will appeal to that liberal perspective. Slowly but surely we're moving the political balance much more to the center. Not to the right. But things are definitely moving our way. We've got some momentum."

One of his confederates, Massachusetts conservative Howard Phillips, believes that Viguerie's mailing lists are at the base of the New Right's sudden influence. It was Phillips's Conservative Caucus that "discovered" Gordon Humphrey in New Hampshire, courtesy of Viguerie's computerized lists. "They're indispensable," he says. "Without assembling that body of names we couldn't have achieved anything. As Jesse Unruh said, money is the mother's milk of politics. Unless you have money you don't have anything. Without the magic of direct mail, conservatives would be relegated to part-time activity. There would have been no fight over the Panama Canal Treaty unless there was a New Right. We helped defeat instant voter registration. If the New Right wasn't involved, the two parties would take the same position and there would be no debate."

Viguerie is the High Tech Lenin of the New Right. He didn't come to the right through disillusionment or defeat. He isn't brooding or starkly resentful. He's relaxed in his corner office, surrounded by paintings of famous golf courses. His head is a gleaming sculpted dome with a few strands of hair brushed across it. He's at ease with himself, not threatened by conversations with journalists. On the contrary, he welcomes these exchanges. He's animated, yet completely self-possessed. He's eager to state his position. He wants challenges. Interviews are exercises, preparatory drills, jogs in anticipation of the long-distance run. He bubbles with optimism.

"If I had been in a lot of the foxholes a lot of the conservatives have been in for thirty years and been shot and shelled and just torn apart and suffered all the defeats and have a what-the-hell attitude . . ." Viguerie shrugs and plows on. "That's just not the attitude of the new conservatives. We believe we will win and prevail. There isn't a Communist leader in the world worth his salt who doesn't feel that Communism isn't the wave of the future. They just believe that they are the stuff of history. There's not a leader I know of in the Free World who believes freedom is the wave of the future. That's what we have going for the conservatives now: the conservatives believe that they will govern America. They see themselves as winners in life. They are totally convinced that they have the ability to govern and that they *will* govern in the foreseeable future. There's an electricity, an excitement that wasn't here six years ago."

Viguerie is a fundamentalist in his political beliefs. What sets him off from mossbacks of previous generations is his sophistica-tion. He knows that without a contemporary approach his ideas would remain ethereal, unconnected to real politics. He wants to win. He's reaching for power. He knows how to work the levers and his intentions are clear. All of this makes him an original American political type, unlike the old rightists who were nur-tured on failure and developed what the late historian Richard Hofstadter termed "the paranoid style in American politics."

Richard Viguerie is a modernist. He may not accept the pre-cepts of the New Deal, but he abides the canons of advertising as if they were eternal verities. He's pragmatic in his use of technique. He wants to use what works. Viguerie has been willing to learn from sources other than fellow rightists. He is an apt pupil of George McGovern, the New Left, and the AFL-CIO, all Satan incarnate to old rightists. But Viguerie is confident that he can truck with the devil without being marked. He emerges stronger in his convictions and surer in how to realize them.

"We've taken close to 100 percent of the left's tactics," he confesses unashamedly. "What we're doing is what they did. We have been thirty years late in realizing how the left did it. We're into making a list of all the things they do and doing the same things." The methods he's adopted are simply common organizing techniques, at least common to the labor movement, the peace movement, and the civil rights movement.

On Viguerie's desk, when I paid him a visit, was a thick book containing copies of the direct mail solicitations from the 1972 McGovern for president campaign, which Viguerie holds in high professional esteem. "I'm studying it," he says. "I'm trying to build a movement. I don't know if you've heard that word much. Among us conservatives that's a word that's used constantly. The movement." Hearing him speak in the shorthand of the left is eerie. The word *movement* resonates oddly when Viguerie uses it. But the right, after all, has momentum. It is in movement. It is a choice, not an echo.

Viguerie's achievement is considerable. He has forged a distinctive New Right, moving it beyond its narrow complaints, melding it into a movement. Previously, the right embraced a politics of nostalgia for a past that never existed; the right expected and needed defeat because defeat certified its opinions. Its politics were concerned with loss of status in a rapidly changing world. Viguerie has helped the right transcend status politics to become a brand of interest group politics, a far more efficacious approach. The New Right often seems to be a collection of motley single-issue groups, very particularized, dependent on the old anxieties. But within the new structures the right is able to have much more of an effect. Viguerie has wedded the substance of status politics to the form of interest group politics. It's a real advance for the right, a signal change in its methodology. Viguerie has pushed the right into the modern era, educating conservatives in the craft of marketing and advertising, essential instruments of American politics. The New Right is much more dangerous because of his pedagogy.

"Years and years ago, I decided that I wanted to do something in a major way to help the conservative movement," he says. "There were different routes I could have gone." He ticks off the names of influential conservative writers. "Bill Buckley, Bill Rusher, Russell Kirk. I could have gone that route. I probably wouldn't have amounted to a hill of beans. That wasn't my nature. I didn't have the educational background for that. What we didn't have, what we had zero people doing, was having someone take the ideas, the writings, the books and market them to the masses. A new cause came along, a new candidate, we didn't really have someone who understood how to market them on a national scale. So I set out for myself to become the best marketer I could be. I wanted to communicate with the masses, to market ideas. And I did that. It may not have occurred to other conservatives. It's not an easy thing to do. It requires certain skills. I had to train myself, to teach myself. I've been doing it a long time, but I've got a long way to go yet. I went to college to learn one profession and then I had to learn a different one. Not a lot of people are willing to do that, put in those kind of hours. I majored in political science at the University of Houston. I went to law school for about a year and a half. I always, always, always wanted to be a politician. I didn't understand *how* I was going to do it. I just knew I *was* going to do it."

An optimistic rightist like Viguerie had to have been born and raised on the cusp of the sunbelt. Richard Viguerie is a sunny new-wave reactionary. He is idea and act, free of cobwebs. He was born in Golden Acres, Texas, a town outside Houston. His father was a middle-level petrochemical executive, his mother a practical nurse. "My parents were the silent majority out there," he recalls. "Their instincts were conservative. We don't disagree on hardly anything philosophical. But there wasn't a situation where I can remember discussing politics in the evening at dinner. It's something I picked up on my own. My philosophy wasn't counter to my parents, but they weren't very political."

When he was very young, perhaps seven, he became enthralled with American Indians. He was very shy and small for his age, even as a teenager. Although he had never actually seen an authentic Indian he was obsessed with their plight. Movies, which mainly portrayed Indians as ignoble savages, perked his interest. He immersed himself in books on the subject. At some point he linked victims of Communism with Indians. The Communists were the white men. The American way of life — entrepreneurial capitalism — was imperiled. It could be wiped out like the Indians. America was the underdog. Communists were closing in. For a boy in Texas, the end of the frontier was vivid.

In college Viguerie had two heroes — "the two Macs" he calls them — General Douglas MacArthur and Senator Joseph McCarthy. When the Army-McCarthy hearings were broadcast Viguerie was riveted to the radio. These hearings, more than anything else, led to McCarthy's demise. During them, Mc-

Carthy's penchant for character assassination and coarse tactics was revealed unadorned on nationwide television. As McCarthy went down, Viguerie, listening attentively in his dormitory room, rooted for him. "Here was a man fighting Communism," he says. "So I became a fighter."

His start in politics wasn't auspicious, a typically undistinguished beginning running the Houston headquarters of Senator John Tower. The following year he moved up the ladder to become the first executive secretary of the Young Americans for Freedom, William F. Buckley's finishing school for future conservative leaders. As part of his job Viguerie was supposed to raise money for the organization. He did not like asking rich people for contributions directly. He decided to write them letters, and his first direct mailings worked. Soon he made the plunge into business. With a $300 investment he rented a one-room office on Capitol Hill in 1965; today he grosses over $15 million a year, a conservative estimate. He was like an oil wildcatter, an independent driller in politics. He sank his lines and hoped for a gusher. It was just a trickle to begin with. Direct mail, while part of an overall political consulting media package, wasn't regarded by most operatives as lucrative enough to base a firm on. It was fine as a supplement to television, but in itself it was patently inadequate. Viguerie kept at it.

Then came three big breaks. The first of these was the 1972 McGovern campaign for the presidency, which demonstrated conclusively the power of direct mail. McGovern's campaign was a sterling example of a faultless direct mail operation. "George McGovern," explains Viguerie, "ran over the Henry Jacksons and the Hubert Humphreys of the world because he understood the new technology. He was a creature of direct mail. McGovern was thinking direct mail from the beginning." The reason McGovern was thinking direct mail was because he had to. He didn't have the backing of the regular Democrats, the AFL-CIO, the urban machines, or the ethnic groups. In early polls his standing with

Democrats wavered between 2 and 3 percent. He had no wealthy supporters. His candidacy seemed particularly farfetched then. He desperately needed a means to nourish his campaign in its lean phase, at least until it could take off. McGovern contacted Morris Dees, the most successful political direct mail operator in the country. Dees, a liberal Southerner, built the biggest direct mail company outside New York and Chicago, sold it, and, when McGovern contacted him, was devoting his time to public interest law and civil rights. (Dees had begun his career as a student at the University of Alabama selling birthday cakes to students' parents.) Dees calculated that the right pitch would enable the McGovern campaign to carry itself through its nascent stages. He wrote a letter asking recipients to contribute $10 a month to the McGovern for President Club. A coupon book for making payments was enclosed; those who signed up were sent an "insider's" newsletter and monthly reminders to pay their "dues." By early 1972 monthly income from the scheme totaled about $100,000. "The club idea proves that Alexis de Tocqueville was right when he observed almost 150 years ago that America was a nation of joiners," Dees declared. Viguerie took notice of Dees's scheme. In his own work, Viguerie began to write fundraising appeals with participatory gimmicks, asking recipients to send in an enclosed poll or an odd dollar contribution for a specific purpose. He was catching on.

His next leap forward was provided by Arthur Bremer. When George Wallace's putative assassin incapacitated the Alabama governor in 1972, Wallace's 1976 presidential campaign was cast into doubt. Wallace had little personal control over the political efforts on his behalf. The collection of money, which would determine if there would even be another run, was farmed out to Richard Viguerie, whom Morris Dees suggested as ideologically compatible. In eighteen months Viguerie raised $2 million and spent as much in the effort. Eventually he garnered $6.9 million for Wallace. Viguerie was Wallace's life support system, sustaining him for one final campaign.

Wallace's campaign was the real making of Vigeurie and the New Right, for it provided a list of 600,000 names, sifted from a larger list of contributors, that was as good as gold. While Viguerie did a lot for Wallace, Wallace was a godsend for Viguerie. His campaign gave Viguerie free-and-clear proprietary rights to the hardcore of the New Right. Unintentionally and indirectly, however, it also contributed to the rise of Jimmy Carter, whose 1976 primary victories over Wallace in Southern states made him the leading candidate, acceptable to blacks and liberals.

The third and perhaps most important boon for Viguerie was Watergate. Besides the removal of Richard Nixon from the Oval Office, the most tangible result of Watergate was a campaign reform act passed by Congress that limited contributions to $1000. Supposedly, this would inhibit arm-twisting of corporate executives by presidential hopefuls, democratize the political process by making parties less dependent on major contributors, and involve more citizens who would feel that their small gifts carried weight. It didn't exactly work out that way. The principal beneficiary of this reform, enacted mainly at the behest of liberal Democrats, was Richard Viguerie.

It was a bonanza for him. With his Wallace list he could sell his services to appropriately reactionary candidates to help them reach the small contributors they now urgently needed. Through a series of campaigns Viguerie piggybacked his list, gathering more and more names, prospecting for the best ones to add to his computer tapes. The list expanded goemetrically. The Wallace campaign itself depended upon these small givers. Watergate made his jackpot seem almost inevitable.

Suddenly, Viguerie was in the big time. But he continued to see everything through an ideological lens. He considered his fortuitous elevation to a position of influence to be more than a simple political victory: it was a triumph of modern marketing. "The left has missed a lot of things," he advises. "They think of direct mail as fundraising. They miss the whole boat if they think that. *It is a form of advertising.* It is not an evil conspiratorial thing. It is just a fact of life, which I haven't found anybody to deny, that the major media of this country has a left of center perspective. The conservatives can't get their message around this blockade, except through direct mail. It's a way for conservatives to bypass the monopoly the left has on the media. It's a way of mobilizing our people; it's a way of communicating with our people; it identifies our people; and it marshals our people. It's self-liquidating and it pays for itself. It's a form of advertising, part of the marketing strategy. *It's advertising.*"

Viguerie began his thrust for leadership of the New Right in 1974, when Gerald Ford nominated Nelson Rockefeller to serve as his vice president. This appointment was the final affront to the New Right. Viguerie moved into action to attempt to block the selection. He telephoned more than a dozen conservative movers and shakers and invited them to his office to formulate tactics. The meeting was a disappointment. "The conservative leaders of America in that room didn't know how to go from point A to point Z," recalls Viguerie. "I saw very dramatically that nobody knew how to organize."

It was then that Viguerie started to develop his theory of leadership, a conception of a counterrevolutionary vanguard that would take command of the right by giving it direction. "There is a lot of planning and communication within the conservative movement that didn't exist half a dozen years ago," says Viguerie. "It's basically happening because of a dozen or so key leaders who are moving in a very bold, dramatic, decisive way. Of all the problems the conservative movement has had over the years it has been lack of leadership that's hurt the most. We've had people who were well known, who were very articulate, who could write very well, could speak, had charisma. Naturally everyone would think that's a leader. But there's a difference between a spokesman and a leader. We've had our spokesmen and now we have our leaders."

Viguerie's desire to form a vanguard is derived from his sense of history. He believes that history is the story of great men, that personalities are the driving force of events. The masses to him are inconsequential compared to their leaders. "This country is here today," he explains, "because of a few dozen people. Maybe twelve. It wasn't the million that demanded the freedom from England. Take away a Washington, a Franklin, where would you be? The same with the conservative movement today. Take away that dozen and you've got problems."

This somewhat imperious attitude, however, generates extraordinary passion in Viguerie. The day I spent with him he was up at four in the morning to write a fundraising appeal. He reserves his most fervent evangelism for his copywriting. His true pulpit is in an envelope. "I feel," he says, "that when I have spent five or six hours writing a letter, I am the audience. I am the person I am writing to. When I am finished I am physically wrung out. I am exhausted because I put myself in there emotionally. I am in my copy. I feel for the people, for the cause. It's very emotional. A lot of my clients don't like the copy because they say it sounds too cornball, too conversational, it's not dignified. But people respond to emotionalism. The successful and effective speakers are emotional."

His feelings aren't wasted. There's more to these solicitations than just a visceral release for Viguerie. Direct mail is part of a grand strategy. It fits in with his theory of the counterrevolutionary vanguard; he believes that a vanguard without a movement is simply a sect. Viguerie doesn't just tender advice to candidates and single-issue groups for a fee. He is building a movement that will support a certain kind of candidate. He is working from the bottom up to create a constituency to back his politics. In the language of the left, he's base building.

Direct mail is not Viguerie's only organizational tool, however. He has created a political conglomerate with satellites spinning around the direct mail operation. Viguerie keeps extending his frontier with a sense of surety; he believes in political manifest destiny. Political action committees (PACs) expedite his missions. They spend millions: in 1972 congressional races, established conservative groups dropped a mere $250,000; but in 1976, with Viguerie geared up, conservative groups raised close to $5.6 million. Viguerie's PACs differ from the corporate PACs in that they're much more ideological. They're also more organizationally minded. Corporate PACs just give their money to candidates they feel best represent their interests. Viguerie wants more than that from his PACs. He wants commitment; he wants more movement activists. So his PACs are designed to train politicians. One of his PACs, the National Conservative Political Action Committee (NCPAC), which helped elect fifty-five New Rightists to office in 1978, prefers to give candidates material services rather than outright grants of money. NCPAC will provide politicians with an ensemble of modern techniques — polling, media advice, and campaign management training. When U.S. Senator Frank Church of Idaho felt threatened by NCPAC support of an opponent in the 1980 race for his Senate seat, he reacted by raising the issue of a Soviet brigade in Cuba in connection with passage of the SALT II treaty. Church was running scared, and thus was influenced by Viguerie's cohorts on this very important matter.

Another of the Viguerie sponsored PACs, the Committee for the Survival of a Free Congress (CSFC) selects the candidates it wants to elect and then runs them through a training seminar. In 1978, CSFC helped elect twenty-six congressmen and five U.S. senators. The key to the success of this PAC is a precinct organization plan, which is presented as a revelation. It calls for an organization of precinct workers to be assigned voter turnout goals and to be supervised by area chairmen. The average twelve-year-old in Chicago could devise a more complicated scheme. But to the New Right this approach is novel.

The group that best reflects the comprehensive Viguerie viewpoint — combining the vanguard with the base, the single-issue campaigns with political races — is the Conservative Caucus. Headed by Howard Phillips, it is located in a rabbit's warren of offices occupied by other New Right groups above Papa Gino's on Tremont Street in Boston. (The offices are rent-free since the owner of Papa Gino's is a New Rightist and on the executive board of the Conservative Caucus: Ideology to go.) Phillips is burly and forceful. Viguerie attests to his political acumen. "Howie's one of the six key people," he confides. In 1978, Phillips ran as a Democrat for the Senate nomination, which struck most Bay State Democrats as ludicrous. Phillips, after all, is a former official of the Nixon administration. But his move indicated the drift of New Right strategy. What happened to his particular candidacy is relatively unimportant. What was meant by it is far more significant.

Phillips's ideas reflect his experience. He doesn't engage in idle theorizing. Obviously, he has a strong impact on Viguerie and the rest of the New Right. He carries weight. "In 1968 I was a conservative Republican," he says. "In 1979 I'm a conservative period." He received his education at the hands of Richard Nixon. When Phillips was a student government leader at Harvard in 1960, he was a fervent Nixon backer. Nixon was his hero. Now he sadly admits, "I'm without heroes." To New Rightists, Nixon is the great betrayer. Democratic presidents simply carried out the tasks they set out for themselves; they were liberals. But Nixon promised something new, fulfillment of the conservative dream, an evolutionary anti-reformism, unraveling the liberal program. They feel he had power in his grasp, but never used it. He shattered their expectations, which were probably somewhat naive to begin with. Nixon was far too centrist for the far right. "He damaged everything I hold dear," says Phillips. "He was the most liberal president in American history, except for Gerald Ford. He's a fundamentally weak man who groveled for Establishment recognition. He just wanted to look good in the history books, have the *New York Times* say nice things about him. At the same time, he hated them. He didn't have the courage of his intestines. I owe him a great deal because I got an education in his administration. My real education is that even presidents are flawed."

In 1974, Phillips formed a group called CREEP II, Conservatives for the Removal of the President. He was afraid that Nixon would make concessions to the Russians as he tried to fend off the Watergate inquiry. After Nixon's abdication, Phillips blueprinted plans for the Conservative Caucus. "I went to Viguerie," he says. "And we sent out material in the mail. Had it not been for Viguerie we couldn't have made much progress. Direct mail has done more than give us money. It gives us a way to get to our people."

Once outside the Nixon administration Phillips explored political options. Perhaps he learned the most from the left. "People in the conservative movement today aren't conventionally ambitious. It's the same way on the left," he says. "A lot of conservatives have read Saul Alinsky. I read all the liberal publications including the *Progressive*, the *Nation*, *Working Papers*. If something works, we're for doing it. In terms of the Caucus, the strategy comes out of trial and error. We need a grass-roots organization and we're developing a system for doing it broadly."

Phillips's Conservative Caucus can take credit for Gordon Humphrey's victory in New Hampshire. Less directly, the New Right has influenced other elections, mainly by creating a favorable conservative climate. "The greatly expanded base of conservative strength permitted Democratic primary upsets," the *New Right Report*, Viguerie's newsletter, gloated. "And the best news is this: This is not a temporary trend. This coalition will be bigger and stronger in 1980."

The New Right strategy calls for support of conservatives, whether they're Republican or Democrat. Before the 1976 election, William Rusher, publisher of the conservative *National Review*, argued, in a book entitled *The Making of the New Ma-*

*jority Party*, for a conservative party to replace the Republicans. For a while, New Rightists embraced the Rusher thesis. Now they've jettisoned it. They're for building coalitions across party lines that maintain ideological consistency. Much of this tack derives from Phillips's experience. "My experience in the Nixon administration persuaded me that parties are less important than I had thought. It doesn't matter which party succeeds. Principles matter."

Viguerie's empire will be at the eye of the coming political storm. Yet he is being criticized by old-style conservative Republicans for his business practices. From three of his PACs, for example, his companies clear 83 percent of the total take. Certainly, he makes piles of money. But it seems out of character for these conservatives to attack a political rival for his entrepreneurial zeal. Isn't that what they're fighting for? Viguerie is an exemplar of economic individualism. He embodies the Ayn Rand ideal, suggested in the title of one of her books, *The Virtue of Selfishness*.

There's more than a touch of Horatio Alger to Richard Viguerie. He's driven to self-improvement, up at four in the morning. But Viguerie isn't a conventional go-getter. He believes that free will is tied to postmortem punishment. "I believe in reincarnation," he asserts. He doesn't know who or what he was in the past, but he's doing his best not to wind up another species next time: if you don't do the right thing you might become a cockroach. Viguerie is hammering himself into line out of fear of metamorphosis. Strangely, he sees this as a liberating concept. "After I began to understand reincarnation," he says, "the idea that we are all responsible for ourselves, that things don't happen to us accidentally, it was exciting. You reap what you sow. Sometimes you're going to reap it in this life, sometimes in the next life. Life is a learning experience. There's a law out there. You violate the law, you're going to be punished. You stick your hand in an electric socket, it's going to hurt. Life is not luck, it's not chance. It's a question of choice. Anything that I do that's not Christ-like I'm going to have to pay for it. This time or the next time. Doggone it, I want to get it right this time."

His mysticism suffuses his politics with confidence. Viguerie's religion gives him a sense of divine direction. More, his religiosity is a justification for his practicality. He feels free to pursue his career, certain that it meets with heavenly approval. He is in control of his life and his machines.

He doesn't fear his computers. "Technology is neutral," he says. "It's just a tool." For him, science is the servant of ideology. Although Viguerie maintains a sure hand on his IBM machines he still reveals doubt about the effect of the new technology on politics generally. "It's seldom that you will find older, established candidates that will be interested in using direct mail. Things you don't understand you don't feel comfortable with. When I'm sixty years old, I may not be any different than they are. It's fear of the unknown. You feel comfortable with what you've done for twenty or thirty years successfully. Why do it a different way? Why change? But there are people doing it a different way and they're running over the older politicians. It's possible to get elected today with the computers and the direct mail and the telephones and not really know how to govern. You can use these techniques to win the nomination and the election, but not know how to govern. That's right, you become a permanent campaigner. Take old Lyndon Johnson. He had all kinds of problems, but he knew how to govern. He knew how to make the bureaucracy work. He knew how to run things and administer things. He wasn't out of place in the Oval Office. The old politicians might understand how to govern better than a lot of the new ones. The new ones are relying on technology that is basically being applied by others. The old ones don't know how to campaign and the new ones don't know how to govern. There might be something to that."

Does this mean that he worries about the depth of commitment of some of the New Right candidates who owe so much to him? He expresses no such feelings. He's upbeat, 1980 promises to be a good year, and after that things look even better. "We're definitely going against the anti-ideological grain," he says. "And we're succeeding." He believes the left is beginning to retreat before his advancing legions. He thinks he can set the order of battle. "If the AFL-CIO wasn't worried about my direct mail, they wouldn't stay up nights worrying about me," he says. "It's a defensive posture by basically older people who don't know how to stop it. You can't stop it. Ask the French how defense works. It doesn't."

"Offense picks the terrain," I suggest.

"Exactly," Viguerie replies. "That's good," he muses. "I'll have to use that."

## CHAPTER THIRTEEN

# SPECTER OF THE LEFT

## RICHARD PARKER

When Richard Parker, publisher of the slick radical monthly magazine *Mother Jones*, appeared at Richard Viguerie's door in the fall of 1978, he was received cordially. Viguerie treated Parker to lunch, lent him his limousine, showed off his computers, and talked about campaigns.

Parker was about to set up shop as an ideological enemy. He believed it was time to organize a response to the right-wing offensive. Parker, a socialist, was abandoning the magazine field to become a direct mail political consultant as a way to reconstitute the left. Within a year after meeting Viguerie, Parker's operation had collected assorted periodicals as clients (the *Progressive*, *In These Times*, *Mother Jones*, *Seven Days*), an ecology group (Greenpeace), a civil liberties organization (Civil Liberties Union of Northern and Southern California), a defense committee (Karen Silkwood Defense Fund), a community organizing effort

(Massachusetts Fair Share), the Institute for Policy Studies, and the campaigns of Congressman Ronald Dellums and Senator George McGovern. Compared to Viguerie with his eight million names, Parker, with less than one million, is a novice. But he's made a start.

"We've decided to become the technological cadre," says Parker. "Technique can partly revive the left. The left has to master technique. This isn't what will turn the political tide. But it recreates a public presence. The media considers the left dead; the media isn't willing to acknowledge it. All other channels of communication have been broken. I don't have a solution, but the computer will be central to the 1980s. Without mastery there's no reason to express a coherent position. For this period, direct mail is appropriate technology. It's a qualified way of reaching people. It makes you think strategically. You have to decide which people will respond to which issues. You have to identify constituencies. You have to identify questions of timing and geography."

Parker counts on the postwar generation — the generation that supported the civil rights movement and opposed the Vietnam War — to once again become the base of a political movement. That generation has grown up, of course. Parker understands this well; he's thirty-two years old. He believes his peers, the prime market for Bloomingdale's and Calvin Klein, haven't discarded their political sympathies. In fact, secure in their jobs and making real money, they might be willing to contribute an occasional $25 to a good cause. The demographics look good, but Parker's thesis will take some time to test.

Richard Viguerie isn't so sure. "Richard Parker is a very talented person and if anyone can pull it off he probably can," says Viguerie. "It's going to be hard for Richard to do this, however, for a number of reasons. He feels that there are a lot of people who were in the streets ten years ago who are now holding jobs, making money, and can give $25. But people who are twenty-five, thirty, forty years old don't make contributions. People who are fifty-five, sixty, sixty-five, seventy years old do make contributions. And they're conservative. The younger people are disproportionately liberal. But they don't have disposable income. They're worried about mortgage payments, sending their kids to school, and buying a car. They're not going out and giving $25 contributions. When you're fifty-five or sixty years old, though, you are. And then you're conservative. So it's going to be a tough one."

Viguerie admires Parker's pluck and understands that the New Right doesn't have a monopoly on technology. But he does think it has a corner on patriotism, his hidden resource. He believes the conservative spirit animates his machines. He doubts that the left has the same stake in America as the right.

Richard Parker's great-great-great-great-grandfather, Captain John Parker, commanded the Minutemen on Lexington Green on April 19, 1775, leading them in the first battle against the British redcoats. "If they mean to have a war, let it begin here," proclaimed Captain Parker. The musket that he fired to begin the American Revolution was handed down from generation to generation. It hung in the study of Richard Parker's great-great-great-uncle, Theodore Parker, the captain's grandson. Of all the great men of New England of his day few had a more profound theoretical grasp of social issues and their relationship to religion and American history than the minister, Theodore Parker. He understood the economic basis of politics and was unwavering in his impassioned advocacy of radical democracy, which he saw as the fulfillment of the American Revolution and the higher laws of God. He fought for women's rights, prison reform, public education, and progressive Christianity. But he achieved his greatest prominence leading the struggle in Boston against the Fugitive Slave Act; he was arrested and tried by the federal government for harboring slaves; and he was an adviser to abolitionist John Brown, aiding him in his attempt to stir the slaves to revolt.

Among those who admired Theodore Parker and sought him out as a mentor was William Herndon of Illinois, an obscure lawyer, junior partner of Abraham Lincoln. Herndon read Parker's sermons closely and passed them on to Lincoln. In one oration, "The Effect of Slavery on the American People," Parker said, "Democracy is direct self-government, over all the people, for all the people, by all the people." In his biography of Theodore Parker, Henry Steele Commager wrote, "It was a good definition, thought Herndon, and he underscored that passage. It might interest Mr. Lincoln."

"Theodore Parker," wrote historian Vernon L. Parrington, "became the embodiment and epitome of New England renaissance. More completely than perhaps any other representative, he gathered up and expressed the major revolutionary impulses of his time and world." Parrington noted that Parker was also "the greatest scholar of his generation of New England ministers."

The Parker family tradition hasn't been muted very much over time. Richard Parker's father is an Episcopal minister. Even growing up in Hermosa Beach, a suburb of Los Angeles, Richard was instilled with the duty to public service as a first principle. "The idea of public service was ingrained in me," says Parker. "It's a very old Protestant notion — you show your virtue by the grace of your works."

External events conspired to disillusion him with the liberal version of public service. Richard knew he was going east to college, but he couldn't decide which school to attend. He had never been East, had never even seen snow, and had no sense of the differences among the Ivy League colleges. John S., his Sunday school teacher, a Dartmouth alumnus, helped him make up his mind. John S. was a good church man, a pillar of the community; he seemed to embody the idea of public service. If John S. was what Dartmouth produced, then Richard wanted to go there. Only when he arrived on campus did he discover that John S. was a Dartmouth rarity. Moreover, he found it increasingly difficult to maintain his naive idealism. "What moved me beyond hopeful liberalism was a realization of Kennedy's high level of moral deception," Richard says. "He lied about being honest."

Coming East was an early encounter with reality. In California, society was so unsettled that he couldn't get a fix on it. The East was different. "I wouldn't have believed in the authenticity of the class structure if I hadn't gone East," he says. "California is more advanced than the East as a sensuous society. The East gave me evidence about the existence of class that in California had only been a suspicion. I was dumbstruck at what had been gotten away with."

His radicalism, which had been at first a glimmering perception of dishonesty and inequality, became the light of illumination when he learned the real identity of his model, John S. "I became aware," says Parker, "that he was a CIA agent. It was the standard pattern. That moment of realization was one of the most frightening in my life. The other was when I handed in my draft card at a protest rally on Boston Common. It was really a jarring event for me. It jelled my radicalism."

This insight into the nature of duplicity gave Parker a mission. He continued his studies in economics at Magdalen College, Oxford University, as a Marshall Scholar. When he returned to America he wrote a series of articles for the *New Republic*, which served as the basis of a book, *The Myth of the Middle Class*, a refutation of the notion that America is a middle-class society. Parker argued that this conventional idea was specious, that classes indeed exist. Although the working class was stratified, it hadn't disappeared; it was still a distinct majority.

He wrote much of his book while a fellow at the Center for the Study of Democratic Institutions, a liberal think tank in Santa Barbara. After completing *The Myth of the Middle Class*, he founded an alternative newspaper, the *Santa Barbara News and Review*, which attracted a circulation of 11,000, impressive in a town of 65,000. From the *News and Review* he moved on to become managing editor of *Ramparts* magazine, once a radical bellwether.

Parker's experience in the left taught him failure and frustration, valuable lessons if you're not defeated by them. Parker, for his part, refused to drown. When he arrived at *Ramparts* in the early 1970s it was engulfed in the turmoil of a disintegrating movement; the magazine was not immune. "Everything was falling apart," he says. "The place had become so democratized that you couldn't make a move. There was no leadership. The high point came when I commissioned a cover on R. D. Laing and the art director's boy friend took a picture of an oil field instead. And so, the article on oil became the cover story. I was against the oil field cover even though it was my piece. There was a tie vote, which they broke by bringing the mail clerk into the room."

When *Ramparts* capsized, Parker and several other survivors rowed back to the dock to begin again. They launched *Mother Jones*, which was initially called *New Dimensions*. "There were continual goddamned battles," he says, "about how to be commercial and about how to interpret the left in the late 1970s." Parker was responsible for the business side. It was he who chose the name *Mother Jones*, after Mary Harris Jones, a militant labor organizer who lived for 100 years (1830–1930). "The name *Mother Jones* came off a list. An adman called me up and suggested it. I changed the name from *New Dimensions* without testing it. It was utter gut feeling. *New Dimensions* was a terrible name. I learned that being forceful got things done. I wrote all the ad copy from day one for *Mother Jones*. Now, it has over 200,000 paid subscriptions according to the audit. It's probably over 240,000. It's in the black, with gross revenue over $2 million a year. From an economic point of view *Mother Jones* is successful. The marketing made it successful. We were offering a way of looking at the world that spoke to people. It was eclectic and that made it attractive. There was an accidental variety that made it an anomaly. It spoke to a generation as a peer." Even the *New York Times*, in a report on the magazine in its business pages, conceded that *Mother Jones* has "a financial stability rare for a left-wing publication."

Parker believes that he can translate his business talents into politics, doing for the left what he has done for *Mother Jones*. He feels prepared for the task. He thinks it's time to help organize a national left constituency by cultivating a broader financial base. He's certain the market is there, but untapped.

Richard Parker's office is on the top floor of the Cannery, over-looking San Francisco Bay. The Cannery is a rehabilitated red-brick complex that used to house a Del Monte fruit cannery. Now it houses a maze of expensive boutiques. This being San Francisco, the bookstore in the Cannery features in its Current Events section a book entitled *Using Plants for Health*. In the Cannery's courtyard, tourists mingle with balloon vendors, mimes and flut-ists. Inside the office, Bill Dodd, the former circulation manager of *Mother Jones* who has joined Parker in the direct mail enterprise, conducts his daily scan of the computerized lists of names. "Lists either work or they don't," Dodd says, sounding like the "tech-nological cadre" Parker aspires to. "It's a time-motion study of people."

Dodd points to a direct mail appeal that the firm has produced, which is pinned to a bulletin board. It is not a mere dunning for funds. It gives the recipient an opportunity to participate. Every-one is a potential activist. Enclosed in a typical appeal is a letter explaining the cause and requesting funds, an envelope in which to mail your check, and a postcard to send to an official to voice your feelings on the issue. "Eco-gram," reads a postcard consisting of three separate preaddressed cards to send to the governor, a congressman, and the group that originated the appeal. "We've copyrighted that title — Eco-gram," says Dodd. "It's effective. We use it on several letters we send out." Direct mail on the left is a form of media, a source of money, and a way to involve a sympathetic audience in activity, even if it's just mailing a postcard. Richard Parker writes most of the copy for the letters. They are to the point, suggesting that there's something practical you can do about the issue. His analysis is not, however, purely functional.

In Parker one can hear familiar strains of New England radicalism, a mixture of clear-eyed realism and moral indignation. Parker himself admits that if he were a pure-bred Californian he wouldn't be capable of undertaking his project. His radicalism is evocative of family and tradition in a way the right would never comprehend. "The crisis is about our peers," he says, inveighing against the dark ages of democracy he believes we're inhabiting. "The liberal myth of the state is dead. It's failed to fulfill its role as a social consciousness. There aren't avenues for conscience in America. People don't want to be invisible. What advertising in America discovered long ago with images of irrational desires is that you can bypass the public function of expressing our rational selves. In high capitalism all becomes erotic; all public contact becomes irrational. Desire is what's played out. It's a specific form of desire — personal gratification, private irrational desires. There's no longer any stage for the rational self. Unless you can crack the codes of the media you're caught trying to hold a Socratic dialogue in Studio 54. You have to make some concessions to it, but you must maintain your own reason and conscience. I'm not sure we've mastered it at all. How do we organize that consciousness in a way that gives us back our public selves?"

The main question Parker must grapple with is the question of the left itself. This differs greatly from the question of the right. The right's appeal is mired in resentment; entrepreneurs like Viguerie seek to heighten and organize that resentment. The left, which may seem narrow and irrelevant, is at its best hopeful, redemptive, and radical in the true sense of the word; its solutions go to the root of society's maladies. But has the left been so fragmented and psychologically defeated in the 1970s that it can't rise to any occasion? And can technique and sheer intelligence help revive the left?

It's pertinent to note that Lenin's *What Is to Be Done?* is, in part, an analysis of media politics. In czarist Russia the state controlled the media; Lenin was an unequivocal advocate of the use of media in order to create a countervailing center of power. In a section of the book called "Can a Newspaper Be a Collective Organizer?" Lenin insisted that publishing a newspaper was the fundamental technique through which the revolutionary organization could be stabilized. Activists would naturally gravitate to it. From its sustained coverage of events, workers would learn to engage in more than sporadic actions and to develop demands that weren't limited to simple economics. In other words, they would gradually gain a sense of politics. Furthermore, through their work on the newspaper, activists would become more professional as political leaders. Provincialism would be overcome, communication increased. On the newspaper there would be, Lenin wrote, "an interchange of experience, of material, of forces and of resources."

A newspaper was appropriate technology in Lenin's day. Direct mail is a contemporary form of media. Through its use, Richard Parker doesn't intend to create a single centralized organization. He wants to provide a coherent framework — financial and political — in which a constituency that will support leftist groups and candidates can be cultivated.

The American left, however, mostly disdains practical politics; it has a self-enforced ignorance of the political system it wants to transform. It casts itself as an outsider deliberately. Being on the outside gives it freedom of action and movement. This approach is often valid because the established order does respond in some ways to outside pressure that isn't compromised. This is a politics of protest, however, not a politics of power. Ironically, the more the left continues its outsider role, the more its effect can only be strictly reformist. The left may adopt a revolutionary credo, but without any inside leverage of its own it can only force ameliorative change. If the left wants to organize the whole of society differently, it must initiate a new practical politics. In order to do that it must begin at the beginning, with so little clout that it always risks being absorbed by the liberal wing of the Democratic party. These are the realities Richard Parker faces. "Left politics," he says, "is locked in ice. Whether it will come alive when the ice melts has us all in suspense."

CHAPTER FOURTEEN

# THE RETURN OF THE KING

## EDWARD M. KENNEDY

The John F. Kennedy Memorial Library is located on the edge of a promontory jutting out into Dorchester Bay, facing on one side the Boston skyline and on the other the open sea. The day the library was dedicated strong ocean winds buffeted the crowd that assembled to remember the past, witness the political clash of the present, and plan for the restoration. It was October 20, 1979, fifty years minus one day after Edward L. Bernays's Golden Jubilee of Light, the ultimate media event of the 1920s. The JFK Library dedication was the Camelot Jubilee, an unprecedented congregation of America's political elite, the opening scene of the 1980s.

As the former cabinet secretaries, advisers, and Kennedy advance men recalled old times, the nostalgia was evident. Politics, they felt, had become much more impersonal since the death of

Jack Kennedy. They savored the rekindled fraternity; it was the ingathering of a traditional society. They had once been part of a blood brotherhood. They compared tie clips, which within this society are equivalent to epaulettes, designating rank and experience. A gold PT-109 tie clip without any inscription signifies membership in the highest order, while a PT-109 tie clip with "Kennedy '60" on it ranks just a level below, but is still distinguished. Exhibiting either of these tie clips means you worked for President Kennedy in his campaign. Other tie clips were on display, too. Clips in the shape of New York State, reading "Kennedy '64," identified those who worked for Robert Kennedy when he ran for the U.S. Senate; clips in the shape of Massachusetts, inscribed "Kennedy '62," proved service to Ted Kennedy in his first bid for the Senate. Anyone who had ever earned a tie clip wore it; literally hundreds of ties were anchored by these symbols of service. Many wondered who would be awarded tie clips reading "Kennedy '80." They questioned what roles they might perform in the campaign and whether they ought to leave it to a new generation.

Although Jimmy Carter and Ted Kennedy delivered speeches, the occasion belonged to the tape-recorded voice of Jack Kennedy, a ghost hovering over the crowd. The mystique of Camelot was recreated: it had its practical political purposes. At the ceremony's conclusion the most sought after man in the audience was Carl Wagner, Ted Kennedy's political aide, who was hiring for the upcoming campaign. While some older Kennedyites had self-doubts about participation because of their age, those eager to sign up buttonholed Wagner. He jotted down phone numbers on his dedication program. It was a perfect Kennedy event. Its ideal sentimental conditions made everyone there think about what they used to think about: Kennedy campaigns.

There had been three schools of thought among Senator Edward M. Kennedy's aides and advisers on the question of his presidential candidacy. The first group was hesitant and cautious, arguing that 1984 would be Ted's year, that it was difficult as well as heretical to run against an incumbent president of your own party, and that it would not be easy to dislodge him, regardless of his standing in the polls. Even if Kennedy did succeed in wresting the nomination, the party might be so rent apart that it would precipitate a Republican victory. At first, Kennedy himself adhered to these precepts.

Another group of advisers was also worried about Republicans. This group, consisting of Kennedy's colleagues in Congress, approached him as early as the spring of 1979. They feared that if Jimmy Carter were the Democratic nominee, the Republicans might capture the Senate and many seats in the House. To these politicians Kennedy was the savior of their committee chairmanships.

Yet another group was disturbed about the direction of the country and Carter's incompetence and conservatism. These were Kennedy's young, liberal aides and his academic advisers, who had once hoped to be brought into the Carter administration, at least for conferences.

As for Kennedy himself, his posture of holding back a decision, so tantalizing to the press, had developed into a strategy itself. He had no campaign, and that was his campaign. It allowed Carter to sink low enough in the polls so that an announcement by Kennedy would be looked upon as an act of mercy. Kennedy's strategy was simply to be Kennedy, an ingenious tack, the ultimate image-making, being yourself. But that wasn't possible any longer. Draft Kennedy groups sprouted in numerous states, and Kennedy's fabled organization could maintain only discreet, distant contact. "I didn't want to go into the army, but I was drafted," said Tim Hagan, chairman of the Cuyahoga County (Cleveland, Ohio) Democratic party. "When your party drafts you, you have to go." But Kennedy was also concerned about the enormous funds the "Draft Kennedy" movement was raising. He was nervous about so much money loosely left in the hands of amateurs.

He was also hurt and angered by the treatment he was receiving from Jimmy Carter's White House. Carter and his aides believed that a show of bellicosity and bad manners could scare Kennedy out of the race. Carter neglected to send Kennedy an invitation to the White House dinner for Chinese leader Deng Xiaoping, and he refused to appoint an old Kennedy friend, former Watergate special prosecutor Archibald Cox, to a U.S. Circuit Court judgeship. Calls from Kennedy's office to the White House were rarely returned, and when they were, they were invariably late. Finally, Jimmy Carter pointedly declared that if Kennedy ran he would "whip his ass," further arousing the ire of the Kennedy family. During a long vacation in August on Cape Cod, sailing his sloop around Hyannis, Kennedy considered his options. His family, feeling insulted by Carter, gave their assent to a campaign.

Kennedy's announcement came on November 7, in Faneuil Hall, the historic Boston site where Sam Adams once addressed revolutionary colonists; the candidate was cheered by family, aides, and a throng of Massachusetts politicians. The timing of the announcement date was hastened as much by Jerry Brown as by Jimmy Carter. Kennedy didn't want to repeat the experience of Bobby, who in 1968 entered after another challenger, Eugene McCarthy, had established himself as a legitimate contender against incumbent president Lyndon Johnson. Jerry Brown, Kennedy felt, might be the McCarthy of 1980. By declaring early he preempted Brown.

His candidacy was also a response to the effect of his image. Kennedy exists on a different plane from other politicians. Observers generally credit this to ethereal personal qualities such as charisma. He also has access to unlimited financial resources and a first-class staff. He presents himself as an ideal to politicians; he has a cerebral surface and a hard political interior. But Kennedy appears as the figure he is, in great part, because of public desire.

The Kennedy candidacy is not a simple dream. Drawn from the frustrations of the past, an incapacity to realize desires in the present, and grand hopes for the future, Kennedy represents the central element in a dream of expectations. He is the object of wish fulfillment. His presidential campaign is fueled by these intensely vivid dreams more than anything else. Consequently, Kennedy doesn't have to manipulate images or sway with every political breeze. He is the symbol himself. If elected president he promises to be our Kennedy.

The common reference in the Kennedy dream is to Camelot, the mythical kingdom of King Arthur and his Round Table. After President Kennedy's death, his widow told Theodore White, author of the *Making of the President* series, that she wished her husband's reign could be remembered like Camelot. She said Jack listened to the record a lot. So Camelot has come to stand for an administration of elegance, youth, and action, in other words, *The Best and the Brightest* without irony.

But Camelot refers to more than a musical comedy version of history. The Arthurian legend is based on a profound myth found in various forms in many cultures. Never before has so compelling a myth been substantiated in American political history. The potency of Kennedy's candidacy has to do with its recurrent quality. The Kennedy story as Arthurian legend makes sense only after the assassination of Jack. The key is not that Camelot was once a "shining moment," but that it has fallen on hard times because the king has departed. The spirit of the absent (or dead) king is still loose, not inhabiting the throne. Yet one day he must return. The kingdom anticipates that his return will be their salvation. The idea of the return of the king leads directly to the cult of the future Kennedy. And Ted Kennedy's candidacy is not the first time the king has attempted to return. He is the returned king in his second embodiment. The recurrence of Kennedys is an essential motif.

The feelings attached to Ted Kennedy are not the result of logical consideration. By speaking out forcefully Kennedy is widely believed somehow to be transversing the otherworld, conjuring the spirit of his dead brothers. By surviving his personal trials, he ensures that the myth remains potent; his suffering certifies it. He surpasses ordinary expectations, confirming the supernatural aura.

In mythic terms the drama of history after JFK's death was supernatural because of the improper transfer of power to a succession of false rulers who didn't possess the king's soul. His assassination commenced a train of strange events concluding with Richard Nixon's resignation. The king was never able to fulfill what was expected of him, and neither were his successors. The king promised great changes and they did not happen. The feeling persists that a supernatural event stopped them. The deaths of the brothers aroused expectations around Teddy. Those expectations aren't precise; they're not a program. They are expectations that *something* of a profound nature will happen.

Ted Kennedy's travails in that light are a series of identity tests. The tests are not of virtue but of power. He is tested on his ability to survive and continue the quest. The airplane crash he survived was a test of fire. Chappaquidick was a test of water, Kennedy's own Vietnam-like metaphor. It involved, like America's involvement in Vietnam, an inglorious escape. His explanation for the accident was patently insufficient, as all official explanations about Vietnam were insufficient. On the surface, this incident seemed to work against him, but within the system of the myth he is strengthened. He bears the burden of the country in the myth, going through personally what is experienced nationally. The myth has a structure and everything in his life seems to fit it. His further trials parallel the disintegration of the country. His son's cancer and his wife's alcoholism prove his calling. He is chosen by his suffering and ability to transcend it.

Whether or not his character is pure has very little to do with the myth. Ted Kennedy is a figure of clarity and power, but not necessarily of redemption. He is a king, but not the messiah. There is nothing indefinite about the messiah. He stops time and starts it all over again; he brings the end of history. The Kennedy myth, however, is about the return of an earthly king. If Ted Kennedy is elected, we enter into the Arthurian myth, which is a certain notion of continuing history.

All the presidents since Jack Kennedy have not been part of the myth. They have been interlopers, intervening chapters. Teddy is the rightful heir, for the crimes of the country were crimes against his family. Would the Vietnam War have been prolonged and would Watergate have occurred if his brothers had lived? This unanswerable question is crucial to our perception of recent American history. To repress the Kennedy dream would be to accept history without remorse, to accept a fatalistic view of events since November 22, 1963, and to deny American optimism. This cannot be done, at least until the last Kennedy ascends the throne of power. A sense of completed drama demands his candidacy.

There are many smaller dreams that make up the larger Kennedy dream, and that of the party regulars has been paramount, since it is they who most desperately seek a Kennedy candidacy. American political parties aren't held together by principle but by fear of defeat and hope of sharing the spoils. Before Kennedy's declaration of candidacy, Carter's failure as a political leader united the Democratic party regulars, bringing them together in a way that hadn't happened in years. With Carter at the top of the ticket they felt their jobs threatened.

The regulars also desired the restoration of the party. They were in revolt against Carter's style of moral uplift, political inconsistency, and closed deliberations. But they don't understand the complexity of the decline of the parties, which only incidentally has to do with Jimmy Carter. To them, Kennedy is a symbol of the old days, when it could be said of national campaigns, as Robert Kennedy did, that Chicago mayor Richard Daley was "the whole ballgame."

When Kennedy speaks to the party professionals they hear

long-forgotten voices, even the voice of Teddy's grandfather, mayor of ragtime Boston, John "Honey Fitz" Fitzgerald. Kennedy takes the regulars back in time to the period before *The Last Hurrah*, when machine politicians were powers to be reckoned with, not quaint objects of sentimental anecdotes. For the regulars, the Kennedy candidacy is a dream of memory, of current convenience, and apprehension of the future.

They regard him with awe and envy. "He can do things, say things, and go places the rest of us can't," says Robert Crane, Massachusetts state treasurer, once a Kennedy factotum and chairman of the state Democratic party. "There are all levels of comparison," he says. "It's like in hockey. On this line are all the hockey greats. And then there's Bobby Orr."

James King, Kennedy's advance man for fourteen years and now head of the National Transportation Safety Board, says, "Regular pols are fascinated that Kennedy's fast moving. What baffles them is his real enjoyment in campaigns. You know a lot of them don't really like to campaign. Kennedy works as hard as anyone I know. He's scrupulous about the kinds of things we regard as staff kinds of things. He understands organization fully. He understands that you have to hire a hall, that there is a committee for the coffee. He's extraordinarily demanding. You never have the feeling you've earned your stars and can take it easy. He has sheer animal energy. That shouldn't be sold short in a campaign. And, this is important, he understands where he's from. When he comes back to Massachusetts you'd think he was 10 points down in the polls with an election in a month. He understands campaigns as educating folks. And I've never been with him when he didn't learn something from the day. He flourishes from the contact."

The Kennedy operation leans heavily on organization and the figure of Kennedy himself — the symbol who doesn't need symbolism. "He presents himself. I just film him," says Charles Guggenheim, the film maker who has produced the senator's political ads since 1970 and who was hired for Kennedy's presidential run in 1980. (Before 1970, Guggenheim made commercials for Bobby Kennedy.) His ads for Kennedy in 1980 employ the techniques he's always used: the candidate as talking head and the voter as man on the street. Guggenheim produces artful ads; he doesn't indulge in packaging gimmicks. With Kennedy he doesn't have to.

Gathered around Kennedy are his Knights of the Round Table, the toughest and the shrewdest. Since the murder of Robert Kennedy, the elders of this mystic circle have pursued adventure in private law practice, government bureaucracies, and the higher echelons of the media. They are bound to Kennedy by primal ties of loyalty, and although they can't abandon their careers, they can be called upon for help.

"There are old foxes around like me," says Gerard Doherty. He wears a tie clip in the shape of Massachusetts inscribed "Kennedy '62." Doherty is a lawyer. He has been a lobbyist for the Greater Boston Real Estate Board and the Roman Catholic Archdiocese of Boston, among other interests. He has lived in Charlestown, a Boston neighborhood, his entire life. The sitting room in his Beacon Street law office is decorated with early-American furniture and paintings. Daily he receives telephone calls from operatives eager to involve themselves in Kennedy's presidential drive; he writes down their names and promises nothing. He is soft-spoken and intense.

"I first met Ted Kennedy in 1958," he says. "I was in the legislature, a young Irish turk. In 1960, I was just getting by; I was in law school. And, in 1961, a friend of mine who was a friend of the Kennedy family, Frank Morrissey, asked me if I would have lunch with Ted Kennedy. When the lunch was over he announced he was running for the Senate. They asked me to set up another lunch for legislators. I got to be his contact person. Then I met with the president and Robert Kennedy and they gave me responsibility for the state convention."

After Ted was elected to the Senate, the Kennedy family carved out a new niche for Doherty. "Teddy had criticism from the cognoscenti, the liberals. They were most interested in party reform. So I became the party reformer. I was state chairman for six years. You just keep handling all the bad problems. It's great for your humility."

Doherty was a valuable Kennedy family asset. He was able to galvanize the troops in distant provinces, winning famous victories. Once he received his marching orders he knew what to do. When Robert Kennedy announced his presidential bid in 1968 his triumph was by no means certain. Lyndon Johnson, the incumbent president, had not yet abdicated. And Eugene McCarthy, carrying the liberal antiwar banner, refused to make an alliance; to the McCarthy followers, Kennedy was a reckless opportunist.

The first primary for Kennedy was in Indiana, where he faced a favorite-son governor, a machine Democrat holding the fort for Johnson. "Teddy asked me to take it," says Doherty. "We had to build around the party organization." Kennedy won, giving his candidacy credence and reinvigorating the legend of invincibility.

Doherty was on his way to organize New York for Kennedy when he received word of the assassination. "I grieved and sorrowed for a while," he says. Then he was back in the fray. "Humphrey asked Teddy for some help." Doherty was the help. He organized Ohio, but Humphrey narrowly lost. "I just came back and practiced law," says Doherty. "I did a lot of lobbying. But I got out of that." Then in 1976 Carter requested aid from Ted Kennedy, who then asked Doherty to run the New York campaign for Carter.

Doherty doesn't think campaigns have changed much over the years, in spite of the new technology. "What's different? I'm older," he says. He doesn't believe he's out of touch. "There are certain kinds of basics. Campaigns are still about developing issues and swaying voters."

To him, Kennedy campaigns are exemplars of political organization. From them one can understand the unyielding, demanding nature of the Kennedy operation and why it has a reputation as a juggernaut. Over time — from Jack to Bobby to Teddy — its principles have remained constant. When he discusses the Kennedy modus operandi, Doherty's voice tightens with determination and excitement.

"Kennedy campaigns are disciplined," he says. "You have a schedule. The candidate is up and goes all day long. There is meaning and substance to the schedule. There's a regimentation. If you were an issues guy you'd be writing a Teddy speech. There'd be somebody slotted to write Teddy speeches on left-handed midgets. There'd be someone slotted to think around corners — where we'll be in three weeks."

But Kennedy's operation differs from a regular political machine. In a machine, the emphasis is on quantity, not quality. As long as there's a precinct captain on the block the machine is satisfied that the territory is covered. Not so with the Kennedyites. They want more than that. "In Indiana in 1968 we found it was disciplined. But a guy running the precinct wasn't necessarily the best guy. We would find second-string people. They were enthusiastic and were given a chance to play first string. We went with what I call one-eyed people," says Doherty, employing his own idiosyncratic terminology. "That's in contradistinction to the beautiful people. With beautiful people you end up in a debate. Too many campaigns turn into internal debates. There are too many smart people who want to debate. But the one-eyed people become pretty good. You give them four things to do and they do them."

The Kennedy operation is based on clear lines of authority, a distinct division of labor, money, and loyalty. But sometimes being loyal isn't sufficient to ensure your place at the Round Table. The case of Robert Crane illustrates how cold necessity can overtake an individual within the structure.

Crane served the Kennedys dutifully in many campaigns and as chairman of the Democratic party in Massachusetts. When he became state treasurer everybody seemed pleased. But he turned into an obstacle when young Joe Kennedy, the senator's nephew, contemplated a run for that office. "Jerry Doherty's role," says Crane, "was to find out if I was interested in running for reelection and to get the message to me that Joe Kennedy was heading in my direction. I had a further conversation with Senator Kennedy. I had an opportunity to express my intentions." The situation became very messy. Crane's side of the story was aired in the *Boston Globe*. Joe Kennedy backed off, perhaps for reasons of his own. Crane emerged as the only dissident to survive a Kennedy coup attempt.

Doherty, for his part, carried on as always, loyal to Kennedy. "When it appeared Joe Kennedy was running I was part of the conversation," he says. "I thought I'd go and tell Crane this thing might happen. I never said, 'I'll punch you in the nose or we'll give you a bag of money.' I wouldn't deliver an ultimatum to anyone. I wanted to have the decency and courtesy to tell Crane. In politics, sometimes you've got to do things you don't want to do."

Ted Kennedy's Washington office looks like an anteroom in the Kennedy library, evocative of tradition. On the walls are pictures of Ted with Bobby, with Jack, with his kids, with his mother, on a sailboat, a picture of Bobby swarmed by ecstatic crowds, a picture of Joe Kennedy, Sr., a panoramic photo of the Boston skyline, and pictures of the birthplaces of Joe Senior (an arrow points to a building on Meriden Street, East Boston), Rose Fitzgerald Kennedy (Garden Street, North End), and John F. Fitzgerald (Terry Street, North End). In the middle of the office stands a Secret Service man, staring into space.

Teddy's bright, young operatives are not those who have experience with the new techniques. They are old-style politicos as young men. The busiest man in Kennedy's office is Carl Wagner, the senator's political aide, hired in December 1978 to fill a position that had been left vacant by Paul Kirk's departure to private law practice in 1976. Kirk's leaving was widely interpreted as an indication that Kennedy wouldn't seek the presidency for a long time; Kirk did, however, join the campaign as a top manager. The hiring of Wagner, in this light, was highly suggestive. He represents the new generation: he's thirty-four years old. His contacts are different from those of the older Kennedy people. He looks to political activists in order to determine who can do what for Kennedy, when they can do it, and how they can do it. Though Wagner is driven by issues and is slightly disorganized, his charm, Kennedy hopes, can cultivate personal loyalty and motivation among the campaign cadres he recruits.

Wagner's day is filled with the endless ringing of the telephone, meetings, and hurrying about town. He eats no lunch and smokes too much. In spite of the chaos in which he finds himself, he isn't frantic and doesn't seem overwhelmed. He's not brash, but self-assured. He appears to possess a sense of balance and buoyancy as he navigates through the political maelstrom.

"Jesus, sorry for being so rushed," he says. Then he's interrupted by another urgent phone call. In order to escape the phones he seeks refuge in a cavernous, empty, unlit Senate hearing room. He bites his nails.

"The argument that the country is moving right assumes a definition of the electorate, that it's divided into left, right, and center," he says. "That's basically incorrect. Characterizing the electorate as liberal or conservative is inaccurate. The overriding sentiment is indifference. People feel indifferent about the institutions' ability to address critical issues.

"There are two deep currents running through American history — a sense of political liberty and a hope of economic opportunity. In 1980, there's a marked difference. There's apprehension. The national debate has to be lifted above legislative issues to a broad discussion of the next decade. The goal of the presidency is to define the goals, gather a group of people to implement the goals, and lead the people. Is there a crisis of confidence? Confidence in what? That's the question. The next five years are going to be difficult. Leadership will be severely tested. Precise goals around which people can be mobilized have to be set. We haven't done that.

"Will the American people respond? Absolutely. And the president must define goals precisely. He must manage the national political debate. The image Kennedy projects is a function of what he believes far more than an assessment of what he thinks is palatable. I work for him because he's the most progressive force in American politics."

Wagner gained his organizing skills working for labor and his practical experience in politics working for George McGovern in 1972 and for Jimmy Carter in 1976. "I learned in the McGovern campaign," he says, "that some of the personnel decisions are of great consequence. I learned that there is a terrific sentiment in the country for statements of conviction. And I learned that in Iowa in January it's zero degrees."

Wagner relies upon instinct, contacts, and organizational savvy. The information he considers most valuable is what he hears, not what the polls tell him. In the course of our conversation he borrowed my pen and notebook and drew a large rectangle and a small circle. He labeled the rectangle "American people" and the circle "Carter." "How does Caddell see it?" he asked, pointing to the distance between the two shapes. "Is this how he sees it? How does he understand the relationship between the president and the people?" Wagner disparages Caddell but doesn't really understand what it is that Caddell does. He fails to comprehend that Caddell's technique can uncover the slightest weakness in Kennedy's posture and telegraph that weakness to just the right audience without the Kennedy operation detecting what is happening.

The Ted Kennedy that Gerard Doherty went to work for is a different man from the one Carl Wagner went to work for. Kennedy was not always a man of achievement, the respected chairman of the Senate Judiciary Committee, and the leading advocate of national health insurance, willing, as he has said, "to sail against the wind" of conventional wisdom. Doherty and Wagner, so different from each other, yet alike in the tasks they perform for Kennedy, span his career.

When Ted Kennedy first ran for the Senate he was inexperienced, living in the shadow of his brothers, and thirty years old. His campaign was managed by Stephen Smith, the Kennedy family executive. In the beginning, Ted was an image without depth, a Kennedy to be sure, but an extension of his family. He was another test case for exercising the Kennedy organization. His was the most lavish campaign ever seen in the state. This occurred, it should be recalled, before the era of campaign spending limits. Ted shelled out $225,000 to an advertising agency, an unheard of sum then. Numerous films and video tapes were produced and aired on television, including one called "Coffee with the Kennedys," about the Kennedys' famous coffee klatches. "Give Teddy a job, elect him to the Senate," joked JFK.

Ted's opponent for the Democratic nomination was Edward McCormack, the attorney general of Massachusetts and scion of another distinguished Boston Irish political family. He was the nephew of House Speaker John W. McCormack. He invited Kennedy to debate him at South Boston High School. At the dramatic encounter McCormack pointed a finger at Kennedy and charged that he had never worked a day in his life. "If his name was Edward Moore, with his qualifications," McCormack said, turning to Ted, "your candidacy would be a joke, but nobody's laughing because his name is not Edward Moore. It's Edward Moore Kennedy."

The next morning, bright and early, Ted and his aides were at a factory gate to shake the hands of workers going in on the day shift. James King, Kennedy's advance man, tells the story: " 'Hey Kennedy,' yelled a worker. 'I hear you never worked a day in your life.' Kennedy tightened. 'Well,' said the worker, 'I want to tell you something. You haven't missed a fucking thing.' I was jumping up and down. 'We won. We won,' I shouted. You didn't need the polls to know that."

Once in the Senate, Kennedy had the perspicacity to introduce himself politely to archtroglodyte James Eastland of Mississippi, a pillar of the Senate establishment. Kennedy observed the Senate's peculiar folkways while compiling the most liberal record. After seventeen years there, he was a powerful figure with many palpable accomplishments. He was not the same Ted Kennedy who entered the Senate as the kid brother of the president. This Kennedy was not merely a candidate of promise. He had a record. He came to the presidential race as something of an elder statesman.

Kennedy, however, entered the 1980 campaign operating on many assumptions that were no longer valid. He had not altered the traditional style of organization his brothers relied upon, which, when it was first employed in 1960, was innovative, a hybrid improvisation of old political techniques. The Kennedy operations were always separate from the party, an implicit recognition that party bosses did not exercise the absolute power they once did. Jack Kennedy was the original practitioner of style over substance, retaining his maneuverability as much as possible. He, more so than Bobby, kept himself aloof from the issues until his commitment could be used for maximum benefit. The Kennedys' keen sense of tactics was the forerunner of today's strategic politics. This particular Kennedy legacy has become the new politics, which confronts Ted Kennedy in the presidential contest. He, however, inherits the family's political methods in an ossified form.

Kennedy's presidential campaign is the last redoubt of the old politics. In the 1980 contest, his image meets its test against advanced strategic politics. His descent from myth to reality in the opening scenes of the race occurred with dizzying speed. His metamorphosis from a heroic character into a mundane politician, seemingly deprived of his mythical dimensions and his magic, was, fittingly enough, triggered by a media event. After CBS broadcast its documentary "Teddy" on November 4, 1979, in which Teddy appeared inarticulate, dissembling, and remote, he fell precipitously in the polls. Governor Hugh Carey of New York called him "a plummeting star." Other party professionals wondered if Kennedy had become enthralled by his own mythology. Tim Hagan, the Cleveland party leader, said, "The idea of the great Kennedy machine — oiled, no squeaking parts, doesn't break down — is all bullshit. They thought the Kennedy glamour was going to carry it. They were playing out the mythology. Bullshit. This is a campaign."

Certainly, Iran's holding of American hostages, creating a mood of national unity and enhancing Jimmy Carter's standing, complicated the early Kennedy campaign. But it was not the sole reason his campaign failed to take off as expected. Much of the trouble stemmed from Kennedy's and his closest advisers' incomprehension of the permanent campaign. Kennedy, in fact, had not run a truly serious campaign since 1962 because his base had always been secure.

In an effort to solve his initial media difficulties, Kennedy brought into the campaign an old family political friend, Herb Schmertz, who as a Mobil Oil vice president is responsible for that company's extensive media campaign. But Schmertz's position on energy was obviously at odds with Kennedy's; in addition, Schmertz's preferred candidate for president was John Connally. "He may be a quick learner, but he doesn't understand political media one iota," says a political consultant who knows Schmertz. "He understands media for a large oil company. And he's very good at that." Another political consultant with vast experience in running presidential campaigns submitted a memo to Schmertz outlining the fundamentals of how a modern campaign, integrating media and polling, ought to be conducted. Schmertz was dismissive. Instead of delegating authority for the media effort, Schmertz devoted his time to writing ad copy. When Schmertz left the campaign after a brief stint of six weeks, the role of media coordinator was assumed by Philip Bakes, previously counsel to the Civil Aeronautics Board, a person with no history of campaign experience.

One of the top-flight political consultants approached by the Kennedy campaign refused the offer. "In October, they said we'd like to consider you for the ads," says David Garth. "In November, they said please, please do the campaign. I thought about it and I said I wouldn't do it. Their approach is from twenty years ago, when reporters didn't ask questions. The Kennedy campaign just opened their doors and said we're doing business. You've got to have a strategy and a vision. They didn't understand media. And what's really shocking to me is that they didn't understand the modern use of polls." When Garth sent two of his in-house pollsters to explain to some top Kennedy advisers the workings of sophisticated polling, the Kennedy men wanted to know why they needed this if they could lay hands early on a television network poll. They failed to understand the difference between horserace figures and strategic calculations.

The Kennedy campaign made a serious bid for Garth's services. Teddy himself met with Garth and so did Stephen Smith, Kennedy's brother-in-law and campaign manager. Garth was impressed with the candidate and Smith, but not with their entourage. "Kennedy gets into problems with his staff," he says. "It's a senatorial staff. They may be very good in their specific issue areas, but they don't understand how to translate that into a campaign." He was also unimpressed with the old knights of Camelot, who apparently mounted opposition to Garth's appointment. "I feel as an emotional decision I'd pull the lever for Kennedy," says Garth, "but I will not accept being knifed from the rear. Smith and Kennedy were not threatened. It's the second-level guys who have a stake in this. They're all there in the woodwork." Garth believes that their political style is anachronistic. "They still think in terms of getting Teddy moving around. But you don't have to stage a barnstorming tour. You have one press conference and one media event a day. What's amazing to me," he says, "is that they were not prepared."

If Kennedy doesn't fulfill the expectations he symbolizes, the dream that supported his candidacy may disintegrate into its raw elements — fear, fatalism, insecurity — which the right can then reassemble. The last time the Kennedy dream exploded, one result was Richard Nixon.

Rightists see Kennedy as a terrifying threat, leftist, the worst of all possible candidates. He is the anti-Christ who will bring on the apocalypse. To the New Right, Kennedy's presidential intentions are received as a declaration of war. "It's ideological warfare," says Richard Viguerie, direct mail tyro of the New Right who works for GOP hopeful John Connally. "With a Kennedy administration we might wake up and there'd be no ballgame. Kennedy might be aggressive in trying to put the New Right out of business. The conservatives are moving along and then they [the liberals] start changing the rules on us. We might not be able to operate. The real danger comes from the left. They will stifle all freedom. Kennedy's committed to socialism. He will be a disaster. It's important to stop him."

On the other side of the political spectrum, Richard Parker, the leftist political consultant, believes that Kennedy needs the left to meet the expectations he arouses. "In order to function he needs pressure from the left to fulfill his liberal agenda," says Parker. "With no pressure there's no room for him to maneuver. He also needs the left because the left, with all its faults, is the only source of dreams. Without the crude dreams of equality and justice, Kennedy has nowhere from which to draw a dream of his own."

In the Kennedy candidacy, dreams of the past and future mingle. "For in every sense," writes Freud in *The Interpretation of Dreams*, "a dream has its origin in the past. The ancient belief that dreams reveal the future is not indeed entirely devoid of truth. By representing a wish as fulfilled the dream certainly leads us into the future."

Even if Kennedy fulfills the dream about himself, his succession will be shaped by the permanent campaign. With the breakdown of traditional constituencies and the trend toward nonalignment, politicians are no longer bred in the same way. Kennedy is who he is because the Kennedy family has been waging their own permanent campaign throughout the twentieth century, positioning themselves as the ultimate Democrats. Ted Kennedy is the last king.